WE BAND OF BROTHERS

$\mathcal{W}$E

NEW YORK, EVANSTON, SAN FRANCISCO, LONDON

1817

BAND OF BROTHERS

by Edwin Guthman

Harper & Row, Publishers

Excerpts on pages 296-297 from a column by Eric Sevareid are reprinted courtesy of Publishers-Hall Syndicate. © 1964, Publishers-Hall Syndicate.

FIRST EDITION

STANDARD BOOK NUMBER: 06-011716-8

LIBRARY OF CONGRESS CATALOG CARD NUMBER: 72-123932

To my wife, JoAnn
who shared all our hopes

Contents

Author's Note

My friendship with Robert Kennedy began in 1956, and I spoke with him in his room in the Ambassador Hotel only a few minutes before he left to claim victory in the 1968 California primary. This book is written out of that friendship. If, among the many other books about him, it has uniqueness, it is that I show him at an earlier time in his career, and that I tend to discount the view that he experienced a great transformation of character and outlook in his last years. I have not tried to provide a definitive account of his life or an objective analysis of his career. I have tried only to set forth experiences we shared, for whatever insight they provide into the kind of man I knew him to be. These are simply my recollections.

Some of my former colleagues in the Department of Justice—William Hundley, Burke Marshall, Herbert J. Miller, Jr., Harold Reis, Jack Rosenthal, Walter Sheridan and Byron R. White—kindly read parts of the manuscript and offered comments and advice that were extremely helpful. I am also grateful to my colleague on the Los Angeles *Times*, D. J. R. Bruckner, for his incisive suggestions and to my former colleagues on the Seattle *Times*, Henry MacLeod, Mae Ryan, Paul Staples and Lane Smith, for their assistance.

I am indebted to Theodore C. Sorensen for his counsel and encouragement.

To Mr. and Mrs. Sidney Bernstein of Pacific Palisades, California, a special note of appreciation, and to Jean Pratt who typed the manuscript.

In doing research a large number of books were invaluable sources of reference. Among these were Robert Kennedy's own works, particularly *The Enemy Within* and *Thirteen Days; Kennedy* by Theodore Sorensen; *A Thousand Days* by Arthur M. Schlesinger, Jr.; *The Making of the President* (*1960* and *1964*) by Theodore F. White; *The Bay of Pigs* by Haynes Johnson; *The Past That Would Not Die* by Walter Lord; and Parts 1, 4, 5 and 7 of the transcript of hearings before the Senate Select Committee on Improper Activities in the Labor or Management Field for the period from February 26 to June 4, 1957.

My son Lester gave me considerable help and I deeply appreciate his editing judgment and his frankness. I am also indebted to Thomas B. Congdon, Jr., of Harper & Row for his invaluable help and editorial suggestions, and to Cass Canfield and Jay Iselin of Harper & Row for the confidence they placed in me.

EDWIN GUTHMAN

Los Angeles, California
February 5, 1971

WE BAND OF BROTHERS

Chapter 1

"Mr. Rogers" Comes to Town

ONE NOVEMBER AFTERNOON in 1956, Clark Mollenhoff, then a reporter for the Des Moines *Register-Tribune*,[1] called me in Seattle from Washington, D.C., to tell me that a Senate committee was going to investigate corruption in the labor movement.

"I've suggested they start with Dave Beck and the Teamsters in the Pacific Northwest," he said. "A young lawyer from the committee would like to come out and see you and I hope you'll help him."

"Who is he?" I asked.

"Bob Kennedy," said Mollenhoff. When I didn't respond, he continued, "You know, he's Senator Kennedy's brother."

I thought for a moment more and then said: "That's fine, Clark, but can you trust him?"

In light of all that was to happen over the next twelve years my response now seems amusing, but that was the first time I was aware that Senator Kennedy had a brother named Bob. In 1956 the name "Kennedy" did not mean much three thousand miles from Massachusetts and Washington, D.C.

I was a reporter for the Seattle *Times* and along with another *Times* reporter, Paul Staples, had been investigating Beck's activities

---

1. Later, special counsel to President Nixon.

for eight years. It began in 1948 when I interviewed Beck while
helping Staples, the paper's labor reporter, cover a strike at the
Boeing Airplane Company. The strike had been called by the International Association of Machinists, and Beck, with his eye on the
large Boeing work force, was trying to organize behind the IAM
picket line and break the strike. Beck lied when I asked him about
what he was doing, and I was somewhat taken aback. When I returned to the newsroom, I told Staples what had happened and then
asked why a man in Beck's position would lie.

"Oh, don't you know?" Staples said. "Beck lies all the time."

"But why?"

"Well, for one thing, I'm pretty sure he is stealing money from
the union," Staples said.

We worked for a Republican newspaper which had been biased
in its coverage of news about organized labor before Staples joined
the staff at the end of World War II. Despite the paper's history,
Staples had earned the respect and trust of the labor movement. He
had excellent sources in many unions, and some who were high in
the Teamsters Union in Seattle had told him that Beck was diverting union funds to his own use. We talked about it and decided to
see if we could get the proof. By the fall of 1956 we were still trying.
The *Times* had published a number of our articles, however, which
at least raised some questions about Beck's activities. They detailed
how Beck had engaged in extensive real estate ventures in the Seattle area; they uncovered the strange circumstances whereby the
Teamsters Union came to buy Beck's lakefront home for $163,000;[2]
and they reported that George Newell, a Seattle insurance executive, was receiving what appeared to be inordinately high commis-
sions (about $300,000 a year) as insurance broker for the Western

2. It later developed that the Teamsters Union not only had bought Beck's home,
but had paid for it in the first place—that Beck had taken $196,000 from the union
treasury to build it. When Staples questioned Beck about the unusual transaction,
Beck said there had been ample precedent. The union, he said, had built a home in
Miami and another in Indianapolis for Dan Tobin, who was president of the Teamsters from 1907 until Beck forced him to retire in 1952. "Yes, Dave," said Staples, "but
the union didn't build Tobin's homes for him and then buy them back." "No," Beck
thundered back, "and Tobin didn't have an eighty-six-year-old mother living with
him either!"

Conference of Teamsters. Newell was a pal of Frank Brewster, who took control of Local 174 in Seattle and succeeded to the presidency of the Western Conference of Teamsters when Beck became the union's international president in 1952. Brewster's careless misuse of Teamster funds also was beginning to surface. The *Wall Street Journal* had delved into Beck's financial operations and written extensively about them. In Portland, Oregon, two courageous reporters, Wallace Turner and William Lambert, of the *Oregonian,* had exposed a brazen attempt, which the Teamsters in Seattle backed, to take over control of gambling and other fringe operations. Staples and I had worked closely with Turner and Lambert.

I had met Mollenhoff in 1954 and we found we had a mutual interest. Mollenhoff had been investigating Beck's counterpart in Detroit, James R. Hoffa. We decided we might be able to help each other and began exchanging information about the two Teamster kingpins. However, when he called in November 1956 to tell me about the committee, I was wary not only because I had never heard of Bob Kennedy before, but because we were respectful of Beck's power and because our experiences with Congressional and legislative investigating committees had not been very satisfactory.

At the time, Beck seemed to be at the peak of his strength. He was president of the nation's largest and most powerful labor union. He had been photographed with President Eisenhower at the White House. He was vice president of the AFL-CIO. The American Legion and other patriotic organizations had honored him for fighting Communism. The City of Hope Hospital and many other religious and civic organizations had paid tribute to him publicly for his seemingly generous charitable donations.[3] He traveled abroad frequently. He had a penthouse in Washington, D.C., and a lakefront estate in Seattle, a city in which he was both feared and respected. He had been a regent of the University of Washington. Business leaders with whom he negotiated wages and working conditions hailed him as a labor leader who lived up to his contract

---

3. The Senate investigation was to disclose that many of Beck's charitable donations were made with union funds.

("Once a contract is signed, I respect it like a Bible," he said), and many newspapers, including the Seattle *Times*, had editorialized that what this country needed was more labor leaders like Dave Beck. The late William K. Blethen, publisher of the *Times*, though no respecter of Beck, had been co-chairman with the publisher of the Seattle *Post-Intelligencer* of a dinner in December 1952 which more than six hundred Seattle business leaders attended to honor Beck on his ascendancy to head of the whole union. Thus Staples and I and the only other persons on the paper who knew what we were doing—Russell L. McGrath, the managing editor, and Henry MacLeod, the city editor—always were wary of Beck. Furthermore, over the years we had developed trusted informants within the Teamsters Union, and so, when Mollenhoff asked whether we would cooperate with a committee of the United States Senate, I was thinking not only about our own skins but also about those of our informants.

In 1948 and 1949 the *Times*, although a conservative Republican newspaper, had strongly and effectively opposed the Washington State Legislature's Un-American Activities Committee when it resorted to very heavy-handed and unfair tactics in probing Communist activity at the University of Washington. The paper also had fought hard and successfully in defense of federal employees who appeared to have been unfairly suspended or dismissed as loyalty risks in the early 1950's. The excesses of the McCarthy Committee's investigation still were fresh and the *Times* had been one of the few papers to speak out strongly against them. Having been much involved in all of that, I explained to Mollenhoff that we had no great interest in furthering a Congressional investigation or in being used by a committee and then being left high and dry.

Mollenhoff, however, vouched strongly for Bob Kennedy as a person who could be trusted completely. He went on to point out that the committee, with its subpoena power, could get Beck's financial records, which we had practically no hope of ever obtaining. That really was the clinching argument, and I agreed to see Bob. Shortly afterward I received a phone call from him. He said he would arrive in Seattle from Los Angeles on November 16 and asked me to reserve a hotel room for him. He requested a room with a bathtub, not a shower, and he suggested I reserve it under the name "Rogers." He would write later in *The Enemy Within* that he did not use a fictitious name to be secretive or dramatic. "Nor was it even with the idea that at this point in our work anyone would care much that we were there," he wrote. "We simply felt that . . . it might be more convenient for us if it was not widely known that we were in town." Certainly, from our standpoint that was correct.

He arrived late in the afternoon accompanied by Jerome S. Adlerman, a staff assistant. I met their plane and had the embarrassing experience of running into my mother-in-law, who was on the same plane and who thought I was meeting her and that it was mighty peculiar when I walked off with two strangers whom I did not introduce to her. We went to dinner in a restaurant near the hotel, and through the dinner and for several hours afterward we talked —somewhat at arm's length—about the situation in Seattle and Portland and what the committee could do. I found that increasingly I was doing more talking than listening. My questions elicited short answers followed by a series of sharp, probing questions.

"How many members are there in Local 174?"

"How many attend union meetings?"

"How many do you think care about what's happening at the top?"

"Why aren't there more who do?"

"What kind of a mayor do you have here?"

We talked a good deal about Frank Brewster as well as Beck. Bob wanted to know about their associates, and he questioned me in detail about what we had published and about Turner's and Lambert's exposé. I wanted assurance that the committee would investigate thoroughly and that our informants would be protected. He promised to see to both. Though his knowledge of the labor movement and the extent of union corruption was not great, he had complete and definite ideas about how an investigating committee of the Congress should operate. He said that a committee should dig so deeply that it could, in effect, vouch for the truth of the testimony and evidence that it made public. Obviously, he said, there might be exceptions, but if an investigation was done skillfully and thoroughly, the facts could be presented in such a way that damage to an innocent person's reputation would be prevented. Since it had been my experience that legislative and Congressional investigating committees had greatly harmed innocent men and women recklessly and needlessly by not bothering to check and recheck what prospective witnesses were going to say at hearings, I was heartened by what he told me. But I did not have authority to commit the paper, and so we left the restaurant with the understanding that I would tell him the next day whether we would help him.

At home that night I drew a line down the middle of a sheet of paper, and in one column I listed the advantages I saw in cooperating with the committee and, in the other, the hazards of doing so. In summary, the advantages centered on the opportunity of having the union's financial records examined, hopefully leading to proof and public disclosure of evidence of corruption and misuse of power. Against this was the risk that the committee would do a careless, halfhearted job or back away from investigating the Teamsters Union—as two previous Congressional committees had[4]—leaving the paper and us and our informants vulnerable to retaliation by Beck. As things turned out, we probably overestimated Beck's appetite for revenge, but people in Seattle never forgot that Beck's organizers often had resorted to force and violence in the past.

The morning after I talked with Bob Kennedy, it was clear in my

4. In 1953 a House Government Operations Subcommittee headed by Representative Clare E. Hoffman, an elderly, outspoken Michigan Republican, heard testimony about labor racketeering in Detroit and Kansas City which threatened to involve Hoffa and some of his chief aides. Dissension riddled the committee. Hoffman was stripped of his power and replaced by Representative Wint Smith (R., Kansas). The investigation was then abandoned. "The pressure comes from way up there and I just can't talk about it any more specifically than that," Smith told newsmen. In January 1954 the committee ordered a new investigation of labor racketeering and put Representative George Bender (R., Ohio) in command. Bender, who was running for the unexpired part of the late Senator Robert A. Taft's term, opened hearings in his home town of Cleveland in September and questioned two of Hoffa's chief henchmen in Ohio. Then the investigation languished, and the Teamsters, who had been backing Bender's opponent, Senator Thomas Burke, switched their support to Bender.

mind that we should help the committee, that as newspapermen we had to go ahead. I talked with Staples and he agreed, and when we recommended this course to McGrath and MacLeod, they did not hesitate. Partly, I am sure, they were motivated by the knowledge that, as Mollenhoff had pointed out, unless some official agency with a reason and the power to subpoena the union's financial records did so, it seemed unlikely that the public would learn the extent of Beck's dishonesty and his misuse of his office. What we did not know was that a wiry, persistent Internal Revenue Service agent, Claude Watson, had been dogging Beck's trail for several years and that Beck, in trying to cover his theft of union funds, had entered into a number of transactions—such as having the union purchase his home—which ultimately contributed to his downfall. Beck almost certainly would have been prosecuted for income tax evasion if the Senate Rackets Committee had not exposed him, but we were not aware that IRS was auditing Beck's books, and in reaching their decision, McGrath and MacLeod had to accept my judgment that the committee would make a complete investigation, that we could trust Bob Kennedy. Neither they nor I ever was sorry that we did. He kept his word to us absolutely.

That was the beginning, the beginning of the relationship which Bob would characterize eight years later in an inscription on a drawing of the Department of Justice: "We few, we happy few, we band of brothers." And it was the beginning of a three-year investigation which prodded Congress to enact the Labor Reform Act of 1959, and which brought Bob face to face really for the first time with labor racketeering on a big scale.

The young man who came to Seattle under an assumed name in November 1956 was just beginning to perceive the extent of the corruption and tyranny that had infected the labor movement. He was only dimly aware that the union racketeers often were in league with crime syndicate hoodlums and that they often were being aided and abetted by lawyers, business executives and financiers. Later, in *The Enemy Within*, writing of that time and about the establishment of the Senate Select Committee on Improper Activities in the Labor or Management Field—which became known popularly as the McClellan Committee[5]—Bob would admit: "It hadn't even started as an investigation of the Teamsters' Union— some notion that it was big and tough and that Dan Tobin, Beck's immediate predecessor as president, had come from my home state of Massachusetts. I didn't know much more than that." Within three years, however, Bob had directed the most sweeping Congressional investigation in the nation's history, and one of the most revealing and effective, in which he commanded a staff of more than a hundred investigators and participated in the questioning of 1,525 witnesses.

The investigation was not his first. He had helped expose corruption among contractors and government officials in the military clothing procurement program. He had participated in Congressional investigations of trade with Communist China and the conflict-of-interest cases that caused Harold Talbott, Secretary of the Air Force in the Eisenhower Administration, and Robert Tripp Ross, Assistant Secretary of the Army, to resign. The military clothing procurement inquiry led to indications that major New York gangsters, including Albert Anastasia and John (Johnny Dio) Dioguardi, were muscling into the labor movement on the East Coast, and the subcommittee had questioned the infamous Dio in closed session in May 1956. But it was the investigation of Beck that opened Bob's eyes, and it was the investigation of Hoffa that revealed to him the depths of the corruption, venality and violence in the ranks of labor and management.

Some observers came to think of Bob as the crusading young

---

5. Kennedy was chief counsel of the Senate Permanent Subcommittee on Investigations, headed by Senator John L. McClellan (D., Arkansas) at the beginning of the probe. In January 1957, when the subcommittee's authority to investigate labor corruption was challenged and attempts were mounted to head off the investigation, the Senate created the Select Committee, specifically to look into corrupt influences in labor-management relations. Besides Chairman McClellan, the original members of the Select Committee were three other Democrats, John F. Kennedy, Patrick McNamara of Michigan and Samuel Ervin of North Carolina, and four Republicans, Irving Ives of New York, Joseph McCarthy of Wisconsin, Karl Mundt of South Dakota and Barry Goldwater of Arizona.

lawyer, struggling with the ruthless enemies of clean unions and honest management. Others saw him as a ruthless opportunist, waging a personal vendetta against Beck and Hoffa. This was the view that Hoffa and his henchmen sought to foster, and despite the McClellan Committee's findings, despite passage of the Labor Reform Act and despite the convictions of Beck, Hoffa and more than one hundred of Hoffa's associates in and outside the union, many people, if they did not actually feel sorry for Hoffa, at best gave Bob scant credit for his record as chief counsel for the committee.

It is true that there were elements of the crusader in the energy and enthusiasm with which Bob went after the labor racketeers. His keen sense of competitiveness could not help but have intruded into the long battle of wits and power that ensued with Hoffa. But "vendetta" means "vengeance," and the pursuit of Beck and Hoffa was not based on any hankering for revenge. There was nothing personal about it. Neither Beck nor Hoffa had done anything to the Kennedys, but it quickly became clear to Bob that they were doing something to the United States. As the committee first unmasked Beck's thievery and then hacked through the massive corruption around Hoffa, it literally became a question with Bob of who was going to control important areas of the nation: rich, powerful hoodlums and racketeers or honest local authorities. By late 1958 he was telling his chief aides and investigators: "We have to be successful because it can't be any other way. Hoffa has said every man has his price, and you have seen his corruptive influence spread to the leading citizens of the towns across the United States, the leading bankers, the leading businessmen, officials, judges, Congressmen. If he can get them to do his bidding, if he can buy them, then you can see what it means to the country. Either we are going to be successful or he is going to have the country."

From the outset Bob appeared to me to be more concerned with what corruption, dishonesty and arbitrary abuse of power were doing to the democratic process and individual morality than he was with the specifics of the crimes that were being uncovered. I noticed almost immediately that as he delved into the activities of

Beck and Frank Brewster he began to identify with the rank-and-file members of the union. He began to express concern that men who worked as hard as truck drivers, gas station attendants and warehousemen were being cheated and being denied not only the right to have a voice in their own affairs, but often the right to a job itself.

Within forty-eight hours after our first meeting, we had put Bob in contact with a group of Teamsters who had been protesting unsuccessfully for years about the operations of Local 174, the largest in the state. They had evidence that Brewster was spending union funds for his personal benefit, particularly for the upkeep of his thoroughbred race horses. We also introduced him to two men who had close knowledge of some of Beck's operations and whose identities, though both men are deceased, I still feel honor-bound not to reveal. One was a Teamster official and the other was a businessman. Both had prospered under Beck and Brewster, but their knowledge of the misuse of union funds gnawed at their consciences. They were troubled men, and they provided information that eventually proved helpful.

Much more important leads were to come, however, from a man of whom Staples and I were not aware. Before Bob left Washington a friend suggested that it might be worthwhile to look up an acquaintance of his who was working in Seattle. Bob did, and this man, whom Bob identified in *The Enemy Within* only as "Mr. X," provided the basis for Beck's downfall. Bob and Jerome Adlerman stayed in Seattle only two days, but within two weeks Bob was back, this time accompanied by Carmine Bellino, the subcommittee's implacable chief accountant. Bellino, within a few months after becoming an FBI agent in 1934, had helped capture John Dillinger, and he went on to become chief of the FBI's accounting section. He resigned in 1946 and in the ensuing ten years had participated in many Congressional committee investigations.

Bob and Bellino registered under assumed names at the Olympic Hotel and dug into the information they had received from "Mr. X" and the others. After dinner one mild November night, while we were walking along Sixth Avenue, Bob asked me: "Guess who has been cheating on his income taxes—Beck or Brewster?"

"Brewster," I answered without hesitation.

Bob smiled slyly at Bellino.

"Wrong," he said. "It's Beck."

Chapter 2

The Matter of McCarthyism

WITHIN FOUR MONTHS the essential facts of Beck's theft and misuse of Teamster funds were laid before the American people. Bob and Bellino presented the results of their investigation in hearings which were dramatic not only for the amount of information that came to light but also for the contrast between Beck's posturing, self-righteous bluster, Senator McClellan's sad-voiced, moralistic pronouncements and Bob's boyish appearance and high-pitched, penetrating questions. The hearings were televised and reported in great detail, and one effect was to make Bob a national figure in a matter of weeks. He was thirty-one years old. He emerged on the national scene amid great controversy and high drama, and there he was to remain—to be tested again and again in the crucible of public life and to be embroiled in controversy to the moment of his death.

He longed to be judged by what he did or did not do, rather than by what someone said or felt about him. However, one of the things he did—serving on the staff of the Senate Permanent Investigations Subcommittee in 1953 while the late Senator Joseph P. McCarthy was chairman—plagued him to the end. Because of it, many persons never fully trusted him. Despite all that he accomplished and all that he stood for in the next fourteen years, his association with McCarthy was the reason batches of voters in the liberal precincts of West Los Angeles, the San Fernando Valley and the San Francisco Bay area gave for hesitating to vote for him in the fateful California primary. In the 1964 New York Senate race, Senator Jacob Javits campaigned with telling effect in support of Senator Kenneth Keating by reminding New York City's liberal voters that Bob owed "an explanation why he chose to make his start in public life by joining the staff of Senator Joseph McCarthy's Investigations Subcommittee in January 1953, at a time when Senator McCarthy's record on civil liberties and reckless charges was already too clear."

It was a fair point to raise, but, like many campaign charges, it was an oversimplification, ignoring one important point: after observing McCarthy's methods closely, Bob had resigned from the committee and had actively opposed McCarthy. However, the record was cloudy. Bob did not break with McCarthy until more than three years after the Wisconsin demagogue became a national figure by making the spurious claim, during a Lincoln Day speech in Wheeling, West Virginia, that 205 (later reduced to 57) "card-carrying Communists" were employed by the State Department. The record was also unclear because after McCarthy had been censured by the Senate in 1954 and had become a pariah to President Eisenhower and most persons in public life, Bob refused to turn his back on him. When McCarthy was buried May 7, 1957, in the cemetery of St. Mary's Roman Catholic Church in Appleton, Wisconsin, Bob was one of a handful of persons who flew from Washington to Wisconsin for the services. He could tell McCarthy to his face that his methods were leading him to disaster; he could write a report highly critical of the Senator. Yet the man's slow self-destruction saddened him, and because of that and because they had enjoyed some good times when McCarthy had been a guest in the Kennedy home, Bob would not turn away from him, especially when McCarthy's career was in ruins and he was being scorned by his peers. So Bob could make a point of talking to him, of being courteous and solicitous and of traveling halfway across the country for the last rites when many a man who had ridden with McCarthy in his heyday remained in Washington.

That was Bob's code, and if his relationship with McCarthy was unclear and uncomplimentary to himself, it was largely Bob's own doing. However, there was a third factor. Almost all authors of books and articles about Bob from the late 1950's on simply accepted as fact that Bob had been an unabashed McCarthy devotee, that it was a black chapter early in his career to be mentioned pointedly but hurriedly, and thus it became a fixed part of the stereotype. David Halberstam in his book *The Unfinished Odyssey of Robert Kennedy* quoted a newsman covering the Indiana primary as saying to one of Bob's speech writers: "What I can't stand about your guy, what I find hard to stomach, is that back right after the war, when I came home, and I led an open housing drive on the campus, and it was a lonely fight, your guy was on the McCarthy Committee. That's what I can't stand. And now he's a big liberal." And Elizabeth B. Drew, the *Atlantic Monthly*'s careful, perceptive Washington contributing editor, would write in 1969 about "the evolving Kennedy, the one who could begin as an enthusiastic McCarthyite and end as the most insistent voice in politics that we could be better." But Bob wasn't an "enthusiastic McCarthyite," nor did he participate in the destructive investigations of Communism in high places that were the trademark of the McCarthy Committee. The McCarthy-Kennedy relationship deserved deeper study than it got, not only in the interest of accuracy, but because closer examination would have provided deep insight into Bob at an early point in his career and would have told a good deal about his character.

He came to the McCarthy Committee after graduating from the University of Virginia Law School, having worked as a young lawyer in the Department of Justice. He also had managed his brother Jack's senatorial campaign, which unseated the incumbent, Henry Cabot Lodge, Jr. It was January 1953. Dwight D. Eisenhower was about to be inaugurated as the nation's thirty-third President, and having this fatherly national hero in the White House held promise of a more peaceful time. But discontent and anger were widespread, not only because the Korean War was grinding through its third year but also because of a blinding fear of Communist adventures abroad and of Communist subversion at home. The years after V-J Day had not fulfilled the wartime hopes for a peaceful world. Instead, the Communist movement emerged as a threatening world-wide force, symbolized by the Iron Curtain, the Communist take-over of China, the Berlin airlift and finally the war in Korea. At home the fear was heightened by the theft of the nation's atomic secrets and prompted an ever-widening hunt for Communist spies, "security risks" and persons in government of dubious "loyalty." Into that pit of fear and frustration stepped McCarthy, an almost unnoticed member of the Senate when he traveled to West Virginia on February 9, 1950, to raise his cry about Communists in the State Department. Quickly his step became heavier and his voice louder, for his charge—that there existed a "conspiracy so immense, an infamy so black as to dwarf any in the history of man . . . [a con-spiracy directed] to the end that we shall be contained, frustrated and finally fall victim to Soviet intrigue from within and Russian military might from without"—found a receptive, growing audi-ence from frightened people looking for a scapegoat. He would be praised by many like the columnist Holmes Alexander, who wrote: "More than any man alive, McCarthy has awakened, alerted and aroused the American people—and through them, their lawmakers —to an implacable hatred of the Communist conspiracy."

Support came gradually, but as it built, McCarthy, with a disre-gard for individual rights, kept flinging charges, naming names and broadening his charges of conspiracy until they included even the revered General of the Army George C. Marshall, who was Eisen-hower's benefactor, President Truman's Secretary of State and, as much as any man, the craftsman of victory in World War II. Though a Senate committee had been unable in 1950 to find any substance to the charges that Communists were rampant in the State Department—not even one, though some there may have been —the more irresponsible McCarthy became, the more he scowled and made charges in his deep, singsong voice, the more he attacked and defeated his critics, the more his power grew. By January 1953 fewer and fewer political figures dared to oppose him openly, and it was a fact, as Richard Rovere later wrote in his book *Senator Joe McCarthy*, that he held two Presidents captive.

With the election of Eisenhower, the Republicans regained control of the Senate. As ranking Republican on the Government Operations Committee, McCarthy became its chairman and also assumed the chairmanship of its Investigations Subcommittee. For a brief period after the 1952 election McCarthy asserted that he was through hunting subversives. He said in an interview, "The picture has so infinitely changed. Now it will be unnecessary for me to conduct a one-man campaign to expose Communists in government. We have a new President who doesn't want party-line thinkers or fellow travelers. He will conduct the fight." But before the year was out, McCarthy announced that, despite the election of Eisenhower, he would continue to expose Communists and fellow travelers in the government, and he embarked on the course that would send him into oblivion.

It was at that time and in those circumstances that Bob decided to become an assistant counsel on the staff of the Investigations Subcommittee. Whether he had been at all troubled or concerned by McCarthy's heavy-handed disregard for basic civil liberties—the issue that so intensely stirred many of McCarthy's critics—is unclear. Probably he had not given much thought to it. He and his brothers had been prodded by their parents to compete, to excel and to serve in the government. They had been taught by a master— their father—how to confront difficult problems, how to analyze their alternatives and decide on courses of action likely to produce the results they sought. They grew to manhood in an atmosphere of wealth, economic liberalism, political involvement and public service. But the political liberalism and the concern for individual rights which marked their careers as public men developed more from what they experienced in later life than from what they learned at home. In Bob's case, working on the McCarthy Committee was an eye-opening experience, one that had lasting impact.

Although Joseph P. Kennedy had for some time been friendly to McCarthy and approved of his Communist-hunting activities, it was not McCarthy but a man whom Bob much admired, the late James McInerney, who recruited Bob for the committee staff. McInerney, a former FBI agent, had been an Assistant Attorney General in the Truman Administration and Bob had worked under him in the Department of Justice. Another ex-FBI agent, Francis (Frip) Flanagan, was counsel for the Investigations Subcommittee, and with a new chairman about to take over, Flanagan was looking for able new faces for the committee staff. McInerney recommended Bob, and Bob joined the staff after being interviewed by Flanagan and talking with McCarthy. John Kennedy didn't think it was a good idea, but Joseph Kennedy did. Unquestionably, his father's encouragement, despite his brother's disapproval, weighed heavily in Bob's decision. Another factor was Bob's strong belief that investigation of Communist activity in the country was needed. The fact that it was the most controversial domestic issue undoubtedly also figured in the decision, triggering that need and desire of his to be where the action was. But it would last only six months, indignation and dismay over McCarthy's tactics soon blotting out any feelings Bob had about the value of the committee's work and the need to be involved in it.

At the time Bob was joining Flanagan's staff, McCarthy set up what was to become a second investigative team and made a fatal mistake by selecting a bright but flawed young New York attorney, Roy M. Cohn, to head it. George Sokolsky,[1] an influential, conserva-

1. From 1953 on, the careers of Robert Kennedy and Roy Cohn were destined to collide sharply and repeatedly. Perhaps nothing was stranger than their relationships with Sokolsky, who was a long-time friend of Cohn's family and who regarded Cohn almost as a son. In 1959 when Cohn engineered a deal which made him chief executive of the Lionel Corporation, the toy train manufacturing firm, Sokolsky invested with Cohn and became a Lionel director. They were leading officers in the American Jewish League Against Communism. Shortly after President Kennedy took office in 1961, Sokolsky wrote Bob asking to interview him. A few weeks later, Bob, while in New York City, visited Sokolsky in his apartment. Sokolsky, though weakened by cancer, diabetes and heart trouble, was still writing three columns a week. They quickly developed a rapport as Sokolsky talked about his experiences in Russia during the Revolution and in later years in China and questioned Bob about the New Frontier. "For the first time since the beginning of the Republic, young men are in control of government," he said. "If you can't make it, this system can't survive." The promise of the New Frontier with its young men in key positions seemed strangely invigorating to the old conservative, and often thereafter Bob, when in New York, would make a point of visiting Sokolsky for long talks that ranged over philosophy, the historic events Sokolsky had witnessed and current problems. Occasionally, Sokolsky mentioned Cohn, particularly in expressing concern over Lionel's deepening financial problems. On December 11, 1962, at the end of an hour-long talk, Sokolsky walked with Bob to the apartment elevator and bade him good-bye with a cryptic remark. "I'm looking closer at Roy," he said. Two days later Sokolsky was dead and, possibly for the last time, Cohn and Kennedy met face

tive newspaper columnist, whose strong anti-Communist views carried great weight with McCarthy, recommended Cohn to him. A precocious student, Cohn had graduated from Columbia Law School by the time he was twenty. He had made a strong record as an investigator and prosecutor in the Department of Justice. The high point of his career at Justice was his participation as an Assistant United States Attorney in the espionage trial of Julius and Ethel Rosenberg, who died in Sing Sing Prison's electric chair after being convicted in 1951 of passing atomic bomb secrets to a Soviet spy ring. But along with a resourceful mind and a flair for prosecution, Cohn also brought to the committee a petulant, arrogant personality and a compulsion to attract attention. He could not, as Bill Henry, the veteran columnist of the Los Angeles *Times*, once wrote, "walk into a drugstore and order a chocolate malt without telephoning half a dozen people, telling the proprietor that he kept the malt and the ice cream in the wrong place, being overeffusive in thanking the soda jerk and getting into a raging argument with half his fellow customers at the counter." And Cohn brought one thing more to the committee—a friend, G. David Schine, a twenty-five-year-old millionaire whose qualifications to investigate Communism seemed limited to having written a brief treatise purporting to define Communism which was placed in rooms of the hotels his family owned and to having prepared an outline on psychological warfare.

With Cohn as subcommittee counsel and Schine as an unpaid "chief consultant," the two quickly launched into eager-beaver investigations which brought considerable publicity to themselves, uncovered little or no evidence of Communist subversion and ensnarled McCarthy in embittering, mounting controversy. They began with a destructive investigation of the Voice of America. In April they dashed in and out of ten European cities in seventeen days in a ridiculous expedition to remove books that were suspect

---

to face. Cohn was standing on the steps of the Central Synagogue in midtown Manhattan when Bob arrived to attend Sokolsky's funeral. Seeing Bob, Cohn stepped down, extended his hand and said, "George would have been glad that you came." They shook hands, Bob nodded and continued up the steps into the synagogue.

from the stacks of U.S. Information Service libraries. It seemed ludicrous then that such half-baked mischief would be taken seriously—that Cohn and Schine would get any appreciable public support, much less backing from members of the Congress—but it was. To Robert Kennedy, the Cohn-Schine show was an appalling travesty of how a Congressional investigation should be conducted. He was at that time working under Flanagan's direction, in an investigation of trade between Communist China and our Western Allies while American and other Allied soldiers fought under the United Nations flag against Chinese troops in Korea. This investigation brought Bob before the subcommittee late in May to testify that Allied nations had engaged in substantial trading with Red China and that two British-owned ships, although flying the Panamanian flag, had transported Communist Chinese troops. The British challenged the charge, but Arthur Krock, the *New York Times* columnist, cited it as an example of the kind of finding that could come from a well-conducted Congressional investigation. By that time, however, Bob had become convinced that McCarthy either would not or could not control Cohn and Schine, and he had decided to leave the committee. McCarthy provided the last straw in June 1953 by kicking Flanagan upstairs to the staff of the Government Operations Committee and placing Cohn in over-all charge of the subcommittee staff. Bob went to McCarthy, protested Cohn's promotion, warned that it would lead to McCarthy's ruin and resigned. Three years later, when I questioned Bob about his relationship with McCarthy, he said: "It was easy for anybody—anybody but McCarthy—to see what was happening. He did not have much use for Schine, but he thought highly of Cohn. He thought he was terrific. And there really was no sense to it all. The way Cohn and Schine were going, not checking anything, not really investigating, McCarthy was out of his mind to go along with them. But he was intoxicated—driven—by all the publicity and they were providing him with headlines. It had to end in disaster, but Joe couldn't see it."

The three Democratic Senators on the subcommittee—McClellan, Henry M. Jackson of Washington and Stuart Symington of

Missouri—also were fed up. On July 10, when the subcommittee's four-man Republican majority voted to give McCarthy sole power to hire and fire staff employees, McClellan, Jackson and Symington took leave from the subcommittee, asserting that they would not return as long as McCarthy's one-man rule remained in force.

That month there was one more occurrence, affecting a member of the subcommittee staff, that would set the wheels in motion for the final drama. The Army drafted Schine. Cohn was beside himself. During the next three months he pressured the Army to give Schine a direct commission and he sought a position for Schine in the Central Intelligence Agency so that he could avoid military service altogether. When these efforts failed, Cohn badgered the Army to give Private Schine preferential treatment, and the record was to show that McCarthy also intervened in Schine's behalf. Transcripts of monitored telephone calls to Army Secretary Robert T. Stevens revealed several statements by McCarthy, including the following:

> I would like to ask you one personal favor. For God's sake, don't put Dave in service and assign him back on my committee. . . . He is a good boy, but there is nothing indispensable about him. . . . If he could get off weekends, Roy—it is one of the few things I have seen him completely unreasonable about—he thinks Dave should be a general and work from the penthouse of the Waldorf.

Schine was inducted into the Army on November 3, 1953, and by that time McCarthy and Cohn's dispute with the Army had broadened into open bickering and browbeating as the subcommittee began investigating Communist influence in the Army, centering on an alleged espionage plot at radar laboratories at Fort Monmouth, New Jersey. On a nationwide television broadcast, November 24, McCarthy accused the Army of "coddling" Communists, and in so doing, barged headlong into an irreconcilable breach with the Eisenhower Administration, for the charge carried with it the insinuation that the President, too, was guilty of "coddling" traitors in the military.

By March 1954, McCarthy, often acting as a one-man subcommittee, was flailing away at the Army with strident demands and accusations of Communist subversion. The Army retaliated by releasing a report asserting that Cohn had threatened to "wreck the Army" unless Schine received favored treatment, a charge which Cohn denied and which McCarthy branded as an attempt to "blackmail" the subcommittee into calling off its investigation at Fort Monmouth. Five days later, the subcommittee, with Senator Mundt as acting chairman, voted to make a special investigation into the charges and countercharges, and on April 22, in the chandeliered Senate Caucus Room, there began one of the most boisterous, disorderly, ludicrous spectacles in the history of Congress—the Army-McCarthy hearings.

McClellan, Jackson and Symington had returned to the subcommittee in January after its procedures were "revised" to require staff members to be hired with the approval of a majority of the members, to give the Democrats a voice in the decision to hold public hearings and to allow them to select a minority counsel. They chose Bob, and when the Army-McCarthy hearings got under way, he sat with them on the minority side of the committee table, a slight figure, with neatly trimmed short hair and horn-rim glasses, wedged inconspicuously between McClellan and Symington.

In 35 sessions, 187 hours of live television over a period of 57 days, McCarthy and Cohn battled with Secretary Stevens and his aides under the klieg lights of the hearing room. Millions of Americans watched with charged emotions. McCarthy's repeated tactic—scornful, almost insolent interruptions: "Point of order, point of order, Mr. Chairman"—became a national colloquialism. The principal participants—Stevens; John G. Adams, counselor of the Army; H. Struve Hensel, Assistant Secretary of Defense; Joseph N. Welch, the whimsical, courtly special counsel for the Army; Ray H. Jenkins, the blunt, earthy special counsel for the subcommittee; and the subcommittee members (Republicans Mundt, Everett M. Dirksen of Illinois, Charles E. Potter of Michigan and Henry C. Dworshak of Idaho; and Democrats McClellan, Symington and Jackson)—came, along with McCarthy, Cohn and Schine, to be recognized in the streets, admired or hated wherever they went.

Bob remained virtually unnoticed. He figured publicly in the hearings only once, and that occurred out of sight of the television cameras—in a sharp and bitter exchange with Cohn. It took place at the end of a session in which Jackson had derided a psychological-warfare plan that Schine had drafted. Bob insisted that Cohn had come up to him and said through clenched teeth, "You can tell Jackson we are going to get him Monday," and threatened to bring out that Jackson had "written something favorably inclined toward Communists." Cohn denied making any threats and said he had asked Bob if he thought it fair of him to be advising the Democrats since he had a "personal hatred" for Cohn. Newsmen heard Bob say, "Don't you make any warnings to us about Democratic Senators," and Cohn reply, "I'll make any warnings to you that I want to any time, anywhere." Senator Potter in his book *Days of Shame* described the encounter as follows:

> As the crowd started out of the Caucus Room, I was watching him [Cohn]. He had sent a staff man out a few minutes before and now the man came back with a file marked "Jackson's Record." I watched Cohn approach Bobby Kennedy, the counsel for the minority Democrats, and there was a heated conversation between them. . . .
>
> Cohn denied that he made the threat and Henry Jackson said that his was not the first one aimed at him during the hearings. It was unfortunate that this exchange between Roy Cohn and the future Attorney General was not beamed out to the television audience. It might have erased the completely false performance of Roy Cohn, boy investigator.

Enough of Cohn's abrasiveness and McCarthy's heavy-handedness did come through on television, however, to materially change public opinion. McCarthy and Cohn were their own worst enemies as they counterattacked recklessly. The culmination came in McCarthy's totally below-the-belt attack on Fred Fisher, a young lawyer in Welch's Boston office, and Welch's moving, memorable reply: "Let us not assassinate this lad further, Senator. You have done enough. Have you left no sense of decency?" It was the moment—if any moment in those turbulent days could be singled out —when McCarthy began to slide swiftly into oblivion. Before the hearings the Gallup Poll found that a sample of the nation's ninety million adults showed that 50 percent had a favorable opinion of

McCarthy and that 29 percent held him in disfavor. By August favorable opinion had slipped to 36 percent, while the number expressing an unfavorable opinion had increased to 51 percent.

On August 31 the subcommittee issued its report in the form of separate summaries and findings of fact by the Republicans and the Democrats. The Republicans held that Cohn had been "unduly aggressive and persistent" in seeking special treatment for Schine, that the charge of improper influence against McCarthy was not sustained but that he had condoned Cohn's efforts and in so doing failed to control his staff. The Democrats asserted that the evidence established that McCarthy and Cohn merited "severe criticism" for "inexcusable actions"—Cohn for misusing and abusing his office, McCarthy for acquiescing in and condoning it. Both criticized the Army. The Republicans said the evidence indicated that Secretary Stevens tried "to terminate or influence" the Fort Monmouth investigation. The Democrats said Stevens sought to block the investigation by appeasing McCarthy and Cohn and, in so doing, demonstrated "inexcusable indecisiveness and lack of sound administrative judgement." Both findings of fact were based on a seventy-eight-page summary of the evidence which Bob prepared. He also drafted the Democrats' report, which was much more detailed and more severe in its criticism than the majority report.

On December 2, after another round of stormy hearings, the Senate voted 67–22 to censure McCarthy for his actions toward a Senate subcommittee which in 1951–52 had investigated his financial dealings and for his abuse of the bipartisan Select Committee that had recommended that he be censured. The vote floored McCarthy. He was through; destined in the two and a half years remaining to him to live in a private hell, discredited with a majority of the people, detested and ignored by President Eisenhower and the other moderate leaders of his party; a man tormented and increasingly ill; a would-be leader of the people, deflated and disabled.

By the standards of conscience and personal conduct to which Bob held himself, he had proved where he stood on the issue of McCarthyism by having quit the subcommittee in protest against the way it was operating; by having served as minority counsel to the Democrats; by having analyzed the evidence in the Army-McCarthy hearing so accurately that it was accepted by the Republicans as well as the Democrats; and by having drafted the unforgiving minority report. It was consistent with everything he did in the next fourteen years that for him those acts themselves would be what mattered, and that he would not feel required to denounce McCarthyism or turn on McCarthy when he was beaten and abandoned. Still, aside from McCarthy's careless, overzealous investigations of Communist activity, there were aspects of his life that were totally out of keeping with Bob's code of conduct, and they must be taken into account. The Senate subcommittee which investigated McCarthy's finances found virtually incontestable evidence that a substantial amount of money collected for "the fight for America" had been used by McCarthy to speculate in soybean futures; that McCarthy received a $10,000 fee from a home-building firm for writing an article and then helped the company obtain a loan from the Reconstruction Finance Corporation; that McCarthy borrowed $20,000 from a lobbyist for a soft-drink firm and then opposed sugar rationing which limited the company's production. When the subcommittee sought to question McCarthy about his financial dealings, he failed to appear on five separate occasions, saying, "I don't answer charges, I make them."

When I realized that Bob not only had worked on the McCarthy Committee but also was on more than just speaking terms with McCarthy, I was deeply troubled. As I noted earlier, the Seattle *Times* had opposed McCarthy and what he stood for, and I had been involved in what the paper did to implement that stand. We had worked to clear a number of federal employees in Seattle who had been caught in the demoniac exorcising of suspected loyalty risks —a postman, a National Labor Relations Board lawyer, a General Services Administration administrator and others. In 1952 I had decided to vote for Adlai Stevenson for President because General Eisenhower failed to speak out directly against McCarthy. Thus I had to get to the bottom of the Kennedy-McCarthy relationship before I could fully trust Bob. In the early months of 1957 we discussed it often. What I found was that Bob in those days had for

McCarthy only one feeling—pity; pity for an acquaintance who could be a pleasant companion but who had made a ruin of his career; pity for the men and women and their families whom McCarthy had forced needlessly and unfairly to live under a cloud.

For me, the final judgment was based on how Bob conducted himself as a Congressional investigator, whether he took responsibility for the testimony of his witnesses, how much effort he made to confirm privately and in advance every statement or charge that was to be presented in public, whether he sought the truth and did not leave it hanging in the balance. And that he did.

Finally, I came to understand why Bob could oppose McCarthy but could not abandon him. It was a quality that underscored all his relationships, that regardless of the passage of time or a change of circumstances he would go to great lengths to help friends or acquaintances, particularly if they were in trouble. This is what he demonstrated with McCarthy, and I was to see it over and over. In the New York senatorial campaign in 1964 I heard Bob give what I regard as the best one-line description of his philosophy in this regard. It came in an offhand answer to a student, and the friend in question was not McCarthy, but Congressman Charles Buckley, then the controversial Democratic boss of the Bronx.

In the tough infighting in 1959 and 1960 for the Democratic nomination for President, the Kennedys had sought the support of Buckley and other powerful Democratic power brokers in New York. Buckley sided with the Kennedys early in the struggle. With two other bosses, he outmaneuvered opposing Democratic leaders to get John Kennedy 104½ votes of the New York delegation to the Democratic Convention in Los Angeles. Without those votes the nomination probably would have been lost.

Buckley was a product of old-fashioned ward politics. He was much more a throwback to the world of John and Robert Kennedy's grandfather, John F. Fitzgerald, the celebrated "Honey Fitz," than he was a proconsul of the New Frontier. He was hard-boiled, irascible and at times profane, but he knew where power was and how to use it. Once committed, he kept his word. He delivered the votes in Los Angeles and the Kennedys never forgot it. In 1962 Buckley's health was failing and his power was declining. He was under heavy attack from the Reform Democrats and the *New York Times*, who regarded him as the embodiment of machine politics at its worst. Nevertheless, President Kennedy and Bob publicly supported Buckley for re-election to Congress. He won. In 1964, when Buckley again sought re-election, Bob journeyed to the Bronx to be the main speaker at a testimonial dinner for Buckley.[2] That fall when Bob campaigned for the Senate, he was asked repeatedly to explain how, if he promised to provide new, vibrant leadership for New York, he could support an old-line machine pol like Buckley. Invariably, Bob would reply that the Kennedys had gone to Buckley in 1960 and asked for his support. "If he was good enough for us to ask for his help in 1960, he was good enough to get our help in 1962 and 1964 when he needed it," was Bob's standard answer. Before a student audience in the field house at St. John Fisher College in Rochester, a young man asked the inevitable question about Buckley, and Bob gave his usual answer. Then he paused and looked thoughtfully at the field house roof for several moments. "You know," he said, looking again at the students, "that's the way relationships between men ought to be."

In the last analysis, the record of the Kennedy-McCarthy relationship shows that Bob was neither a devil for having worked for McCarthy nor a saint for not having turned his back when McCarthy became an outcast. It shows further that by his conscience and his conduct he was never a McCarthyite.

2. Buckley was defeated in the Democratic primary. He died January 22, 1967, at the age of seventy-six. Bob, of course, went to the funeral.

Chapter 3

Moving In on the Teamsters

IF ANY GOOD came out of the McCarthy debacle, it was that McCarthy's and Cohn's tactics so disgusted and angered the Congress and so degraded the legislative process before the eyes of millions of citizens that reforms were forthcoming. Under pressure of public opinion, the House in 1955 amended its rules to provide for minimum standards for investigative committees. The rules defined procedures and guaranteed the accused greater protection, including the right to counsel and the right to have defamatory or incriminating testimony heard in closed session. In the Senate, committee chairmen made more of an effort to see that the excesses of the McCarthy era were not indulged in. It is never possible to fully protect against an unfair question being asked or a witness blurting out unverified, damaging testimony, but the fact is that after 1954 McCarthy-type abuses occurred less often not only in Congressional hearings but also in those of the state legislatures.

When the Democrats regained control of Congress in the 1954 election, Senator McClellan took over the chairmanship of the subcommittee and Bob became chief counsel. As they directed first the subcommittee and later the Rackets Committee, McCarthy's mishandling of his investigations and his demagoguery were never very far from their minds. Both had left the subcommittee in protest against McCarthy's methods. When McClellan led the Democrats off the committee, it was not an idle, feeble protest, considering the atmosphere of 1953 and the fact that a majority of McClellan's constituents in Arkansas were pro-McCarthy. It was an act of political courage. When Bob wrote *The Enemy Within* in 1959, he referred to the antics of McCarthy, Cohn and Schine as examples of how an investigating committee should not operate:

Much of the criticism of Congressional committees could be avoided by sound investigative work before a case is presented. I was an assistant counsel to the Senate Permanent Subcommittee on Investigations when Senator McCarthy was its chairman. I lasted only six months. With two exceptions, no real research was ever done. Most of the investigations were instituted on the basis of some preconceived notion by the chief counsel or his staff members and not on the basis of any information that had been developed. Cohn and Schine claimed they knew from the outset what was wrong; and they were not going to allow the facts to interfere. Therefore no real spade work that might have destroyed some of their pet theories was ever undertaken.

Neither McClellan nor Bob needed to have observed McCarthy and Cohn at close range, however, to have conducted their investigations over the next five years more even-handedly. McClellan and Bob were concerned primarily with facts and evidence and were willing to work unusually hard in pursuit of the truth. Furthermore, long before McCarthy had appeared on the national scene, McClellan was urging Congress to make rules for its investigations which would ensure that witnesses received fair hearings and a chance to answer charges made against them.

Born in rural Arkansas and destined to a life of struggle and tragedy, including the death of all three sons—one of spinal meningitis in World War II and two in accidents—McClellan had risen to a position of respect and power in the Senate by dint of careful preparation, inner restraint and hard work. He brought to his committee work a hard-shelled concept of justice which *Time* described as "the personal code of a man who has had to learn the hard way to control his strength, who has had to beat down wild winds of temper, and learn that the law—in whose cold virtue he once sought escape from a world that used him cruelly—must be tempered by understanding." He had been elected to Congress first in 1934 largely on his record as prosecuting attorney of Arkansas's 7th Judicial District. The first time a Democratic whip sought to tell him how to vote on a bill, McClellan told him: "Look, you don't know me and I don't know you, but we're going to get to know each other pretty darn quick. I vote as I please." If he was anything, he was his own man—outwardly cordial, but a loner; a conservative, never a New Dealer or a New Frontiersman; a rugged protector of Arkansas's interests and an implacable battler against waste and corruption in government.

Thus by the mid-1950's McClellan was highly respected in the Senate as a solid, even-handed, relentless investigator, and in Bob, despite the twenty-nine-year difference in their ages, he found the perfect partner for the work that lay ahead. Later, they were to draw apart, for McClellan's concern for the rights of workingmen did not extend to the rights of black men. In the sixties they were to be on opposite sides in the fight for civil rights, on such issues as immigration reform and the Supreme Court's decisions in school desegregation and in protecting the rights of the accused, and especially in the controversy over the Kennedy Administration's decision on the multibillion-dollar contract award for construction of the TFX tactical fighter plane. Bob and McClellan would retain a warm personal respect for each other and remain closely allied in trying to blunt the power of organized crime, but they would never be as close as they were when they formed one of the most formidable investigative teams in the history of Congress.

In the fall of 1956, as their investigation veered into labor racketeering, the extent of the corruption which they began to unearth bound them to a common purpose. The situation, particularly in the Teamsters Union, was far worse than they had suspected. They soon came to believe that the structure of representative government and individual liberty in the United States could hardly be challenged more fundamentally from within than by the misuse of enormous amounts of union funds and by the abuse of union power which Beck and Hoffa came to represent—malignancies which had to be exposed and opposed unremittingly.[1] They concentrated on the Teamsters because the union's nationwide control of transportation gives it enormous economic power and a key position in the labor movement. "When there is corruption at the top and a close association with the underworld—this kind of power is a threat to every decent person as well as to the very foundation of our democracy," Bob wrote later in his book *The Pursuit of Justice.* Other Congressional investigators had backed down under pressure after lifting the lid slightly on corruption in the Teamsters Union. With McClellan and Bob, pressure from Beck and Hoffa had the opposite effect. The more evidence of improper financial transactions, gangland connections and oppressive use of power that they found, the harder they investigated and the more determined they became to see that law violations were prosecuted and that new laws were enacted to curb the expanding power of corrupt union leaders.

They were much alike in their rugged concepts of honesty and in their particular disdain for men who accepted positions of trust and then violated those responsibilities. Neither shrank from investigating where friends or powerful interests were involved, although it must be pointed out that McClellan's later investigations of organized crime skirted inquiry into the extensive gambling operations that had thrived for years in Hot Springs, Arkansas. Without a constituency, Bob had no regional or personal boundaries to worry about. However, when he was Attorney General, he still did not back away from investigations that threatened to embarrass or give his brother's Administration discomfort because friends of the Kennedys or influential persons or organizations were involved. This, as much as his skill as an investigator, won first the respect and then the binding loyalty of the men who worked with him— men like Carmine Bellino, who said in 1958, "Bob is the only man

---

1. This conviction was held by many persons who looked into union corruption or who had their faces pushed into it—workers, union officers, shopkeepers and businessmen who refused to knuckle under; honest law enforcement officers, public officials and newsmen. Between these people and the investigators a bond of trust and common purpose formed that held fast throughout Bob's life and which continues today among those who worked with him.

I've met in government who is willing to go all the way, all the time." By that time Bellino had been involved in federal investigations for twenty-three years—eleven with the FBI and twelve with committees of the House and the Senate—and nothing happened in the next ten years to cause him to change that statement.

The basic purpose of a legislative investigation is to obtain information and evidence bearing on whether a new law is needed or an old law should be amended. A secondary purpose is to focus public attention on a situation so that remedial action may be taken, and this is a legitimate reason for a legislative hearing. Supreme Court Justice William O. Douglas in his book *We the Judges* wrote:

> The investigative function is sometimes turned to publicity purposes with the aim of making political capital out of somebody's misfortune or mistake. But the fact that power is often abused does not detract from its importance.
>
> The right to ask a question and the right to demand an answer are essential to the democratic processes. I have often thought that without those rights any government would be intolerable. Certainly modern government is so complex and involved that opportunities for machinations within the bureaucracy flourish. Only the pitiless light of publicity can restrain them. That is why the embarrassing question from the Senator or Congressman sitting at the end of the table serves a high function. His right to demand an answer spells in a crucial way the difference between the totalitarian and the democratic regime.

Justice Douglas was referring in that instance to government, but what he said would apply as well in our system to any concentration of power—in business, labor, education, communications, transportation or wherever it exists.

When a legislative committee undertakes an investigation, it takes on the responsibility to determine the truth and to present all the facts. It must also make every effort to protect individuals and organizations from false or misleading accusations and from infringement of a man's right not to be punished for his beliefs or to be compelled to give self-incriminating evidence. It is not only that the lives of individuals and the well-being of organizations are at the mercy of the committees. The quality of the legislation that might be enacted and the reputation of the Congress or the state legislature are at stake, too. McClellan and Bob understood clearly the implications of their investigation. They understood what McCarthy and Cohn did not—that what is required is a dedication to the truth and the willingness to search for it regardless of the obstacles or time involved.

In taking stock of the Rackets Committee's record, Bob reported in *The Enemy Within:*

The reason I attempted to know as much as possible about what witnesses could and would testify to, and consequently what answer they should give, is that in no other way is an orderly presentation of evidence and testimony possible. It was our job to present the facts so that members of Congress could see clearly the areas in which legislation was necessary. If we had allowed witnesses to come before the Committee with no real idea of what testimony to expect from them, without first interviewing them, studying and checking their information, we should have had utter chaos and confusion, plus many inequities. At best, every hearing would have turned into an endless fishing expedition or a guessing game, a tremendous waste of time. We should never have got anything done.

However, the most important advantage of checking and rechecking testimony is that it lessens tremendously the possibility of damaging an innocent person's reputation. A prospective witness who intended to make a charge against another person had his story checked from every possible angle. On quite a number of occasions, after checking, we did not permit him to testify.

In our investigation into the vice rackets in Portland, Oregon, we had the essential information from one witness, Jim Elkins. Because he was an ex-convict, we spent three months checking and rechecking his story before permitting him to testify in public. . . .

It is usually possible to find a witness who will testify to almost anything about a person who has been active in public life or who has taken a stand on issues; such a man is bound to have made enemies. . . . You cannot put a man—or a woman—on the stand, allow him to hurl accusations indiscriminately and, when his testimony is found to be untrue, disown him and accept no responsibility. Of course, a witness may make statements that you could not possibly have anticipated; that happened a number of times before our Committee. But at least there should be a painstaking effort to confirm everything you think he will include in his testimony. In my estimation it is not enough merely to permit the person he accuses to come in and answer the charges after they have been made; the charges should be verified and corroborated before the witness is permitted to make them. . . .

Looking back over the record, I do not know of any witness whose reputation was besmirched by our Committee. An examination of some fourteen million words of testimony shows no instance where the regular staff presented a case that was not fully and factually established and documented. We made mistakes, certainly, but in three years of hearings I can think of no case that the regular staff[2] presented for which the Committee need apologize. However, I know the record would be far different if we had not spent so much time verifying testimony and obtaining documentation.

This was the committee's record as Bob saw it, and in later years it would always rankle him that those who criticized him for having worked six months on the McCarthy Committee never seemed to take into account that there was a good deal of difference between the way the McCarthy and the McClellan committees operated. This was understandable, at least in part, because from 1957 to 1960 McClellan and Bob faced the American people as persistent, hard-driving prosecutors. If people were sickened by the corruption that was brought to light or took satisfaction in the downfall of powerful men like Dave Beck and Frank Brewster, there also was sympathy for them and there was some fear of the committee. Still, the fact is that the Rackets Committee did much to protect civil liberties by investigating deeply and carefully and by documenting and exposing abuses of power in labor and management that were infringing on the rights of thousands of workingmen and women and many other citizens. It is one thing to make speeches defending civil liberties. It is much more difficult to act effectively to halt abuses of those liberties. The motivating force behind the Rackets Committee investigation was a determination to expose an alliance of big labor and big business that was operating with comparatively little regard for the rights of union members, that was betraying the American people and corrupting our system of self-government.

My home town, Seattle, had been under Beck's thumb for twenty

2. Twice in this paragraph, Bob took pains to emphasize that he was referring to work done by the "regular staff." He took responsibility for what his investigators and his witnesses said or did, but he could not and did not take responsibility for questions asked by Senators which did result in faulty or unfair testimony being aired publicly.

years. The day of reckoning began at 10 A.M., Tuesday, February 26, 1957, when the Rackets Committee convened for its first public hearing. McClellan called the committee to order in the ornate Caucus Room of the Old Senate Office Building. He gave a brief statement outlining the committee's goals, and then the first witnesses, Wallace Turner and William Lambert of the *Oregonian*, came forward to testify. They told how they had begun investigating reports of a Seattle-directed attempt by the Teamsters to take control of pinball machines, gambling, punchboards, after-hours night clubs and protection in Portland. Turner said:

"As newspapermen, we long ago reached the limit of our ability to bring about changes that would halt the misuse of the economic power of this organization [the Teamsters Union]. Time and again we have been visited in secret places at night by honorable workingmen who complained of their inability to take action to stop the improper activities of their union leaders. Without exception, they were in terrible fear that their visits to us might become known to their union's bosses. The fear of retaliation is one of the most potent weapons to silence criticism from within the Teamsters Union in the Pacific Northwest. That fear pervades this organization."

"What do you mean by that?" McClellan asked.

"I mean the members of the union are scared to death to get out of line," said Turner. ". . . A newspaper can only go so far. Local, city, county and state officials are hampered in the performance of their duties by union power. The only hope of exposing a disgraceful condition which impairs the political and economic freedom of a city like Portland rests in such a congressional body as this one, free from such pressures."

Dave Beck had been born on June 16, 1894, in Stockton, California, and brought to Seattle four years later by his parents, who, like thousands of others, thronged into the city hoping to share in the riches of the gold strikes in the Yukon. But, unable to raise funds for the passage to Alaska, Beck's father, Lemuel, turned to his trade as a carpet cleaner and his mother, Mary, worked in a laundry. In the years of his affluence, Beck would recall waiting often with his sister outside the laundry at night for his mother, who had left home at 6 A.M. to go to work. The riches from the Yukon that transformed Seattle from a small seaport town into a bustling Western city never touched the Becks, and young Dave sold newspapers on the street after school to help make ends meet. He left Broadway High School in his junior year and found work driving a laundry truck.

The Seattle in which Beck grew up reminded Mark Twain of a character in a Horatio Alger story. Returning from a Western tour, Twain told friends that Seattle was the only city he had ever been in where you could actually feel the straining and striving of the city, as well as of its inhabitants, to grow big. Less endowed with Eastern financial backing than its two principal rivals, Tacoma and Portland, Seattle became the dominant city in what its Chamber of Commerce calls "The Evergreen Empire," largely on the daring and the energy of self-made, single-minded men. Every child in Dave Beck's day knew the story, for example, that when the Northern Pacific chose Tacoma as its terminus in 1872, threatening to keep Seattle forever in its small-sawmill-town status, the townspeople— there were less than three thousand of them—organized and began building with their own hands a rival line, the Seattle, Lakeshore & Eastern, and ultimately won for Seattle selection as the terminus for both the Great Northern and the Milwaukee Road. True, destiny nudged Seattle when the steamer *Portland* tied up at the Schwabacher Dock on July 17, 1897, with a ton of gold from the Yukon; still, it was a city that time and again made its own destiny. During Beck's formative years it was a city of boom and bust and boom again; a city of pleasant homes and unmatchable scenery; a union city with a lusty history in which radical and conservative forces contended vigorously and in which prevailed a chip-on-the-shoulder provincialism born of the frontier and of being in the northwest corner of the nation, separated by a snowcapped mountain range and three thousand miles from the center of things.

In 1936 all the economic strains and political forces in the city combined to create conditions which enabled Beck to become something much more than a successful labor leader. His dominance of the city can be dated from that year.

He had gone to war in 1918, serving in the Navy as a gunner aboard seaplanes patrolling the sky over the North Sea to repel German zeppelins. When he returned to Seattle to resume his laundry truck route, the city had not yet settled down from the tension caused by the first general strike in an American city. For five days, beginning on February 6, 1919, sixty thousand Seattle workers left their jobs, halting almost all activity throughout the city. The strike started in the shipyards, and when the Metal Trades Council asked other unions to go out in sympathy, most of the city's labor leaders were attending a rally in Chicago. Rank-and-file members in local after local—110 in all—voted to strike and formed a general strike committee which delegated power to an executive committee, later known as the Committee of Fifteen.

Soldiers were summoned to the city, but there was no violence. The strike ended as quietly as it had begun.

Returning to the city after leaving the Navy, Beck thought the strike had been a pointless outrage. He was against strikes. Even as a young truck driver before the war, he thought a strike of the laundry drivers was wrong, and, though he participated in it, he grumbled later, "You lose more in pay than you get from the raise in years." But he would remember the general strike, and so would everyone else. It was to remain a presence in the city through the prosperous twenties and in the grim, gray years of the thirties. Those who lived through it could never put it entirely from their minds. They could not forget the inconvenience or the incredible quiet, nor could they forget the fear of revolution or the uncertainty that hung over their lives for five strange days.

In the early 1920's, Beck quit a laundry truck route that was earning him $100 a week—good money in those days—to become a union official. In 1925, a few months before Bob Kennedy was born, the Teamsters gathered in Seattle for their international convention. Beck, rising through the ranks of Laundry & Dye Drivers Local 566, had just been elected president of the local. His enterprise and his organizing talent had caught the eye of the union's international president, Dan Tobin, and during the convention Beck became a part-time organizer for the international, retaining his position as president of Local 566. From that point on, determinedly reaching for respectability and financial security in the city where he had grown up in poverty, Beck methodically expanded his power through skillful organizing and hard bargaining, surrounding himself with cronies and young toughs. The creed which he preached wherever he could—at union meetings, at the bargaining table, at gatherings of civic, business and fraternal groups—could be spelled out in one word: stability. Beck favored stability backed by improved wages and working conditions for the workers; profits and secure contracts for the bosses and proscriptions against strikes, turmoil and radical ideas. He was clearly a new kind of labor leader. He appeared to many citizens to be a bulwark against the radical influences that played a spiritual, if not guiding, role in the general strike; that had long been strong among the lumber workers; that were rising on the waterfront under the leadership of the San Francisco Longshoremen's leader, Harry Bridges. And clearly he was more energetic, more inventive and more solicitous of management than the more doctrinaire, battle-scarred trade unionists who had dominated the Seattle Central Labor Council since Beck drove a laundry truck.

Beck was among the first labor leaders in the nation to go outside the traditional vertical boundaries of the American Federation of Labor to organize the unorganized regardless of the nature of their jobs. He was also among the first, if not the first, to insist that union leaders should travel in the same style as the business executives with whom they negotiated. In the early days he would compare his standards with those of the head of a laundry. Later, it would be those of the president of Frederick & Nelson, Seattle's leading department store. Still later it would be those of the head of General Motors. If the head of the laundry or Frederick's or GM drove a Cadillac, said Beck, then the head of the Teamsters in Seattle should drive a Cadillac. He provided his aides with expense accounts, encouraged them to travel like business executives and to be active in civic and political affairs so that when they dealt with any employer —however important—they did not have to go hat in hand. He himself became a force behind the scenes in Washington politics, albeit an increasingly controversial one. He became Exalted Ruler of the Benevolent and Protective Order of Elks, a member of the state parole board and ultimately president of the Board of Regents of the University of Washington.

When people met Beck for the first time, they always remembered his small, darting, pale blue eyes, his smooth pinkish cheeks and his changeable voice, which could be cajoling, threatening, commanding, solicitous or exceedingly self-righteous, shifting easily from one mood to another. As he matured, his red hair thinned until he became quite bald; his sturdy build became portly. But he did road work and exercises and kept fit. He did not smoke or drink.

Beck's new brand of union leadership showed, too, in his preference for negotiating with employers' associations. The pattern was taking shape as early as 1927 when he negotiated a contract with an association of laundry owners that gave his drivers $18 a week and commissions of 12 percent on everything they delivered. The commissions were based on a standardized price list for the laundries. The Teamsters were charged the following year with conspiring to fix prices. They were acquitted, and through the years any suggestion that the Teamsters were engaged in fixing prices would exasperate Beck. "Any intelligent person knows Dave Beck can't fix prices," he would retort. And yet as he organized the unorganized —bakery workers, gas station attendants, brewery workers, warehousemen, retail clerks, automobile salesmen and many others who did not drive trucks—retailers, no matter how small, fell victim to picket lines, stink bombs or worse if they cut prices. During the 1930's the Teamsters were accused from time to time of doing violence to shop owners who cut prices, but the Teamsters were seldom brought to court. Except for a grand jury subpoena which caused Beck not to set foot in the State of Oregon for twenty years to avoid being questioned about labor violence, he stayed above the battle. But his methods were effective. For example, the breweries on Puget Sound did not have competition from Budweiser, Schlitz, Hamm's, Pabst Blue Ribbon or other nationally distributed Eastern beers for years because the Teamsters refused to unload freight cars hauling those brands. Eastern Washington farmers were stopped at the summit of Snoqualmie Pass or Stevens Pass and required to take on union truck drivers if they wanted to sell their products in Seattle. By 1936 not much moved on wheels in Seattle and not much was sold over the counters that did not have some form of blessing from Beck's headquarters.

On August 13, 1936, the American Newspaper Guild struck the *Post-Intelligencer*, a Hearst newspaper, over the firing of two long-time employees for union activity. The Guild's picket line was quickly augmented by Longshoremen, members of other unions and individual citizens. The *P-I*'s management attempted to continue publication with supervisory and nonunion help but gave up as violence swirled outside the plant. Beck moved his Teamsters in to support the strikers, and the *P-I* was sealed off, the first large newspaper in the world to suspend publication because of a strike by its editorial staff. The paper was unable to publish during the rest of August, through September and October and into November. Feelings and positions hardened, and the business establishment shuddered with anger, foreboding, frustration and fear. The voice of the establishment, Colonel C. B. Blethen, publisher of the *Times*, thundered editorially: "How do you like the looks of Dave Beck's gun now?" That sentence was to cost the *Times* $10,000 in libel damages, and, though it was not literally correct, it was an accurate reflection of how the city's business leaders felt. In mid-November Beck moved to end the strike.

"What are your terms?" asked Harvey Kelly, a Hearst labor relations man, and Beck replied: "A partnership between management and labor with labor getting a better cut of the profits. We'll keep the radicals out of the picture."

The *P-I* resumed publication, and the Newspaper Guild won recognition, a contract and an impressive victory that spurred Guild organizing efforts in many other cities. But Beck was the big winner. When he backed the strike and then was instrumental in ending it, the business establishment got the message: *If he can close the* P-I, *whom can't he close? But he respects profit-making. He keeps his word and he'll keep Harry Bridges on the waterfront.* Colonel Blethen stopped writing anti-Beck editorials, and so did the *P-I.* Oh, individual Teamsters brought actions from time to time alleging abuses of power, and in 1938 a young councilman, Arthur B. Langlie, defeated Beck's candidate for mayor, John F. Dore, but after the *P-I* strike by and large Beck did about as he pleased in dealing with businessmen and other unions and Harry Bridges never did get a foothold off the waterfront.

By 1937 the Chamber of Commerce labor relations committee had public praise for Beck and he could speak around the city telling businessmen that he was going to organize their truck drivers whether they liked it or not, and they would cheer him.

With his home base secure, he began to look beyond Puget Sound. In 1937 he originated a new concept in the Teamsters Union by bringing the district councils and all the locals in the eleven Western states, Alaska and Hawaii together within the benevolent confines of the Western Conference of Teamsters. Beck was elected president and, with a staff of organizers and an increasing number of local officials beholden to him for their jobs, he mediated intra-union problems, pushed organizing the unorganized, helped when needed to win higher wages and better working conditions and vastly increased his power, not only in the West, but also in Dan Tobin's office and in the councils of the AFL.

It was also at about this time that he began to use his talents in a serious way to make money for himself. Later, he would say it was the $10,000 he collected in libel damages from the Seattle *Times* that got him started. His first loan of any size recorded in the files of the King County auditor's office was for $21,000 from the Seattle–First National Bank. The year was 1939, and the loan enabled Beck and Brewster to buy a service station across Denny Way from the Teamsters headquarters—a station where Teamster cars would be gassed and serviced thereafter.[3] The loan also secured a comfortable relationship between Beck and the Seattle–First National, the state's largest financial institution, which established a branch across the

---

3. From 1950 to 1955 the station grossed $164,589 in Teamster business, and during those years Beck and Brewster split income of about $6,000 annually from the station.

street from Beck's office while he began to acquire property nearby.[4] And something else happened: At some point, probably during World War II, he began to regard the union's treasury as his own. The outward manifestations were an increasing number of dealings in real estate and his move from a bungalow in the University District, where he had lived for many years, to a grand estate on the shore of Lake Washington. But the full extent of his dipping into the union's funds would remain masked until 1954, when Claude Watson, Internal Revenue agent, began checking Beck's income tax returns. Beck then scurried to restore the money he had taken and attempted to give an appearance of legality to what he had done.

I have sketched Beck's background and rise to power—it would take a book to deal with it fully—because it is necessary in any assessment of Bob's conduct as chief counsel of the Rackets Committee. The confrontation with Beck was to be repeated with Hoffa and other labor moguls—Maurice Hutcheson, president of the Carpenters Union, James G. Cross, president of the Bakery and Confectionery Workers Union, and many others—avaricious men of enormous power who answered to no one. In each instance, as in the case of Beck, the early discoveries of corruption or abuse of power would challenge Bob and spur him on. There was never a sign that Bob even fleetingly considered backing off or going easy, though this was a time when probes of labor had never gone very far in Congress, nor were they very popular in those halls.

In the winter of 1956–57, as I watched the investigation of Beck gather force, two things impressed me very much. One was the skill with which Bob, Bellino and the other investigators went about their work and the effort that they made to get the facts regardless of what roadblocks were put in their way. In the case of the Teamsters in Seattle, financial records were destroyed, potential wit-

---

4. Two of his lots, adjacent to the headquarters, purchased for $39,000, were later bought by the union for $135,000.

nesses were unavailable or dropped from sight, the committee's subpoenas were ignored, and Beck postured and puffed. But the committee reconstructed the records, enforced its subpoenas and found the witnesses. I remember in December 1956, when Bob and Bellino, having overcome a good deal of delay and maneuvering, first questioned Brewster about evidence that indicated that he had used union funds for high living—not on the scale of Beck, but involving nearly $100,000. The meeting was in Brewster's office in Seattle, and that night I asked Bob how it had gone.

"All right," he said. "We covered a lot of ground and he got pretty sore. At the end he said we had no business investigating him and that he'd done nothing wrong. I told him we'd be a lot more impressed if we didn't know that he'd lied to us on several matters."

"How did he take that?"

"He took it."

The second thing that struck me was the surgical judgment the committee used in deciding which persons were to be questioned in the public hearings. The committee could have torn Seattle apart with the information it uncovered about Beck, the power he held, the people he corrupted and the amoral climate that permitted him to operate without opposition. There was no pity for the men and women who were caught up in Beck's net, but neither did one sense that Bob and the others either felt vindictive toward them or reveled in their predicament. There was an investigative professionalism that I had not seen before. Beck and Brewster had been found diverting union funds for their own personal gain. The committee concentrated on that issue alone and documented what they had done, and then it moved on to Hoffa and the others. But it could have spent more time profitably bringing other Seattle associates of Beck in for questioning. Beck was the most powerful labor leader in the nation, and the number of people in Seattle who were in his pay or in his debt ranged from leading newspapermen to some of the most important businessmen; the committee could have generated headlines and sustained public interest by questioning them. But to what purpose? These individuals, while corrupted or compromised by Beck, had not been directly involved in the misuse of the funds. The committee documented fifty-two ways in which Beck "misused his authority, position and trust as president of the Western Conference of Teamsters and subsequently as president of the International Brotherhood of Teamsters" and then turned its attention eastward.

With the memory of McCarthy still fresh and the misconduct of other committees very much in the public eye, the way Bob, McClellan, Bellino and the others went about their work was refreshing. They didn't fish for information. They weren't speculating when they called a person to testify in public. They knew the answers to most of the questions. Often witnesses said they knew less about their own financial affairs than the committee did. Not infrequently there would be an exchange such as occurred when McClellan was questioning George Newell about the use of Teamster funds to pay for Beck's and Brewster's personal insurance policies. Newell, outwardly gruff but likable, had become wealthy on the premiums he collected for placing Teamster life and health and welfare insurance policies, and he had owned race horses with Brewster.

"How long has this been going on," asked McClellan, "that you have been writing policies for these individuals and collecting from the Teamsters' organization, either a local or the Western Conference?"

"I have no way of knowing, Mr. Chairman, because I don't handle any money, personally," Newell replied. "It comes into our bookkeeping department."

"Your records would reflect it."

"Apparently they do."

"Will you check your records and submit to this committee the number of policies for the last five years, or, rather, beginning in 1950, that you have written for these individuals, and have received the money . . . from any source of the Teamsters, so that . . . the Teamsters, when they get representation and somebody to look after their interest, might recover this money?"

"I will be glad to, if our records show it. Do they show it, Mr. Bellino?"

"Yes," Bellino said.[5]

I had never seen anything like it before, not in the hearings of state or Congressional committees that I had covered nor in anything I had read about.

---

5. Newell subsequently supplied a list of the policies. There were 13, and the amount of money involved totaled only $753.39. Seven were for Beck, and one premium for a building he owned with his doctor was for only $36, but he let the Teamsters pay it.

Chapter 4

Dave Beck's Downfall

THE UNMASKING of Beck began as soon as Turner and Lambert finished testifying. Beck's financial affairs were enormously complicated and, though the committee now knew the basic elements of his misdeeds, it needed time to document the case. McClellan and Bob decided to lay the groundwork publicly by going into the Teamsters' abortive effort to get control of pinball machines and other fringe operations in Portland, setting up Brewster for questioning about what he knew about Beck's finances.

The first witness was Albert J. Ruhl, secretary for thirty-two years of Teamsters Local 690 in Spokane, Washington. Ruhl reluctantly disclosed that he had loaned $3,900 of the local's funds to Thomas A. Maloney to open a cigar counter and restaurant in Spokane. Maloney, a fat hanger-on in Brewster's circle of friends, had been one of two men dispatched to Portland to arrange for the Portland takeover. Ruhl said he loaned the money to Maloney because he felt sorry for him and because he was a friend of Brewster. Then Ruhl admitted that he had loaned $17,000 in union funds to Sam Sellinas, a gambler in tax difficulty who also was a friend of Brewster, and that he had loaned $30,000 to Richard Klinge, a friend of Dave Beck, Jr., and a protégé in the union of Beck, Sr., for the purchase of a tavern in Seattle.

In light of what was to be disclosed, Ruhl's three loans were small, but they indicated that the dues money of the Teamsters in Washington State had been handled loosely, and, as Senator John F. Kennedy would understate a few days later, it all did not seem "completely proper." Rapidly, the committee brought out that Teamster money had been used to pay expenses for the men who trained Brewster's horses; for his jockey; $4,000 for a down payment on Brewster's home in Palm Desert, California; $93,650 for Campbell Soup stock and stock in a Canadian gold mine; for expenses for Tom Maloney and his associate in the Portland escapade, Joseph P. McLaughlin, a Seattle card-room operator.

Many other questionable expenditures came to light. One involved the $3,115 purchase of a car in 1954 for Mary James, a girlfriend of Terry McNulty, a Teamster business agent whose principal duty was to walk Brewster's horses in the early morning hours and haul them in a truck to various California race tracks. Brewster was unable to explain most of the expenditures, pointing out that he signed union checks in blank and that someone else, probably two associates who had died—Gordon Lindsay and John Sweeney—were responsible. When Brewster was questioned about the purchase of a car for Mary James, he expressed incredulity. "I don't believe that, and I would have to look at the record for that," he said. "I know that we never bought Terry McNulty's girlfriend an automobile!" But the Teamsters had.

Some of the questionable expenditures were as small as $15, but the total came to $409,309.98. Ultimately, auditors decided that Brewster personally owed the union $88,000. He paid back the money, although he began to do so only after the committee's investigation was under way.

Brewster was embarrassed and at times contrite over the disclosures. A husky, vigorous, urbane man, Brewster had not coveted great wealth like Beck nor sought power or consorted with important racketeers like Hoffa. His weakness was a liking for the high life, and he dipped loosely into the Teamster treasury to pay for his extravagances. It should be noted that after Bob first confronted Brewster, under strained circumstances, they got along increasingly well on a personal basis. Unlike Beck and Hoffa, Brewster had a sense of humor, and he did not appear to hold a grudge. After five days of intensive questioning, Bob thought Brewster had borne his embarrassment well and admired him for it. Brewster apparently respected Bob's candor and seemed to take the attitude that Bob was only doing a job. A relationship developed between them, and long afterward, including when he was Attorney General, Bob always picked up the phone when Brewster called. When John Kennedy delivered a Jefferson-Jackson Day speech to Washington State Democrats in Seattle in June 1959, most labor leaders boycotted the dinner because of his sponsorship of labor-reform legislation and Bob's work on the committee. But Brewster and his wife were there, along with other officers and trustees of Joint Council 28.

The change in the Kennedy-Brewster relationship was not an isolated case. Repeatedly throughout his life Bob was able to develop a candid and often friendly relationship with enemies. Besides Brewster, for example, there was the late John J. O'Rourke, the tough, dapper Teamster leader in New York. In 1956, Hoffa, with underworld help, sought to take control of New York Teamsters Joint Council 16 and install O'Rourke as president. The attempt failed when a federal court invalidated the election, but O'Rourke won without opposition the following year. In 1958, O'Rourke pleaded the Fifth Amendment before the committee when Bob sought to question him about the establishment of seven "paper locals" that had been created to rig the 1956 election. Before and after his appearance before the committee O'Rourke, whom Hoffa had also made fifth vice president of the International Brotherhood of Teamsters, conferred with Bob. They had several conversations thereafter. There was no noticeable change in O'Rourke's allegiance to Hoffa until 1962, when he defied Hoffa's efforts to bargain on a national scale for the Teamsters. Later he was instrumental in denying Hoffa further use of union funds for legal fees to defend himself against the government's charges. When Bob ran for the Senate in 1964, O'Rourke's Teamsters worked openly and very effectively for him, and on election night O'Rourke was one of a handful of outsiders invited to be with Bob and his family as the returns came in.

Brewster returned to the witness table in the Senate Caucus Room for the fifth day on Friday, March 22, 1957, and in midmorning Bob shifted the questioning from Brewster's personal expenditures and his conduct of union affairs.

"Mr. Brewster," he began, his voice slightly higher-pitched and betraying excitement. "I now want to go into a matter of considerable importance that perhaps does not involve you directly, but you have firsthand information about it, or more information perhaps than anyone else . . . that is the question of the loans to Mr. Beck. Do you know of any checks made payable to Dave Beck which were considered as loans for any year from 1949 through 1952?"

Brewster conferred with his lawyers, squared his shoulders, leaned forward and answered: "I could not identify and remember any checks that were made out to Dave Beck as a loan. As I explained before, I signed checks in blank. But as far as my memory serves me, I do not remember [any] of the checks being made out when I signed them."

"Did you consider any of the money that went to the public relations account in Los Angeles as loans to Dave Beck?"

"I did not."

Bob then asked whether Brewster knew about transfers of Teamster funds to Nathan Shefferman, a Chicago labor-management consultant who was a friend of Beck's. Did he consider the money that went to Shefferman as money borrowed by Beck?

"I have no knowledge," Brewster said. ". . . That was strictly between Dave Beck and Shefferman."

Bob asked about a payment of $146,678 in Teamster funds in 1951 and 1952 to John Lindsay, a Seattle contractor who built Beck's lakefront estate.

"Were you ever told by Dave Beck that monies that were being given or sent to John Lindsay were, in effect, loans to Dave Beck?"

"I was not."

Carmine Bellino was called to testify. He reported that examination of Teamster financial records in Seattle did not turn up any record of loans to Beck from 1948 to 1952, that $250,000 or more had been taken from Teamster bank accounts and used for Beck's personal benefit and that since 1954 Beck had repaid the union $270,110.16.

"And there is no record whatsoever of monies going out as loans to Mr. Dave Beck?" Bob asked.

"That is correct," said Bellino.

"And we found in many instances, did we not, that the monies went to third parties and ultimately ended up for the benefit of Dave Beck?"

"Yes, sir."

Brewster, appearing to be concerned and subdued, returned to the witness chair and McClellan took over the questioning.

"You've heard the testimony of Mr. Bellino," McClellan began. "During this time did you have any knowledge that Mr. Beck owed . . . loans amounting to $250,000?"

"I did not," Brewster answered in a low voice.

"You never knew it?"

"No, sir."

"When did you first learn about it?"

"I don't remember when it was—when he paid it back, I believe."

Brewster said he had assumed Beck had borrowed the money properly but said he had no thought that it would be that much. McClellan sternly demanded to know whether it was not Brewster's duty to know about the loans and see that proper records were kept.

"Mr. Senator, I trusted the man," Brewster answered earnestly.

"I'm not talking about that. I am talking about your duty," McClellan said.

"Well, duty and trust are probably different. My duty I neglected, the trust I did not."

"Your trust has been misplaced, do you feel?"

"Do I have to answer that?"

"No, you don't."

With those questions, the committee established on the record that the Teamster official who should have known whether Beck had been borrowing money from the union, as Beck said he had, could not support Beck's story. Brewster's mood was tense and somber as he sat through the ordeal, able to give his long-time associate in the union no aid—only discomfort. But by noon Brewster had relaxed and brightened. He was through being questioned, at least for the time being, and he had heard that Beck had been ordered to appear before the committee the following Tuesday.

"Boys," he said jovially to newsmen, "wait until the main event."

"You can write it in your book," said Dave Beck on Tuesday, March 27, 1957, "that every time I've ever received money, it went on my income tax returns." He was standing outside the Senate Caucus Room, talking with reporters while waiting to appear before the committee. He was head of the nation's most powerful labor union, a man with entree to the White House and a close connection with other powerful political figures, a man feared, respected and courted by some of the nation's leading business executives, and he was about to plead the Fifth Amendment privilege against self-incrimination in refusing to answer any questions about his financial dealings or his conduct of union affairs. He would even have to refuse to tell a committee of the United States Senate what he had told the newsmen for fear of opening the door to questions that he did not want to answer under oath.

Beck had lost some struggles in his time, but he had never been humiliated. Now, though outwardly his demeanor was defiant and confident, he was about to be humiliated, and the whole prospect of what was about to happen must have seemed surreal to him. He had been maneuvering desperately for three months to avoid this moment. He had consented to see Bob and Bellino on January 5 in his suite in the Waldorf-Astoria Hotel in New York, and he had lectured them, shouted at them, and been extremely patronizing, but he had not shaken them. Now the whole country was watching.

Beck faced the committee with an air of assurance and indignation which appeared to convey the feeling, "You can't do this to me!" He challenged the committee's authority to question him, and when McClellan demanded that he hand over his financial records, he refused, invoking the Fifth Amendment for the first time.

McClellan had stated at the outset that the committee had evidence which clearly indicated that from 1949 through March, 1953, Beck had misappropriated over $320,000 of union funds. When the committee asked Beck whether, in light of this evidence, he did not have a duty to the members of the union that transcended his right to take the Fifth Amendment, he pleaded for the first time that he was only doing so on "the 100 percent unanimous advice" of his counsel, mainly former Senator James H. Duff of Pennsylvania. It was to introduce a comic-opera aspect into the hearing. Of course, Beck was in deep difficulty with the Internal Revenue Service. He expected to be indicted for income tax evasion and he was only protecting himself, but obviously he thought hiring a former member of the Senate would cause the committee to think better of him and to show some sympathy for his position. Instead, it had the opposite effect. Senator Duff did not accompany Beck to the hearing. He was attended by three other attorneys. Again and again, Beck invoked the name of the absent Duff, and each time the audience laughed a little louder, but the Senators were not smiling.

"If I go up to the hospital and hire a doctor, I intend to follow his advice," Beck said. "When I hired Senator Duff, I intended to follow his advice."

Beck had used this kind of logic to win many an argument, but the Senators saw it differently.

"You attempt to shift the responsibility for pleading the Fifth Amendment from yourself to your very fine counsel," said Senator Ervin, after praising Duff for advising Beck to exercise his right against self-incrimination.

Beck reddened and replied: "Senator . . . I am only doing it on the advice of my chief counsel, Senator Duff, who occupies or did occupy a position of honor in the United States Government comparable to what you now occupy."

Finally, Beck was reduced to answering, almost pleadingly, "I'm only following his advice," and the next day in the Washington *Evening Star* Mary McGrory wrote a memorable lead in her account of the hearing. "Dave Beck," wrote Miss McGrory, "yesterday became the first man to plead innocence by association."

Beck jousted heatedly at times with the Senators and exchanged philosophies with them for ninety minutes. Then Bob began asking a series of questions charting the course Beck had followed in dipping into the treasury, starting out with relatively small sums, totaling $36,000, to pay off bank loans in 1946. The questioning turned to evidence that Beck took $4,812.39 from the Western Conference in 1949 and deposited it in his own bank account, and that from 1949 through 1953 he paid John Lindsay $196,516.49 in union funds for work done at his estate. Beck took the Fifth Amendment. Bob began asking whether during that period Beck also had not siphoned $85,-119.92 in union funds to pay his personal bills through his pal Nate Shefferman, who worked for Sears, Roebuck & Company, and other employers. There occurred at this point an exchange between Bob and Beck that produced the rapid-fire, combative questioning that was to become Bob's trademark with the public; that showed his preparation, persistence and courage, but which also laid the foundation for the stereotype that he was ruthless.

"What was his [Shefferman's] position with Sears, Roebuck?" Bob asked.

"I can't answer that," Beck said.

"You don't know what Mr. Shefferman's position was with Sears, Roebuck?"

"No, I cannot."

"You have no idea?"

"No, I do not."

"You have no idea?"

"I do not have any idea of his official position; no."

"Do you know what services he performed for Sears, Roebuck?"

"Well, let me answer it this way. I don't know where you are going or where you intend to go—"

"Yes, you do, Mr. Beck," Bob interrupted.

"And I say I don't!" Beck shouted. "I am not contradicting you. Don't say that I know when I do not answer the question."

"Then answer the question," Bob said evenly.

"All right," Beck said, his voice rising. "I tell you I do not know."

"Answer the question."

"All right, I am not going to answer the question because I don't know. I am going to answer the question in this manner: I must decline to answer the question because this committee lacks jurisdiction or authority under Articles I, II and III of the Constitution; further, I decline to answer because I refuse to give testimony against myself, and invoke the Fourth and Fifth Amendments; and further because the question is not relevant or pertinent to the investigation."

"Answer the question."

"I have answered the question. Do you want me to read it again? I will. I must decline to answer the question because this committee lacks jurisdiction . . ."

Beck was asked to step aside temporarily, and Shefferman was called to testify. Beck started to leave the room, but McClellan called him back.

"I want you to be here while Mr. Shefferman testifies," McClellan commanded.

"Fine, fine, fine," said Beck, taking a seat.

Shefferman, a white-haired, garrulous, seventy-year-old Chicagoan, had known Beck since 1934. He had been a labor consultant for Sears for thirteen years and in 1948 had opened his own consulting business; his clients were mostly department stores. At the witness table, he lauded Beck as "a terrific personality" and hemmed and hedged and talked, but in the end he answered the committee's questions. He admitted that he had purchased $85,000 worth of goods and services for Beck. He said he did not know where the money came from when he was reimbursed, but the committee did. At least $29,000 came from a public relations account that Beck had established in Los Angeles, and the rest came from other union funds.

There was a cheap tone to it all because many of the items were for very small amounts: $7.50 for a tie, $9 for undershirts, $9.68 for diapers, $3.50 for a bow tie, as well as larger items such as $4,534.94 for landscaping at Beck's home. When Beck was questioned later, he had to take the Fifth Amendment even as to whether he had used union funds to purchase five dozen diapers.

The questioning of Shefferman also brought out that he and his son Sheldon, Dave Beck, Jr., and Norman Gessert, a cousin of Mrs. Beck, Sr., shared in profits of $200,121 from the sale of toy trucks to Teamster locals—which Beck, Sr., promoted—and from the sale of furniture for the Teamsters' gleaming new headquarters which Beck built in Washington with a view of the Capitol. Shefferman also admitted that in 1948–49 he gave Beck $24,000. He said it was for "services, friendship," and because he "hadn't ever done anything" for Beck, but he was not being entirely candid. Later, it was to come out that when the Teamsters purchased the property for their Washington headquarters from the American Legion, Shefferman had wedged himself into the negotiations. Although he in no way affected the outcome of the negotiations, he later submitted a claim to the Teamsters' executive board for a $12,000 commission, asserting that he had saved the union more than $65,000 in the deal. The board paid the commission. Shefferman deposited it in his checking account and five weeks later sent Beck a check for $8,000.

When the hearing adjourned for the day, Beck pushed through the crowd to reach Shefferman's side, saying he had not seen him before he came forward to testify. They started to leave the room together, but as photographers attempted to get pictures of them, Shefferman backed away.

"What's the matter?" Beck said to his friend. "You haven't done anything wrong."

But Shefferman lagged behind, saying, "You go ahead, Dave."

As much as anything, that told how far the international president of the Teamsters Union had fallen in just one day. Beck strode out of the room and headed for an elevator followed by a swarm of photographers.

The next day, again hoisting the shield of Duff, Beck told the committee there was no doubt that he would be able in a court of law to provide full, final and satisfactory answers to the questions being raised. Meanwhile, anticipating that his day in court might not be far off, he would continue on Duff's advice to exercise his constitutional rights in refusing to answer the questions regardless of public opinion.

"I am big enough and broad enough and able to take it," he said. But he wasn't.

Late in the day Bob introduced evidence which disclosed that in 1954 Beck, in scrambling ahead of the income tax investigators to make restitution to the union, had borrowed $200,000 through Roy Fruehauf, head of the Fruehauf Trailer Company; then, to repay Fruehauf, had sold his estate to the Teamsters for $163,215, notwithstanding the fact that he had already stuck the union $196,000 to build it. Outside the hearing room Beck had been claiming that any money—he estimated that the total was between $300,000 and $400,-000—he got from the union had been in the form of bona fide loans. Now this evidence, coming on top of Brewster's testimony that he did not know of any loans, buttressed the committee's contention that Beck "took" rather than borrowed $320,000 in union funds; that when he repaid the Teamsters $200,000 with the Fruehauf loan, he did not know how much he "owed" the union. And Beck would not explain it. Reading through heavy-rimmed glasses, he appeared subdued and weary for the first time as he intoned his reasons for taking the Fifth Amendment.

As a final blow, McClellan dressed him down, asserting he had shown "flagrant disregard for honest unionism" and "arrogant contempt for the 1,500,000 honest" Teamsters. Beck reddened but did not attempt to reply. He was dismissed, to return to Seattle exposed as a cheap, greedy fraud, a leader totally insensitive to the responsibilities of his office and, what was worse, incredibly vulnerable. Waiting to oust him were the forces of James R. Hoffa. And, of course, the committee was not through with Beck, nor was the IRS.

The committee had seven investigators, including Pierre Salinger, who later would be President Kennedy's able press secretary, checking records and interviewing witnesses in Seattle. Bob and Bellino arrived on April 7 to join them. It was Bob's third visit to the city since November. On the first two he had arrived unheralded, had registered at the Olympic Hotel under the name of

"Rogers" and had worked without attracting much attention. Now, because of the widespread news coverage of the hearings—we had printed very detailed accounts in the *Times*, and KING-TV had broadcast Beck's appearances live—he was recognized wherever he went. As he walked along the downtown streets in the soft spring showers, passers-by grabbed his hand and motorists lowered their windows and shouted greetings to him. Everywhere he went the people of Seattle said to him, "Congratulations," and many of them urged him to "keep going." He responded with a quick smile, a shy wave or a brief "thank you." He expressed surprise at the warmth of his reception, but it elated him.

I had come to like him very much. The committee by its actions had dispelled our fears that we might be used and abandoned, that it might investigate sloppily or be insensitive to the rights of the people it brought before it. It had accomplished far more than we had expected in bringing Beck and Brewster to bay. Bob had kept his word that he would protect our sources within the union. I appreciated that, and I respected the skill and tenacity with which he and his investigators went about their work. But it was more than that. I enjoyed being in his company. Though he sometimes was withdrawn or laconic, I usually found him easy to talk to. When he was working, he was very serious, but his sense of humor, wry, needling and often self-depreciating, was never far below the surface.

At Hickory Hill, his home in Virginia, a casual, cheerful atmosphere prevailed. He invited me and other visiting reporters to dinner often while we were in Washington covering the hearings. If it was a large party, invariably some kind of parlor game, like charades, was played. I remember when my wife, JoAnn, came with me in May for Beck's second appearance before the committee, and we went to dinner at Hickory Hill together for the first time. The other guests were the late Henry Suydam, a reporter for *Life*, and his wife, Marjorie, and Stanley Tretick, a United Press photographer. It was about 10:30 or 11 o'clock when we finished eating and the night was warm and muggy. We all took a walk on the broad lawn that sloped away from the rear and one side of the house. As we were walking and talking, Ethel Kennedy said, "Let's have a race." Jo and I had never done anything like that at a dinner party, in Seattle or anywhere else. But that night, somewhat self-consciously, we did. It seemed crazy then and it still does, but in a small way it typified the sense of participation, competition and exuberance that one experienced at Hickory Hill.

There was one thing more that drew me to Bob in those days. It was that as a reporter I had never encountered a person in public life who answered my questions as candidly and completely as he did. Often he would go out of his way to be helpful, and the people in his office and his investigators also were friendly and helpful. The night Hoffa was arrested on charges of attempted bribery of the committee[1] it was Ethel Kennedy who roused us out of our beds at midnight so that we didn't miss being at the United States Courthouse for our papers when Hoffa was arraigned. So the atmosphere for the press around Bob and the committee was easy, open and conducive to good reporting. When hearings were in progress, Bob would brief us each night about what to expect the next day. Except on a few occasions when especially sensitive information was to come up, Bob would disclose to us in considerable detail what evidence was going to be presented. He would explain the nuances of a particular question or line of inquiry so that, for example, when he began asking Brewster about Beck's "loans," we immediately understood the significance of it. As a result we were able to write with far greater accuracy and insight than if we had not been briefed, and, of course, the committee benefited because this kind of informed writing and radio and television commentary led to greater public understanding of its work.

1. It seemed that night that the FBI had an open-and-shut case against Hoffa. A New York lawyer, John Cye Cheasty, had alerted the committee that Hoffa had asked him to spy on the committee's work. Under the eye of the FBI and with the committee's knowledge, Cheasty turned over some documents to Hoffa and received $2,000 in cash outside a Washington, D.C., hotel. But the following summer a jury of eight Negroes and four whites acquitted Hoffa. Two factors seemed to have been crucial in the decision. Hoffa surprised the government and testified in his own defense, and the government lawyers were caught not well prepared to cross-examine him. The second factor was the appearance in the courtroom of ex-heavyweight champion Joe Louis, who conspicuously made a show of friendship for Hoffa.

I do not know of any instances—though there may have been some—when the confidence of the briefings I attended during the Beck-Brewster phases of the hearings was breached. Bob measured the newsmen who came to them, found those he could respect and trust, and he developed a special relationship with most of them that continued through the years. They would always have access to him, and any time he could tip them to a story, verify some information for them or help them with personal problems, he would go out of his way to do so. Besides Clark Mollenhoff and the *Oregonian* reporters, Wallace Turner and William Lambert, this group included the late Edward F. Woods of the St. Louis *Post-Dispatch;* Don Irwin, New York *Herald Tribune;* Joseph A. Loftus, *New York Times;* John Seigenthaler, Nashville *Tennessean;* Paul F. Healy, New York *Daily News;* Cecil Holland, Washington *Evening Star;* the late Edwin A. Lahey, Chicago *Daily News;* labor columnist John Herling; David Kraslow, Miami *Herald;* Edwin W. O'Brien, St. Louis *Globe-Democrat;* John F. Van Camp, Baltimore *Sun;* Don Shannon, Los Angeles *Times;* and Robert Thompson and Alvin A. Spivak, International News Service.

In later years, some of these men, particularly Mollenhoff, would write critically about the TFX decision and other actions of the Kennedy Administration and probe hard into its activities. Yet in that delicate relationship between newsman and public official, the trust, formed so early in Bob's career, might be strained but it would persist.

On the afternoon of May 8, Beck returned to the Senate Caucus Room to be questioned further under circumstances far different from when he had testified in March. It was evident immediately, as he entered the room, slowly and reserved, not jauntily as a few weeks before. The Duff ploy having failed, he was accompanied by a new counsel, the prominent Washington, D.C., defense lawyer, Edward Bennett Williams. He was under pressure now from within the union to resign, and in Tacoma, Washington, a federal grand jury had indicted him on charges of income tax evasion. He had been summoned for two reasons. First, after testifying in March he made headlines nationally by indicating that he had done nothing wrong but had taken the Fifth Amendment only "to protect a lot of fine people" and that he would have "blown the lid right off the Senate" if he had testified freely. The Senators wanted very much to question him under oath about that. Second, the continuing investigation in Seattle had turned up considerable evidence of Beck ventures into the business world that seemed anything but at-arm's-length deals.

Williams protested that Beck's rights to a fair trial in Tacoma might be prejudiced if he were interrogated about any financial transactions and asked that his appearance be postponed. However, McClellan explained that the committee would not question Beck about improper use of union funds but would concentrate on his improper use of power. It was a fine line, and in retrospect it is evident that the committee went deeply in public into transactions which were to figure in Beck's income tax trial. Whether in actuality the testimony over the next seven days added substantially to the weight of unfavorable public opinion is open to argument. It was only part of the avalanche that was falling on Beck. Through the summer and fall, the grand jury in Tacoma expanded its probe; a King County grand jury in Seattle indicted him for embezzlement;[2] and Hoffa pushed him aside unceremoniously and took over as president of the Teamsters. Certainly, the testimony would not do him any good. Yet it was important for Seattle because it enabled the people to see more clearly, through the details of Beck's snug associations with businessmen, what happens when power unchecked becomes the power of self-indulgence and power without a purpose; and that whatever largess Beck dispensed for civic or charitable benefits, there usually was a catch: Beck was benefiting

2. A three-year statute of limitations prevented local authorities from doing anything in 1957 about almost all of Beck's misappropriation of union funds, they having occurred before IRS began investigating in 1954. However, Prosecutor Charles O. Carroll found one item—Beck had sold a used Teamster-owned Cadillac for $1,900 and pocketed the money—and with a good deal of skill and tenacity made it stick. A jury convicted Beck of grand larceny in December 1957, and he was sentenced to serve from two to fifteen years in prison, but the sentence was made to run concurrent with the time he served on McNeil Island.

financially, too. For the committee the testimony was important because it put into the record for the first time a pattern of unsavory involvement between big business and big labor that was to recur disturbingly through the hearings and figure in the passage of the Labor Reform Act. And there was the matter of whether Beck could blow the lid off the Senate.

McClellan asked Beck whether he had been quoted correctly and Beck replied: "I decline to answer on the grounds that the answer might incriminate me." McClellan pointed out that the committee was giving Beck an opportunity to talk. Beck said he understood but preferred to remain silent. Williams interjected a doubt that the question was relevant to any legislative purpose. McClellan said with impatience that Beck had insulted the Senate and had implied that he had a lot of information and "I'm giving him the opportunity to spill it." Blinking impassively, Beck had nothing to say, and a few minutes later he was reduced to invoking the Fifth Amendment when asked if he knew his son and to hearing the spectators laugh derisively as he did so. The committee had been looking for young Beck and three other men for weeks to subpoena them. What must be the thoughts of a man who finds himself saying, "I decline to answer because it might tend to open up avenues of questioning which might tend to incriminate me," when asked if he knows his only son?

For the next week the committee questioned a dozen men who had been involved in or had knowledge of his business deals, including the bookkeeper of the Western Conference of Teamsters and Joint Council 28 Building Association, who appeared to have been picked for the job precisely because he had not been trained as an accountant. He just kept the books and did what he was told.

As mentioned earlier, for many years the Teamsters had kept Eastern-brewed beer out of the state by refusing to haul it. When Beck finally allowed Eastern beer to be sold in Washington after the war, it wasn't long before he acquired an interest through his son and wife in a Seattle distributing firm, the K. & L. Beverage Company. The testimony disclosed that the Anheuser-Busch Company of St. Louis then gave K. & L. the largest territory it allocated in the country; that Anheuser officials endured a great amount of aggravation in dealing with Beck about the company's business to keep him placated and went to him on at least two occasions for assistance in labor disputes in Chicago and Los Angeles. Beck also put up money for a concealed interest in Sunset Distributors, Inc., after arranging through Emil Sick, president of the Rainier Brewing Company, to obtain a distributorship for the locally brewed Rainier beer.

The committee went into the details of the Fruehauf loan and then focused on a small Seattle firm, the National Mortgage Company, which came into being in September 1953—after Beck became international president—to handle the investment of about $15 million of union funds in real estate—principally in GI home mortgages—in the Seattle area, California, Arizona and Michigan. About three-fifths of the money, $9 million, flowed into the Seattle area in three years. Outwardly, it appeared that Beck's only interests were to make money for the union and to stimulate the economy of his home town in the process. Of course he did, but he was also making money for himself—money he probably couldn't have laid his hands on if the union funds had been invested elsewhere.

National Mortgage was headed by a Seattle mortgage banker, Donald F. Hedlund, and the committee uncovered the fact that Beck owned a one-third interest in the firm through his nephew, Joseph McEvoy. The testimony produced an interesting clash of ethics between Hedlund and Fred P. Loomis, a Seattle investment counsel, that was to put all Beck's dealing into perspective. Beck had hired Loomis in 1947 to advise him on investments. When Loomis learned that Beck was going into business with Hedlund in the investment of Teamster funds, he wrote Beck cautioning him not only to avoid a conflict of interest, but also to avoid the appearance of one. In reply, Beck, writing with about as much candor as he was capable, bared the philosophy that was guiding him:

> I am very sorry if Don told that I was going into the mortgage business with him. As you will recall, I told Don in our office that morning that I would not be in the firm as a partner, it would be in another name. . . .
> I repeated I can see no valid objection to my rewarding my friends with

our business rather than just acquaintances.

I have not and I will not be a party directly or indirectly to creating any situation or dealing with anyone to the injury of our international union. I insist that the international union get the advantage in every respect that would accrue from any purchase, but in buying it has to go through some broker so the international union is not injured whether it be through Don's associates or some other mortgage company. . . .

I am anxious to aid some of my associates to successful business development if I can do so without penalty to the . . . union.

That sounded all right, but it didn't work that way. He had to push and control everything he got involved in. A true measure of Beck was his son, Dave, Jr., a heavily built but weak man who had been so dominated by his father that he had done nothing in his own right.[3] Beck, of course, probably did not understand that he had all but destroyed his son, just as he could not see anything wrong in concealing his interest in National Mortgage by putting it in McEvoy's name. But, like Dave, Jr., McEvoy, a truck driver, didn't get to do anything. Like so many other persons close to Beck, he was just a front. It was even questionable whether the National Mortgage arrangement was serving the best interests of the union. There was no competition for the mortgages, and experienced financial men, like Loomis, felt the Teamsters' investments were overly concentrated in Seattle.

Beck's remarkable financial transactions were so numerous and so complex that it was to take certified public accountants hundreds of hours to determine how much he had taken from the union. After years of work they would admit privately that they were by no means sure that they had accounted for every dollar. Many people knew bits and parts of Beck's dealings, but he did not permit anyone, not even his closest confidants, to know about all of them. He was always in debt, but he was always able to borrow large sums at favorable interest rates from the Seattle–First National Bank or from the Occidental Life Insurance Company, which underwrote health and welfare and life insurance for the Teamsters throughout

---

3. Beck, Jr., also was convicted of grand larceny in the sale of a Teamster-owned Cadillac. He was fined but not sent to prison.

the Western Conference. Loomis advised Beck to simplify his financial operations, get out of a lot of his businesses and pay off his debts. In 1955 Loomis learned that National Mortgage was to receive a kickback of $7,500 in financing the construction of an apartment house in Honolulu with Teamster funds. He promptly submitted his resignation and advised Beck to have a prominent Seattle lawyer explain to him his responsibilities as the trustee of other people's money. Beck accepted his resignation.

Hedlund thought his association with Beck was an admirable arrangement. He stiffly denied that he or Beck had done anything unethical. He blandly told the committee that though he had been in mortgage financing for twenty years, he did not know that it was a well-established principle of our system of law that a trustee is at no time allowed to obtain "any personal benefit, advantage, gain or profit" from funds he administers. So a Don Hedlund would go along while a Fred Loomis would not; an Episcopal bishop, the Rt. Rev. Stephen F. Bayne, Jr., would speak out[4] while an Emil Sick, the brewer and civic leader, would not; a prosecutor, Charles O. Carroll, would feel duty-bound to act on the committee's disclo-

---

4. In 1946, Beck summoned some Seattle business leaders to a dinner and raised about $150,000 on the spot to help pay off a $250,000 mortgage on St. Mark's Cathedral, seat of the Episcopal diocese, which had been foreclosed in 1941. Beck was not a member of the church or even an Episcopalian. Emil Sick was. Mr. Bayne became bishop in 1947, and when the committee probed into the Teamsters, his was the strongest voice raised locally against what Beck and Brewster had done and what the city had countenanced. "We do not know how much of what he has done is legally wrong, and how much is simply an extraordinary conception of public trust," Bishop Bayne said. "But the plain evidence thus far is of a moral irresponsibility so far-reaching as to be almost incredible. . . . How one wishes for a dime's worth of honesty in all the complicated maneuvering to save this management or to insure a period of labor peace. . . . What all these Beckadillos underline is the fact of irresponsible power . . . wielded by cynical men who are above any law except the income tax. . . . Of what good is it to preach church membership or Christian belief if we can make no useful connection between that belief and the world we live in and the people who live in that world?" A few weeks after Bayne spoke, Paul Staples and I interviewed Beck in Seattle, and at one point we asked him, of all the difficulties he had encountered before the committee, what had bothered him most. He said it was that of all the people and organizations he had helped no one had come forward to speak in his defense. He ticked off twenty charitable groups or more—the Boy Scouts, the Children's Orthopaedic Hospital, the Red Cross and on and on. Then he paused. His small eyes narrowed. He pounded his fist on his desk and said: "And then there's that Goddamn Bishop Bayne!"

sures while a Major Gordon Clinton, upright attorney and ex-FBI agent, would decline to help the committee.

Hedlund steered Beck into one deal that was to be Beck's ultimate undoing. In the fall of 1956, about the same time the committee was gearing up its investigation, Beck, in his lust for money, stooped to enrich himself by handling a $76,000 trust fund for the widow of his friend and union associate, Ray Leheney. Beck had raised the money for the trust fund, as a memorial to Leheney, from contributions and Teamster assessments. Acting as the fund's trustees, Beck and Hedlund invested Mrs. Leheney's legacy, using it to buy mortgage contracts which they had acquired with union funds. Then, without having risked a penny of their own money, they pocketed the difference between what the mortgages cost the union and what they had made Mrs. Leheney pay for them, a profit of $11,585. Committee investigators discovered the deal while examining Beck's books, and the committee put all the details of it into the record while questioning Hedlund.

When the hearings began in March, Beck had repaid the union $270,000. The committee had been able to document that Beck had taken at least $320,000. By the time Hedlund took the stand, Beck had borrowed $150,000 from Seattle–First National, out of which he reimbursed the union an additional $100,000, bringing his total repayment to $370,000. Amounts of money of this size and much larger had been mentioned throughout the hearings, but it was the relatively small sum of $11,585 that people remembered and that stuck in their craws. It stripped away Beck's remaining pretenses —he would even make a profit for himself as trustee of a widow's funds—and that more than anything caused rank-and-file Teamsters and all but a handful of retainers to turn against him, if they had not already done so.

Beck was convicted by a jury on February 10, 1959, on four counts of evading income taxes totaling $299,000 in the early 1950's. He also was convicted on two counts of subscribing to false tax returns filed by the Teamsters Joint Council 28 Building Association and sentenced to five years in prison. On appeal, he pleaded that the government had not proved he had not stolen the money from the union and that therefore he should not be required to pay taxes on it. The Supreme Court sustained his appeal but upheld his conviction of filing false returns for the Building Association. He entered McNeil Island Federal Prison in Puget Sound on June 20, 1962, and he was released on parole December 11, 1964. His wife, Dorothy, whom he married in 1918, had died. He returned to Seattle to live on his $50,000-a-year pension and manage his business interests.

We can look back now, and each of us can make his own judgment about the value of the committee's work. Was the national interest served? Did the Teamsters Union benefit? Is Seattle better off?

The answers are rooted really in the answer to another question. What would have happened if the committee had not come along to expose Beck, Brewster, Hoffa and the other errant labor leaders and businessmen? The odds are overwhelming that they would have continued what they were doing unchecked, accountable to no one. For example, men in the Internal Revenue Service and the Justice Department who were involved in Beck's income tax evasion case have told me there was justification for their fear that Beck had enough clout to prevent criminal prosecution. But once the committee moved in on Beck, there was no way the case could be pigeonholed, and grand jury action by the government was soon forthcoming. Local authorities had no stomach for investigating Beck until the committee's revelations created a public demand for action that could not be ignored.

Near the conclusion of its hearings on Beck, the committee made public a list of thirteen points which, it asserted, documented that Beck "took" rather than "borrowed" more than $300,000 from various Teamster bank accounts in Seattle. It followed that with the list of fifty-two ways in which Beck assertedly "misused his authority, position and trust" as president of the Western Conference and subsequently as international president of the union. Beck would say, "In my judgment, I haven't done a single, solitary thing wrong," and he would say repeatedly, "If I had to do it all over again, the only thing different I would do would be to keep better [financial] records." But two juries in his home territory found him guilty of felonies, and the courts upheld those convictions. It was arguable whether the unfavorable publicity generated by the hearings created a climate of public opinion which infringed on his right to a fair trial. Two trial judges and the appellate courts thought not. But Beck might have survived the prosecutions. The Teamsters were to hold their international convention in October 1957, and their tradition was to go along with a brother caught in the toils of the law at least until he went to prison. Beck was only under indictment when the Teamster convention delegates gathered in Miami. Hoffa willing, Beck would have been re-elected to a second five-year term. The evidence is that Beck would have continued operating as in the past. Federal investigation had not put any fear into him. His obsession for money overrode all else, and he had come to prefer associates like Don Hedlund to the more ethical Fred Loomis. What brought him down was the extent of the committee's investigation, culminating in the disclosure that he had made money from a widow's fund.

In toppling Beck from office, the committee created a situation which enabled Hoffa, a far more daring and far more dangerous man, to come to power. Though Beck commanded considerable influence and power, he turned out to be a paper lion, a feudal lord with courtiers but no army. His sin was avarice. Hoffa did not covet money solely to enrich himself, as Beck did; he used it, rather, to consolidate and expand his power. He believed with the utmost cynicism that every man could be bought. In grabbing power and in using it boldly and in forming open alliances with some of the toughest, most unsavory racketeers alive, the ever-defiant, muscular little giant from Detroit made Beck and Brewster look like small-timers.

Thus the hearings increased Hoffa's power and did not lower his standing among the nation's truck drivers, despite his arrest on charges of attempted bribery of the committee. His acquittal on that and other charges[5] served to strengthen him in every way and raised

5. Besides the bribery acquittal, Hoffa and two co-defendants were tried twice on federal wiretapping charges. The first trial ended in a hung jury, and Hoffa was acquitted in the second. Hoffa and two associates were charged with federal mail fraud involving alleged misuse of union funds in a Florida land development scheme, but the charges were dismissed on grounds that the grand jury was selected improp-

the question whether the law ever would catch up with him. He would also withstand disclosure after disclosure by the committee of dishonesty, violence and arbitrary abuse of power involving him directly or indirectly. And despite these disclosures he would use millions of dollars from the reserves of the Teamsters' Central States, Southeast, Southwest Pension Fund to finance and enrich his shady associates. He would be emboldened to resort to a massive assault on the jury system to avoid going to prison. He was elected Teamster president in an election of questionable validity—Bob called it "rigged from start to finish"—and moved remorselessly to deprive the local unions of what independence they had. However, the committee's work was only the beginning of a grinding, resolute effort, led by Bob, which hampered Hoffa and ultimately sent him to prison, although in 1957 that day of reckoning was ten years in the future.

It seems beyond challenge that had it not been for the committee Beck might have continued in office, Hoffa willing, and that Hoffa would have continued to gather power without effective opposition anywhere; that both would have become so entrenched and so enormously powerful that Bob's fear that "either we are going to be successful or they are going to have the country" was not farfetched. Perhaps some other dedicated public officials would have come forward to expose and prosecute them, but the evidence is all against that probability. The fact is that little or nothing had been done to curb them or the other dishonest labor leaders and the businessmen who were going along with it all, though the circumstances cried out for action.

We can see some tangible results of the hearings. The Labor Reform Act made embezzlement of union funds a federal crime, and it prohibited offering or accepting bribes in labor-management relations. It provided for fair election procedures, including a secret ballot for union members, and it required that detailed financial and

---

erly. In 1962 a federal grand jury indicted Hoffa on charges of collecting more than $1 million from an employer in violation of the Taft-Hartley Act. The jury was unable to reach a verdict, and it was out of this case that jury-tampering charges were brought against Hoffa on which he was convicted in 1964, and sent to prison in 1967.

administrative reports be filed with the Department of Labor, making conflicts of interest and misuse of union funds harder to conceal. Beck and Brewster put back the money they had used. The Labor Reform Act now prohibits much of what Brewster did, but there was no strong evidence on which he could have been prosecuted under existing laws. However, he made restitution, assigning to the union his home, his interest in the service station he owned with Beck and other assets. The union's treasury benefited in other ways, too. For example, George Newell, who had made a profit of one million dollars from 1952 through 1956 as insurance "broker of record" for the Western Conference, cut his commission from 2 to 1 percent. In a larger sense, there was a stirring throughout organized labor. The AFL-CIO, at considerable cost to itself, expelled the Teamsters, and many corrupt union officials within the Teamsters and in other unions eventually lost their jobs. Ultimately, in the effort which Bob mounted as Attorney General, Hoffa and more than a hundred of his associates went to prison on charges ranging from jury-tampering to embezzlement of union funds.

As for Seattle, we cannot gauge the effects precisely, but we do know that greater balance was restored to the contending forces in the city. The fall of Beck removed a corrupting influence from the economic and political life of the community. Along with that and Brewster's chastisement, the way was opened for the late Don Ellis and other leaders, less flamboyant and less interested in personal glory, to take control of the union's affairs. The rank-and-file Teamsters had greater opportunity than before—if they chose to use it—to have a voice in the affairs of the organization that had such an important bearing on their lives. They also had the knowledge, for whatever it was worth to them, that their government could act effectively to protect their rights and the use of their monthly dues. For the Teamsters who cared and for the citizens of the city in general, there was some reassurance that evil did not always triumph.

There is a final reflection to mention about the rackets investigation. It was a major factor in John Kennedy's election as President. It not only kept the Kennedy name in the forefront of public opinion for three years preceding the Presidential campaign, but it was to measure accurately the character and spirit of the Kennedys. Other politicians who sought the Presidency—particularly Democrats—would have hesitated to risk antagonizing the leaders of organized labor by participating in such a searching investigation of union corruption, or by having a brother be a part of it.

"He knew it meant risking his good relations with organized labor—and that at least two other Senators with national ambitions, Henry Jackson and Stuart Symington, had declined to serve," Sorensen would write later in *Kennedy*.

There had also been hints of national Teamster support for his Presidential candidacy if only Bob Kennedy would "play smart."

But whatever the political pitfalls, Kennedy was interested. Internal union safeguards had intrigued him since his Taft-Hartley studies in the House.[6] As chairman of the Senate Labor Committee's Subcommittee on Labor Legislation, he knew he could hardly avoid involvement in any legislative proposals growing out of the hearings (although he also declined an opportunity to leave the Labor Committee for a position on another committee). The well-known antilabor views of many of the Rackets Committee members already selected, and particularly those of South Carolina's Strom Thurmond, who would eagerly take his place if he declined, underlined both the difficulty and the necessity of his accepting.

He decided to join the committee. He sponsored the resulting labor reform legislation. For the first time in his Congressional career, he concentrated intensively and almost exclusively for a period of years on a single piece of legislation. He was, said the *Christian Science Monitor,* "burning his bridges" to labor support for the Presidency. And the Senator, in one of those subsequent moments of detached self-appraisal which reflected neither boasting nor complaining, noted that it was "certainly the toughest political job any Presidential candidate could ever take on."

Like Bob, John Kennedy believed there was a job to be done. If the leaders of labor were displeased, he would, in the last analysis, go over their heads and make his case with the people. But at the same time he antagonized the leaders of big labor, he also gave the leaders of big business reason to regard him with resentment be-

---

6. Kennedy served on the Labor Committees in the House and Senate throughout his Congressional career. In 1947, as a freshman Congressman, he had strongly opposed the Taft-Hartley Bill which labor found so restrictive.

cause the committee exposed management's involvement with labor corruption wherever it found it—even in the executive offices of the *New York Times.*[7] John Kennedy's was the strongest voice on the committee in pointing out management's transgressions. Before the committee finished with Beck, Kennedy ticked off some of the largest companies that had been drawn into the investigation—Anheuser-Busch; Fruehauf; Associated Transport, the nation's largest trucker; Occidental Life Insurance; and Montgomery Ward—and said:

"Although I think Mr. Beck, as a trustee of the union funds, was culpable, I think these men who came before this committee and saw nothing wrong in any of these things that they did are certainly not equally responsible, but are responsible. While there is no law against it, I think the committee should take cognizance of the attitude that they took before this committee and recognize that they have a responsibility as well as rights in this matter."

And so he would speak out against both big labor and big business and he would play a major role in the shaping and the enactment of the Labor Reform Act. The country watched, and when Kennedy went to the people through the difficult primary route in the winter and spring of 1960, many people were with him, in no small part because of his conduct on the McClellan Committee.

The investigation also was a major element in the fire that forged a closely knit group of tough-minded men behind his cause. It is no accident that some of John and Robert Kennedy's most trusted aides —men like Pierre Salinger, John Seigenthaler, Carmine Bellino, Kenneth P. O'Donnell, James J. P. McShane and Walter Sheridan —came out of the rackets investigation.

7. The committee disclosed that during a Teamsters strike in 1948 the *Times* had paid $35,000 to Harry Gross, an ex-convict-extortionist, and Cornelius Noonan, president of Local 1730, International Longshoremen's Association, to get its Sunday magazine section, which was being printed in New Jersey, delivered. The *Times* cooperated with the committee, and Amory H. Bradford, vice president and business manager, testified before the committee. "This is not the kind of payment that we would make today," he said.

Chapter 5

The Way to Washington

A FEW MONTHS after President Kennedy's death, Jess Unruh, one of the most powerful Democratic figures in California and former speaker of the California Assembly, told a reporter that "the Kennedys are the only people in American politics who have not built their careers on massive ingratitude." I would not have gone that far, but I would have to say that long after the Seattle *Times* could be of any further help to the committee, Bob did not forget the paper. It made an impression on us because we had not often seen that trait in the public officials with whom we dealt.

Whenever the committee came across information in which Bob thought we might be interested, he would call to tell us. He knew, for example, that since 1951 we had been probing and watching the activities of Frank Colacurcio, a Seattle pinball machine and restaurant operator who was becoming a power among interests that operated on the fringes of the law and who appeared to have connections in the Democratic Party. Occasionally, the committee came across Colacurcio's tracks outside Washington State and once his name figured briefly in a hearing. Each time Bob called to fill us in.

In October 1959, Bob came to Seattle as a favor to the *Times*. W. J. Pennington, comptroller of the paper, was also president of the Rotary Club of Seattle and asked me if I could persuade Bob to speak. Bob said he would. He arrived some weeks later about 3 A.M. aboard the *Caroline*. I found him asleep curled under a blanket in the rear of the plane. As we drove along the dark, wet, deserted streets toward my house, he shook his head. "Just tell me one thing," he said. "How did you talk me into doing this?"

"I didn't," I said. "This is one of the few cities in America where the people don't think you're ruthless. You must have been dying to come out here."

"Sure," he said, "thanks a lot." We rode on home in silence.

The following noon he addressed the Rotarians. It was the first time I heard him speak in public, and he appeared somehow to be smaller and younger as he stood behind the lectern. The words came quickly and easily, and, speaking without notes, he discussed the new labor-reform legislation and praised it, reviewed the committee's work and advocated a central federal intelligence bureau to pool information on crime across the nation. Finally, he reminded the business-minded Rotarians that "I can't think of a case where a union became corrupt by itself. Management always is involved, too." It was the same speech that he had been giving to other civic and fraternal groups, and he had polished and memorized it. Many in his audience had felt the heavy hand of Beck and they liked what they heard, but perhaps no more so than the businessmen of Birmingham, Alabama, and other cities where he had spoken. Because of his role on the committee, he was much in demand in those days as a speaker before businessmen's groups. Later, he would remember those appearances with irony as the businessmen who had applauded him for racket-busting and investigating labor corruption blasted him for enforcing the antitrust and civil rights laws.

Late that afternoon he met with a group of Seattle men and women who were interested in supporting his brother. In the evening we had a party at our house for him, and were introduced to a Kennedy idiosyncrasy. At midnight the party was in full swing, but Bob, though he was the guest of honor, having had little sleep the night before, excused himself politely and went upstairs to bed. He left the following morning, and the next time I saw him was in

Los Angeles, two days before the opening of the Democratic National Convention.

Washington is a run-of-the-mill state as far as national political conventions go. Although among the eleven Western states only California has more votes, Washington's votes can become crucial in a convention only because it is near the bottom of the alphabetical roster: In a close run, it is one of the states, along with West Virginia, Wisconsin and Wyoming, whose votes can put a candidate over the magic figure or cause him to fall short.

In 1960, as John Kennedy trudged from factory entrance to high school gymnasium to main street in hundreds of towns whose names he would never forget—in New Hampshire, Wisconsin, West Virginia and Oregon—his brother, Edward, and a small corps of backers foraged through the nonprimary Western states to find delegates where they could. Washington would have fifty-four, each with one-half vote. The Kennedy forces would find them hard to win over.

Senator Warren G. Magnuson, a long-time member of the Senate's inner establishment, was with Lyndon Johnson. Like him, many of the older leaders of the party in the state, with ties back to Harry S. Truman and FDR, supported Johnson. As a fallback, they favored Senator Stuart Symington. Among the younger Democrats and in the liberal wing of the party, there remained deep affection, respect and support for Adlai Stevenson. Senator Henry M. Jackson, a popular, potent vote-getter in his own right, was a Kennedy man. The Stevenson and Kennedy forces had been organizing from the district level up while Magnuson was busy in the Senate and elsewhere. As the two sides battled with mixed results, Governor Albert D. Rosellini, who would lead the delegation and have a say about its makeup, remained uncertain and uncommitted. He knew he faced a difficult campaign for re-election, and he was reluctant to alienate any source of support. But in the selection of the Democratic candidate for President religion would influence him more than anything. He was the first Catholic to become Governor of Washington, a state whose voters are predominantly Scandinavian Lutherans. What was more, his lieutenant governor, attorney general, house speaker, insurance commissioner and several other state officials were Catholics, and all would be on the Democratic ticket. Would it help in a state like Washington to have another Catholic at the head of the ticket? Rosellini thought not, but kept silent.

It was impossible to tell how the Washington delegation would break. On the paper we tried to keep close tabs, and during March, April, May and June Bob called us about once a week. "I understand we've got nine and a half votes out there now," he would say, and we would say, "No, the way we count, you've got four." Each time he called, he would have a higher figure for his brother than we did.

John Kennedy came to Spokane for the state convention late in May, but so did Lyndon Johnson and Stuart Symington, and the Stevenson forces were still going "madly for Adlai." So no bandwagon rolled through Spokane that weekend, and the delegation went to Los Angeles uninstructed and wrangling. By this time the Washington votes were becoming "crucial." By Bob's calculations, if Kennedy's vote topped 700 when the roll call came to Washington, there was a good chance for nomination on the first ballot. Bob would instruct his floor managers to be ready at that point to apply the little extra pressure that might be needed to reach 761 and victory. And now there was another factor: between the state convention and the national convention "Scoop" Jackson had become a serious candidate for Vice President and was campaigning openly for it.

When I arrived in Los Angeles on Saturday, July 9, I was surprised to find Jackson's top aides and the agency executive who had handled his campaign advertising for many years setting up a campaign headquarters in the Statler Hotel. There had been some talk in Seattle earlier in the week about Jackson as a possible running mate with Kennedy, but it had not received serious consideration in the press. When the Jackson aides told me that what they were doing wasn't for prestige or publicity but that Jackson could get the nod, I knew where I could find out for sure. I found Bob in Suite 8315, the Kennedy headquarters in the Biltmore Hotel. It was about

3 P.M., and he was eating a turkey sandwich and drinking a glass of milk.

"He's my choice," he said, "and Jack likes him. I'd say he and Symington have the strongest chance. Orville Freeman[1] is another possibility. It depends on how things develop. Scoop would help us in the West, but between now and Thursday he is going to have to convince some of the Midwestern and Eastern leaders like Daley, Lawrence and Bailey[2] that he can help the ticket the most. We've told him that, and he understands it. I hope he can do it."

"Does it make any difference how the Washington delegation votes?" I asked.

"Well, it would be nice if Scoop could deliver it all," he said. "It would help. But getting broader support outside the West counts more."

It was not the most important development in Los Angeles that day, but it would be the most interesting to the readers of the Seattle *Times*. I went back to the Statler and told the Jackson people that they were right and then called my managing editor. My story led the paper the next morning, and my assignment for the convention became: "Stay with Jackson all the time." I did, except that Bob had volunteered to meet me each morning and keep my feet under me. We met in the Biltmore between 7:30 and 8 o'clock, and he not only gave me the latest assessment of Jackson's chances but told me in detail what was happening in his brother's fight for the nomination. On Saturday he had been optimistic. On Monday morning, with the news that Illinois would give Kennedy 59 of its 69 votes, he was confident of victory, though it was not yet known how three important states—California, Minnesota and Pennsylvania—would vote.

Within the Washington delegation, the fact that Jackson had a chance to be Kennedy's running mate changed nothing but the emotions of the delegates. An attempt Monday afternoon to bind the delegation unanimously for Kennedy was beaten down in a tense caucus, despite support even from Johnson's man (and Jack-

1. Governor of Minnesota and later Secretary of Agriculture.
2. Mayor Richard Daley of Chicago, Governor David L. Lawrence of Pennsylvania and John Bailey, Democratic boss of Connecticut.

son's friend), Senator Magnuson, who indicated he would switch to Kennedy to help Jackson and said: "We've got a real good chance [to nominate Jackson], and I know whereof I talk." But the Stevenson delegates could not be budged, and Rosellini remained noncommittal. He plugged Jackson's campaign but refused to endorse Kennedy, saying: "I'm going to watch it for another day." Tuesday saw little change in the delegation, and on Wednesday forenoon— the day the voting would begin—Johnson came before the Washingtonians to plead for help to "stop Kennedy." He said he was entitled to their support, and he tore into Kennedy, casting doubt on his physical fitness and attacking Kennedy's liberal credentials. He assailed Joseph P. Kennedy, inferring not too subtly that the ex-ambassador had been soft on Hitler and was anti-Semitic. "I was never any Chamberlain-umbrella-policy man. I never thought Hitler was right," Johnson thundered.

By Washington State standards, it was a low political speech —and it did not change any votes. But it caused Jackson's aides to put in a frantic call to Bob, who hurried over to the caucus and disclosed that Jackson was his personal choice for second place on the ticket.

"My brother has the highest regard for Jackson," Bob said. "He is my personal choice for the Vice Presidency, but that is not going to determine who is selected. If I said that Jackson would be the Vice President if my brother gets nominated, I would be misleading you. But when the decision is made, a representative of Jackson will be there."

The net effect of three days of intense pressure on the delegation was that Kennedy picked up Magnuson's vote and a few of those previously uncommitted, including Rosellini's, but lost as many delegates, who resented the pressure. And so the delegation took its place in the rear of the arena, behind a television tower, still divided, still leaderless and very much on edge. When the roll call reached Washington, Kennedy had 697½ votes—just short of Bob's prediction—but obviously ample for a first-ballot victory. At that point, the political thing for Washington to have done—if only to further Jackson's chances—would have been to cast all its votes for

Kennedy. The state chairman, Luke Graham, hesitated at the microphone. Delegates shouted at him to poll the delegation again. Aides pleaded with Jackson to intercede, but he refused to budge. Just as stubborn, the Stevenson backers glared adamantly at Graham. The chairman, with a last look at Jackson, turned and announced the vote as: Kennedy, 14½; Stevenson, 6½; Symington, 3; Johnson, 2½; and Rosellini, ½.

A few minutes later, Wyoming proudly cast all 15 votes for Kennedy, and that did it. I pushed my way out of the Sports Arena and waited with other reporters outside the Kennedy cottage, one of several which had been built for the candidates on the arena grounds. The curtains on the front picture window were drawn back and we could see the elders of the party—Daley, Lawrence, Bailey, Governor Mike DiSalle of Ohio, Averell Harriman of New York, Governor Abe Ribicoff of Connecticut, Governor G. Mennen Williams of Michigan, Representative John McCormack of Massachusetts, Representative William Green of Pennsylvania, Mayor Robert Wagner of New York, and many more—arrive alone or in groups to wait for the candidate's arrival. Soon we could see the lights of a police escort flashing in the darkness. A cavalcade moved swiftly down a ramp, and in a few minutes Kennedy was walking quickly toward the cottage. Bob was waiting on the porch and stepped down to greet him. They nodded and shook hands firmly. If they spoke, we could not hear it. Then Kennedy walked into the cottage, and we could glimpse him moving among the men inside.

The next morning when I met Bob, I asked if anything had been decided.

"No," he said. "It's between Symington and Scoop."

There have been many accounts published now, by persons more knowledgeable than I, about how John Kennedy chose Lyndon Johnson to be his running mate. What I know is that when Bob said it was between Symington and Jackson, he believed that to be the case. In the predawn hours Thursday, he and his brothers had discussed with their father whether to offer the nomination to Johnson. The next morning, though Bob knew the possibility was being explored, it seemed—and later he would use these words—"so inconceivable" to him that Johnson would accept that he did not think it worth mentioning.

In April 1964, he told me: "There were only three persons who knew the whole story, and now one is gone. I guess it will have to wait until Lyndon and I write our memoirs." I suggested that the versions might differ. "They might," he said.

Bob made these comments after reading a draft of an article on the selection of Johnson which Philip Potter, chief of the Washington bureau of the Baltimore *Sun,* had sent to him for his approval. Potter, who had been close to Johnson for many years, had interviewed the President, Bob and others. In a note attached to his manuscript, Potter wrote:

> I am holding up submission of this until I hear from you. The President has authorized me to quote him. I believe it is essential, in the interest of authenticity, to quote you, and pray that you will agree. I do not think the story can be told otherwise, and I feel it is about time that a thorough account be published to lay forever the many distorted and inaccurate accounts of that day's happenings.

Bob asked Potter to make very few changes. It is worth noting that he did not disagree with Potter's findings, which were set forth at the outset of the article, as follows:

> It was not an unfriendly Robert F. Kennedy, but the telephone—and Lyndon B. Johnson's penchant for keeping it in constant use—that almost upset the arrangements for a Kennedy-Johnson Democratic ticket in 1960.
>
> This fact has emerged from a series of interviews with the President, Attorney General Robert F. Kennedy, Senator Edward M. Kennedy and the late President Kennedy's principal political lieutenants, Kenneth O'Donnell and Lawrence F. O'Brien, both of whom served Kennedy and now are serving Johnson as special White House assistants.
>
> Their recollections of the hectic negotiations between Kennedy and Johnson after the Massachusetts senator's nomination for President late on the night of July 13 repudiate completely conjectures that Kennedy offered his principal rival second place only as a "gesture"; that Robert Kennedy tried to sabotage his brother's decision to name the Texan; that the Johnson camp took the initiative in getting him on the ticket.
>
> The decision, say the Kennedy brothers and the Kennedy lieutenants, was Kennedy's own and was based on his political acumen and judgment after he weighed on his own nomination night the qualifications of various

prospects, including Senator Symington of Missouri, Senator Jackson of Washington and then Governor Orville Freeman of Minnesota.

Bob asked Potter to make only two changes of importance. One was to delete a sentence in which Potter wrote that Bob recalled that he had been "actively in favor of putting Johnson on the ticket." The second had to do with the beginning of a statement denying reports that he had tried to block Johnson's selection. Potter quoted Bob as saying: "It's a lie and unthinkable." Bob crossed it out and wrote: "It's untrue and of course really makes no sense." The rest of the quote, which Bob did not change, was:

"I was not operating independently. I was Jack's agent. And no one knew that better than I. It was unimportant whether or not I concurred in Jack's decision. Jack was definitely happy to have him on the ticket. That was enough for any of us."

For Scoop Jackson, Thursday would be long, worrisome and ultimately terribly disappointing. He began the day feeling sanguine about his chances. He had made some progress with the Eastern leaders—not enough, probably—but he had support inside the Kennedy camp and he felt he was very much in the running. About 9:30, John Salter, Jackson's administrative assistant, was called to Suite 8315 to confer with JFK and Bob. The candidate asked Salter to list "the vital reasons" Jackson would be best for the ticket, and Salter gave four:

1. Jackson had increasing national stature as the Senate's expert on defense, atomic weapons and scientific matters.

2. Jackson would unify the Western Democrats, particularly in California, which also had split its votes bitterly between Kennedy and Stevenson.

3. Jackson would have support in the East primarily because of his role in the Army-McCarthy hearings.

4. Jackson would magnify Kennedy's image as a "youthful, vigorous, winning leader."

The Kennedys were noncommittal, and two hours later Salter and Jackson, thinking they would learn the decision, returned to the suite and conferred with JFK for fifteen minutes. But they found that no decision had been made, and Kennedy explained that personal preference was one thing but that now he had the job of reconciling differences among the party leaders. He said nothing that indicated Johnson was in the picture.

Jackson walked the four blocks back to his headquarters in the Statler, thinking he would know the answer in forty-five minutes. Nearly three hours later, Kennedy telephoned and told Jackson that it would be Johnson—that a number of the leaders thought Johnson should be on the ticket and that he also had come to that conclusion. As a consolation, he asked Jackson to be Democratic National Chairman. Jackson asked for time to think it over but promised that he would do everything he could to help win the election. I remember how shocked I was when Jackson told me. After what I had heard Johnson say about the Kennedys, he was the last man I thought would be on the ticket. I had a lot to learn.

A few days after the election, I was interviewing Jackson in his office in the U.S. Courthouse in Seattle when Bob called him. After their conversation, Jackson said, "I have a friend of yours here," and put me on the line. I congratulated Bob and we chatted briefly and then he said: "Would you be willing to come back here and work in the Administration?" I asked what he had in mind. "I'm not sure," he said. "There are fifteen or sixteen things you could do. I'll call you back."

The next time I heard from him it was the middle of January, two days before the inauguration. I had gone to Olympia to cover the legislature, and he reached me there. Without amenities, he said: "How would you like to do my press work and handle public information for the Justice Department?"

"I'd like that," I said. "I'll do it."

"Don't you want to come back and talk about it first?" he asked.

"Sure," I said. "I'll be there Saturday [the day after the inauguration] or Sunday."

Because of fog in Seattle and snow in the East, it took me more than forty hours to reach Washington. I arrived on Monday afternoon and went directly to the Attorney General's office on the fifth floor of the Justice Department. Packets of mail and packages were stacked high on tables and littered most of the floor space in the reception room. An attractive brunet receptionist took my name. The phone rang frequently. Men and women strode purposefully in and out of the inner offices. I watched the action like a spectator at a tennis match. I don't know what I expected—a dignified law office, I guess—but I remember thinking, "My God, it's just like the Biltmore Hotel!" After thirty minutes or more, Angela Novello, Bob's personal secretary, appeared and I was relieved to see a familiar face. She guided me into the Attorney General's walnut-paneled, vaulted office. Bob, in shirtsleeves, grinned and said: "Howya doing? Do you think it's big enough?"

Bob called in John Seigenthaler, who had become his administrative assistant in the campaign and would serve in the same capacity at Justice. A minute later Byron White, the Deputy Attorney General, entered, and in shaking his huge hand I sensed what I was to learn later—that he was one of those rare, highly touted persons who live up to all their advance billing. I sat down between White and Seigenthaler, and Bob took a chair facing me. He turned it around and sat, tilting it forward, with his arms folded on the back. The conversation lasted only fifteen minutes, and during most of it Bob outlined what he wanted me to do. He said that the public relations office had a chief, an assistant and four secretaries and that its work had been confined to routine answering of press inquiries and to putting out news releases. He thought that a great deal more could be done to inform the public about the Department's activities. It would be essential to develop as broad an understanding of the Department's actions as possible, he said, and not only because civil rights and organized crime would be areas of controversy. Since his appointment had not been received "with unanimous approval," he pointed out, there would be great attention on everything that Justice did. He said he wanted the Department to speak with one voice on basic policy matters. I asked if he meant that the Assistant Attorneys General would have to clear with me before agreeing to see a reporter. He said not necessarily. He intended to be more accessible to reporters than his predecessors had been, and he wanted his top aides to be, too, but he didn't want differences over policy aired in public.

I said that his reputation for truthfulness held him in good stead with the reporters who knew him and that this was a good foundation on which we could build. Seigenthaler agreed. I asked how soon he wanted me to come to work.

"Right away," he said.

"Tomorrow?" I said. He nodded. I told him I had to give the *Times* two weeks' notice and could be on the job between the sixth and tenth of February.

"You can be here on the sixth," he said with a smile, and it was on this small point that I experienced for the first time directly the combination of friendly needling, stimulation and authority that characterized his leadership. "I'll be here on the sixth," I said.

White had watched me closely but had not said anything. As he stood to leave, he shook my hand and said, "I'm glad you're coming. We'll knock a few corners off of you, but then we'll all have a few corners knocked off us before we're through here."

Bob invited me to spend the night at Hickory Hill, and about 7 P.M. I accompanied him home from his first day in the Attorney General's office. The only time I saw him evidence any newness in the job was when we stepped into a black, chauffeured Cadillac limousine. He appeared a bit embarrassed by its elegance. "The government provides them for all Cabinet officers," he explained. "It rents them for about $500 a year, which isn't a bad deal."

As we drove across the Memorial Bridge and turned into the George Washington Memorial Parkway, the headlights reflected off the snow stacked on the side of the road. Bob asked about my family and what I had been doing and talked about his hopes for the Justice Department. He thought the Department had been negligent in pressing its cases against Hoffa. He said he did not know why, but that he was going to have each case reviewed thoroughly and would make a full effort to bring Hoffa to justice. He wanted the Department to prosecute cases of significance rather than amass an enforcement record that was high in the number of cases brought, but low in impact. When we reached his home, Ethel greeted him at the door and with an innocent look asked: "Was there enough for you to do?"

"Hardly," he said.

Paul Fay, President Kennedy's friend from PT 109 days, who had been appointed Under Secretary of the Navy, was staying at the house. The evening was spent in warm recounting of their activities during the inauguration weekend. At one point, I remember saying to Bob, "While you were making history, I did one thing I'll bet you wish you could have done."

"What's that?" he said.

"Coach a Little League football team." He looked at me speculatively for a moment and then said softly: "Yes. I'd like to do that sometime." That I could have mentioned it that night—that in the slower tempo of life in Seattle I had had the time to coach the team —is some measure of the great changes that were to occur in my life.

The next day driving into Washington, we dropped the three oldest boys, Joe, Bobby and David, at Our Lady of Victory School, an appropriate name, it seemed, that splendid, chilly morning, for a school attended by the nephews of John Kennedy. At the Department, Bob told me that he would announce my appointment in the afternoon, but that I would have to write the press release. Later, he introduced me to the man I would succeed, Luther A. Houston, who had been a respected, veteran Washington correspondent for the *New York Times* before going to the Justice Department in 1957. I asked Houston if he would stay on the job for at least two weeks after I started to teach me the ropes. He agreed to do so, and I always was grateful for his cordiality, kindness and sound advice in those early days. Houston gave me a brief tour of the public information office, and I stopped by to tell Bob I was leaving. As I was going out the door, he called out: "Say, Ed, what's Charley Smith doing these days?"

When the Beck hearings were at their height, Charles O. Carroll, the King County prosecuting attorney, sent a young deputy, Charles Z. Smith, to Washington to comb the committee's files for evidence on which to prosecute. Smith, a man of great integrity and high intelligence, studied the records for two weeks with Bob's full cooperation. Later, Smith's legal scholarship was to make a large contribution to the conviction of Beck and Dave Beck, Jr., for grand larceny. In 1959, Smith, then thirty-one, wanted to enter private practice, and Carroll and several other friends interceded in his behalf with the leading law offices in Seattle. Young members of the firms who had worked with Smith in Carroll's office or had seen him in action reacted enthusiastically. However, their senior partners invariably demurred on one of two grounds: They thought either that it might be awkward when they all went to lunch at their private clubs or that some of their clients might be resentful. Smith is black. He set up an office with two other young attorneys, but their practice was small and consisted mostly of divorces and police court matters. I told Bob I thought Smith was having a hard time.

"We're going to have a special group of lawyers to review the Hoffa cases," Bob said. "Charley would be of tremendous help. Do you think he'd be interested?"

I thought Smith would, and Bob asked me to call him before I went back to Seattle. I went into another office to make the call and took a phone from its receiver. Then I put it back and returned to Bob's office.

"Before I make that call," I said, "there's one thing you ought to know. Charley was head of Lawyers for Nixon in King County."

Bob looked at me with a somewhat pained expression.

"I'm not interested in his politics, only what he can do as a lawyer," he said, nodding his head several times to emphasize the point. In a few weeks, Smith went on duty in the Criminal Division and became a valued member of what was to become known as the "Hoffa Squad," which Walter Sheridan headed. As with Beck, Smith played a major role in the conviction of Hoffa for defrauding the Teamsters Central States, Southeast, Southwest Pension Fund.[3]

There was one more thing I did that day before flying back to Seattle. The Department of Justice building is a massive, gray granite structure built in the Hoover Administration. It occupies a block of the Federal Triangle, bounded by Pennsylvania and Constitution

---

3. Smith now is a Superior Court judge in Seattle.

avenues and Ninth and Tenth streets. It is about midway between the White House and the Capitol. I started from the Attorney General's office and walked through the Department's labyrinth of hallways. Circling from the fifth floor down to the first, past solemn portraits of previous Attorneys General, I jotted in a small notebook the location of the various divisions, whose names were painted in gold letters on wooden standards.

I would come to know the men and women who worked behind those formidable doors and become familiar in detail with the work they did, but I would still be making wrong turns in the maze of corridors after working there three and a half years. That first day I felt awed, somewhat bewildered and unsure of myself.

Aboard the plane my mood changed. We landed briefly in Chicago and then flew westward over the frozen lakes and snow-covered fields of Wisconsin, the Dakotas and eastern Montana. The land below looked barren and lifeless, but in a day I had felt the exhilaration that abounded in Washington at what seemed to be the beginning of a new era. In the dusk, the land seemed alive with hope. Pride in being chosen for the job, confidence and an eagerness to start work displaced the lonely thoughts of the afternoon.

Chapter 6

We Happy Few

THE EBULLIENT, STIRRING START of the Kennedy Administration ended with a thud in the fiasco at the Bay of Pigs. In the chastening, soul-searching aftermath, Bob ruefully recalled the earlier time that had seemed so stupendous. "Those were the days," he said, "when we thought we were succeeding because of all the stories on how hard everybody was working."

From the beginning the news media had concentrated on the vigor and the style of the new President, his family and his men. Writers and television commentators dealt with "The First Hundred Days" as though there were something compelling and magical about them. Invariably they compared Kennedy's first weeks with Franklin D. Roosevelt's "First Hundred Days," when a series of dramatic actions rallied a people hungering for leadership in the depths of the Depression. The atmosphere around the White House was so contagious that only ten days after Kennedy took office a group of distinguished writers and photographers undertook to document what was happening for a book—*Let Us Begin*—which was to appear as soon as possible after the hundred days had passed. Unfortunately for the publisher, the Bay of Pigs intervened and the book, like everything else, had to be revised hastily.

Looking back now, all the fuss about the "First Hundred Days" seems to have been much overdone, and yet it had a certain validity. The Kennedys were activists by nature and by instinct. John Kennedy did not have anything like FDR's landslide mandate for change. Still, he viewed the Presidency, as he so often expressed it, as "the vital center of action," and he believed it was important to make a favorable first impression. So he was both doing what came naturally and at the same time constantly buffing his image as he sent an unprecedented number of messages and bill drafts to Congress, held the first Presidential press conferences televised live, organized the Peace Corps, sent messages to foreign leaders and dispatched aides overseas, reorganized the White House staff, made public speeches and moved informally but purposefully through Washington.

Furthermore, many people believed in 1961 that the nation faced crises and challenges more demanding than any since 1933, though the circumstances had changed greatly, and the problems were vastly different and more complex. Eisenhower's soporific second term had ended with Castro taking over Cuba; the shooting down of a U-2 spy plane over the Soviet Union; a calamitous summit conference in Paris; and riots and violence in Japan, South Korea and Turkey. The British author and foreign affairs analyst, Barbara Ward, touched a chord of common concern when she wrote that the world's problems had gathered momentum so rapidly in the 1950's that only the "liveliest, most far-sighted statesmanship" could keep the 1960's from disaster. And she expressed a widely held worry when she wondered whether Western man, "while gaining affluence, may not have lost his vision and his soul." But now new spirit, fresh ideas and boundless energy emanated from the White House. All said they had no illusions about the future. Yet it seemed in those early weeks—that brief moment—that through the President's words alone the nation's spirit had been lifted, its purposes rediscovered and its future charted. The enthusiastic response to the Peace Corps seemed proof enough that the American people could be counted upon to respond when their President called for service and dedication in an hour of national peril and national opportunity.

If there was more spirit than substance to it all, still the miracle of the "First Hundred Days" seemed real enough. The writers and commentators were not alone in believing it. The New Frontiersmen, reflecting the glitter from the White House, took up their jobs with zeal and unlimited confidence. It seemed that, with John Kennedy leading us and with all the talent he had assembled, nothing could stop us. We believed that if we faced up to the nation's problems and applied bold, new ideas with common sense and hard work, we would overcome whatever challenged us and that during the next eight years the nation would make great progress at home and abroad. We were neither foolish nor naïve. We had grown up during the Depression. Most of us had been enlisted men or junior officers in World War II or in Korea, and most of us had experienced months of combat. We knew we faced a precarious, unstable world in which a Bay of Pigs blunder could happen or one man's bullet could break our hearts forever. I suppose we might have thought about that, but in those heady, early weeks we did not have time.

Outside the White House, nowhere was the new tempo or the new ways of doing things more evident than in the Department of Justice. And nowhere, outside the White House, was the new Administration more on trial. As Bob had put it, his appointment had not met with "unanimous approval."

Later, when speaking to groups of lawyers in the Department, Bob had a story to tell about how he became Attorney General.

"I started in the Department as a young lawyer in 1950," he would begin. "The salary was only $4,000 a year, but I worked hard. [Pause.] I was ambitious. [Pause.] I studied. [Pause.] I applied myself."

Without fail, the lawyers would be laughing before the punch line: "And then my brother was elected President of the United States!"

The President-elect disclosed from the steps of his home in Georgetown in December 1960 that he intended to appoint his brother to be Attorney General. There must have been many critics, judging from the tone of their comments, who believed the decision had been made just about that simply. More controlled but nonetheless vocal opposition was raised by the bar over Bob's limited experience as a lawyer. He never had been in private practice nor tried a case in court. Nepotism always should stir editorial writers, and it did. Furthermore, many expressed concern that Bob's experience as mentor of his brother's campaigns inevitably would inject political considerations into the administration of justice which should be outside the arena of politics, even if it hasn't always been.

Bob anticipated the criticism, and because of it and for personal reasons, he resisted the appointment. He knew that if he did an effective job, particularly in civil rights and antitrust enforcement, he would be unpopular and even more controversial than he was, and he felt it would place an unnecessary burden on the President. He considered sub-Cabinet posts in State or Defense, but realized his relationship and his access to the President would present unsolvable problems for his immediate superiors. He thought about returning to Massachusetts with the intention of running for governor in 1962. He sought advice from Senator McClellan, FBI Director J. Edgar Hoover and his old friend, Justice Douglas. McClellan and Hoover urged him to become Attorney General. Douglas counseled that his career would be better served by doing something else, such as becoming president of a university. Finally, he decided to take at least a year off to study, travel and write. But his brother persisted with persuasive arguments. He said he had relied on Bob's advice in the past and would need it as President. He said that since others were making sacrifices to serve in the Administration, Bob could not refuse to serve. In the end, Bob agreed without saying so in so many words. He didn't have to, such was the closeness of their relationship.

When I heard the announcement, my first reaction was that it was a mistake. I felt it smacked too much of nepotism, and that with the name of Kennedy there was no way Bob could administer the Department of Justice without embroiling himself and the President continually in hot water. It was obvious that no matter how good an Attorney General Bob would be, he might become the Administration's Achilles' heel. He would have to do the job better than it had ever been done. What I didn't fully appreciate, and what most critics did not understand, was the relationship between the President and Bob—that it was remarkably close even for brothers; that John Kennedy felt a need to have his brother's counsel; and that he perceived rightly that a man of Bob's leadership and organizational abilities would be stifled in a staff role but would thrive in a command of his own.

The wisdom of having Bob as Attorney General began to dawn on me very shortly after I began working in the Justice Department. Bob had moved swiftly to implant his brand of leadership. The 31,700 career employees in Justice wondered, undoubtedly not without some skepticism, what kind of an Attorney General he would be. By the evening of the second day they had a pretty good inkling.

President Kennedy's second Executive Order upgraded the Food for Peace Program. The Department of Agriculture and the State Department had been jointly responsible for the program, but the order established the office of the new director, George McGovern,[1] in the Executive Office of the President. In preparing the order, a White House aide called Bob about 6:30 P.M., to check some legal points, and Bob called the Office of Legal Counsel for advice. The top career men in the Legal Counsel's office and elsewhere in the Department—by and large an impressive group of skillful, experienced and dedicated lawyers—had been accustomed to burn the midnight oil under Bob's predecessor, William P. Rogers,[2] and other Attorneys General, but with no crisis apparent, no one was in the Legal Counsel's office when Bob called. Harold F. Reis, first assistant in the office, was reached at home, and he returned to the Department to prepare a memorandum for the White House's guidance. Before leaving to return home, Reis, a short, wry man, poked his head into Bob's office and said: "Mr. Kennedy, I just want to tell you one thing."

---

1. Now U.S. Senator from South Dakota.
2. Now Secretary of State.

Bob looked up, expecting Reis to complain about being called back.

"As long as you're here," Reis said, "there'll be somebody on duty in our office every night until you leave."

News of incidents like that has a way of traveling swiftly through the bureaucracy, especially when it happens again the very next night. At 6 P.M., Bob, Byron White, John Seigenthaler and several other members of the staff had gathered in Bob's office to watch on television the President's first news conference. Midway through the conference, a reporter asked about the Portuguese cruise ship *Santa María*, which a group of Portuguese rebels had hijacked in the Caribbean four days earlier and were sailing toward Brazil. A number of American tourists were aboard. Navy planes kept the *Santa María* under surveillance as destroyers sped to intercept her. The reporter asked, could the Navy board her when it made contact? The President hedged.

"The *Santa María* has been located," he said, ". . . and the position is approximately six hundred miles north of the mouth of the Amazon River. . . . Now, there are Americans involved . . . but we have not given any instructions to the Navy to carry out any boarding operations."

Bob put in a call for Reis. The Legal Counsel's office was only down the hall from the Attorney General's and Reis appeared in seconds. As Reis walked into the room, Bob asked whether the Navy had a right to board, adding that the first Cabinet meeting was in the morning and the question was likely to come up. The problem was new to Reis, and he didn't know what to say. As he hesitated, someone declared, "Well, it's piracy, isn't it, and under international law any country can fire on or board a pirate ship. Isn't that so?"

Reis replied that while he had been in the Department a long time, he had arrived well after the old piracy days and so he didn't really know the answer. The taciturn White, permitting himself a trace of a smile, told Bob that it was ridiculous to assume that Reis could furnish the answer without research.

"Well," Bob said, "I'd like a paper on it in the morning."

Reis watched the rest of the press conference and then returned to his office. The question was not one readily answered. He called the State Department's Legal Division and the Navy Judge Advocate General's office and a number of private attorneys who he thought might help. He also summoned three other career Justice lawyers—Harry Sellery, Mary Lawton and Leavenworth Colby—from their homes. At 3 A.M. they finished a three-page memorandum concluding that as a matter of international law the Navy would have the right to board the *Santa María*. Reis handed the memorandum to Bob at the White House shortly before the Cabinet meeting began. That was the way it would be.

Like Reis, I found myself swept immediately into Bob's pace. On Friday I had been a reporter in Seattle. On Monday I was press officer for a major federal department about which I knew very little. The change felt awkward. I had a lot to learn, and Bob didn't wait. He expected performance immediately. I learned as I went, and on the third day I learned something most important: that I would never be able to go to Bob and plead ignorance about something because I had not been informed about it.

The President was going to announce that he would ask Congress to create fifty-nine new federal judgeships to relieve congested court calendars. The Attorney General's office would supply the details about where the proposed judgeships would be located. Bob called me into his office and asked me if the press release was ready. I hadn't even heard about it and told him so. He didn't say anything, and he didn't have to. The frown on his face communicated the message.

I talked to John Seigenthaler about it, and he advised me to do what he did: watch Bob's schedule closely, observe who was in his office, who was waiting to go in and what was going on—and then show up or do what had to be done whether asked to or not. I did from that moment on. In the next three and a half years, I don't recall Bob saying very often that he was going to have a meeting and that he would like me to attend or that he was going somewhere and wanted me to accompany him. He expected us to anticipate his needs and act accordingly. He did not stand on ceremony, and if we had—if we had said, "I should have done that, but you didn't tell me to, I didn't know"—we wouldn't have been much help to him and we wouldn't have been around very long.

And so the pace would be swift and the new Attorney General would be demanding. That much was clear throughout the Department.

The young attorneys who came to take command of the Department's various divisions and offices were highly motivated men, incorruptible, low-keyed and forceful, and they were extremely bright. Two, Byron White and Nicholas deB. Katzenbach, Assistant Attorney General in charge of the Office of Legal Counsel, had been Rhodes Scholars. Only a few had been in government before. Katzenbach had been in the office of the General Counsel of the Air Force from 1950 to 1952. Solicitor General Archibald Cox had served in World War II in the National Defense Mediation Board, the office of Solicitor General, the State Department and the Department of Labor and was chairman of the Wage Stabilization Board during the Korean War.

They did not fear the government. They welcomed the chance to serve in it. Like John and Robert Kennedy, they had fretted and become restless during what they regarded as eight years of national drift and inaction, of failure to face the nation's problems. They viewed the government as a means to rekindle the nation's spirit, to shape a peaceful world and to make a new start in dealing with the problems of prejudice, poverty and urban congestion at home. They came determined to do their part in those endeavors, and as lawyers they came with a special feeling for the law, an unyielding commitment to see that the rule of law would be upheld and that justice would be administered evenly.

They were young. The oldest was Lee Loevinger, who left the security of the Minnesota Supreme Court to be Assistant Attorney General in charge of the Anti-Trust Division. He was forty-seven. Ramsey Clark, Assistant Attorney General in charge of the Lands Division, was the youngest—thirty-three. I remember late in 1961 realizing reluctantly during a staff meeting in Bob's office when White, Cox and Loevinger happened to be absent, that

I was the oldest in the room. I was forty-two.

Politically, they were near the center. Herbert J. Miller, Jr., Assistant Attorney General in charge of the Criminal Division, was a Republican. The rest were Democrats. Loevinger had been a contemporary of Hubert Humphrey and Orville Freeman in the struggles of the Democratic-Farm-Labor Party in Minnesota. Joseph F. Dolan, who, along with William A. Geoghegan, was one of White's two deputies, had been a member of the Colorado legislature. The rest had not been greatly active in politics until John Kennedy made his run for President, and then only White, Cox, Dolan and John R. Reilly, who became head of the Executive Office for United States Attorneys, had played significant roles in the campaign. Katzenbach had been in Switzerland on a research project in international law during the campaign and did not even vote. Politics figured to any extent only in the appointments of Clark and Loevinger. Clark, whose father, Tom, was a justice of the Supreme Court and former Attorney General, was, as a Texan, close to both Lyndon Johnson and Speaker Sam Rayburn. Loevinger[3] was put forward by Humphrey and Sargent Shriver, who was in charge of recruiting talent for the new Administration.

White brought most of the others to Bob's attention. The influx of Harvard men into the Administration was enough to cause James Reston of the *New York Times* to quip that "Harvard will have nothing left but Radcliffe when Kennedy gets through raiding his alma mater." But in the Justice Department Yale predominated. Two of the Assistant Attorneys General—Katzenbach and Louis F. Oberdorfer, who became head of the Tax Division—attended Yale Law School with White. Burke Marshall, who became chief of the Civil Rights Division, also was a Yale Law School graduate and William H. Orrick, Jr., who headed the Civil Division, did his undergraduate study at Yale, but White knew them only by reputation.

3. Loevinger left in June 1963 to become a member of the Federal Communications Commission. Clark remained throughout Bob's term. He became a trusted member of Bob's inner group of advisers and served as Deputy Attorney General and Attorney General under President Johnson.

Bob fully recognized his limitations as a lawyer and the criticism which his appointment had aroused. As a consequence he sought to enlist men who were recognized within the legal profession as being particularly able in a variety of specialties, not only for the posts of Assistant Attorneys General but for responsible positions throughout the divisions and in the offices of the U.S. Attorneys. By and large, he succeeded. He brought to the group exceptional talent for command and bruising experience in Congressional committee work, one area to which no one else except Dolan had been exposed. The others represented a broad spectrum of legal experience, and no single anecdote reveals more about Bob's instincts about men and his process of selecting them than why and how he chose Burke Marshall.

After the election, it was widely believed in the Kennedy camp and in the press that the sensitive post of Assistant Attorney General in charge of the Civil Rights Division would go to someone prominent in the civil rights struggle. Most speculation centered on Harris Wofford, a former Notre Dame Law School professor, who worked on civil rights matters for John Kennedy from 1959 on. Wofford would have been an excellent choice. He had experience in Washington on the staff of the U.S. Civil Rights Commission as well as his service on JFK's staff. His credentials as a lawyer and as an activist in the cause of equal rights were beyond question. His appointment would have been a plus with blacks and white liberals.

But as Bob and White looked ahead to the role the Justice Department would play in the gathering struggle over civil rights—that Justice would be at the center of federal action, bearing the greatest responsibility and receiving the greatest amount of criticism and opposition—they felt that the only proper course for the Department would be to proceed in strict accordance with the law, avoiding any appearance of pitting one social point of view against another. They decided that someone who had been in the forefront of any rights or racial cause might be handicapped by ideology or past associations in civil rights enforcement. Therefore, they began looking for an outstanding lawyer, someone no less sensitive than

Wofford[4] to the cause of equal rights but not identified with it. The search led to Marshall, who was practicing antitrust law in a leading Washington, D.C., firm, Covington & Burling.

Probably no man ever came into the United States Government with looks that were more deceiving than Marshall's. Behind a solemn, self-effacing manner, a slight build, spectacles and a creaky voice were a brilliant mind, a great amount of exceptionally penetrating logic and a terse, dry sense of humor, and he possessed more physical courage than most men twice his size. Marshall was so self-effacing and so laconic that when he came for an interview with the equally laconic Attorney General, the meeting was notable only for long periods of dreadful silence. When it was over, Marshall, who wanted the job very much, left believing that he had blown his chances. Bob was not impressed and doubted that he ever could establish a relationship with Marshall. They were to become the closest of partners and the closest of friends, deeply trustful and respectful of each other.

"I picked him on his reputation," he explained. "I asked a dozen people, and they all said Burke was the best young lawyer in Washington."

As with Marshall, White and Loevinger, the legal credentials of the other men were impressive. Cox, a respected arbitrator in labor cases and an adviser to John Kennedy in drafting the labor-reform legislation, was a Harvard Law School professor. Oberdorfer had been a clerk to Supreme Court Justice Hugo L. Black and was a partner in a leading Washington law office. Katzenbach, an expert on international law, was a University of Chicago Law School professor. Miller, a graduate of George Washington University Law School, also was a Washington lawyer of growing reputation.

The fact that Miller was a Republican who kept an autographed photograph of President Herbert Hoover in his office added a nonpartisan color to the group, and Bob felt it would help mute charges that the Administration was being political when Republicans were

---

4. Wofford served on the White House staff and then directed the Peace Corps in Ethiopia.

prosecuted. But those were minor considerations, and, as it turned out, the Kennedy Administration prosecuted many more prominent Democrats than Republicans. In selecting the head of the Criminal Division, Bob's overriding concern was to find a first-class lawyer as the first step in upgrading the practice of criminal law. He had been critical of Justice Department prosecutions in the past, particularly in the Hoffa bribery case, and felt strongly that the presentation of government cases needed to be strengthened. From what he had seen, he also was concerned that rights of defendants often were poorly protected by sloppy defense work. If lawyers of top ability could be persuaded to work in the Criminal Division, he reasoned, promising young attorneys might be inspired to practice criminal law, instead of gravitating to the more lucrative specialties. Miller came to Bob's attention when he served as a lawyer for the Board of Monitors, which was supposed to keep Hoffa on a straight and narrow path. Though the board was somewhat less than effective, Bob measured Miller's strength of character, ability and hard idealism and liked what he saw.

These men were, as John Kennedy said in his Inaugural Address, "tempered by war." Like so many of the New Frontiersmen, they had spent from two to five years in the service—a mark of the Kennedy Administration that was not well understood and was often overlooked. Theodore H. White was the first to catch the essence of it when he noted in *The Making of the President—1960* that control within Kennedy's convention force was "precise, taut, disciplined—yet as casual as that of a veteran combat army, blooded in battle, which has learned to know all of its own component parts and recognizes the full reach of its skills and courage." And White quoted one of Kennedy's lieutenants as saying "I think we learned something during the war about how to do things; we learned to work in a way the generals didn't understand." Thereafter, few observers perceived how much World War II service influenced the actions of the Kennedy men.

Their youth and their style were noted often, but it was not only that the New Frontiersmen were the youngest group of men to come to power since the early days of the Republic. They also were the first group of GI's, deck officers and platoon leaders to come to power this young since the Civil War. It was part of their style, and it separated them from the men of Lyndon Johnson's age, who had not heard a shot fired in anger, from General Eisenhower and from the old liberals of the New Deal era.

It was something felt inwardly; something hard to discern perhaps, and even harder to describe. Havoc and death, gallantry and fear, days of waiting and nights without sleep, the yearning for home—all these had bred impatience with mediocrity, instincts for action and distrust of convention. But having survived the war, they had self-confidence and were inclined to be more hopeful than fatalistic. Still, having seen strong countries devastated and proud peoples shattered, they were always aware that, as President Kennedy said in his first State of the Union address, "We shall have to test anew whether a nation organized and governed such as ours can endure. The outcome is by no means certain."

Outwardly, the experiences of World War II were most apparent in the way they reacted quickly in a crisis. They had spent such a long time in the service that their instincts as soldiers, sailors or airmen never left them. They were disciplined and knew how to work together. They had no time for red tape and cut through it with pleasure and vengeance. They understood logistics and the need to keep communications open. When it was necessary to raise a nonmilitary force quickly to protect the Freedom Riders in Alabama or to mount a complex operation to ransom the Bay of Pigs prisoners, they improvised. They organized easily. All the things a junior officer or a noncom has to think about besides fighting— moving his men, feeding them, keeping contact, getting supplies, finding a place to sleep—came naturally.

Lastly, the war left them all with a healthy skepticism of the brass. As the U.S. marshals were gathering at a naval air station in Memphis during the crisis at the University of Mississippi in 1962, plans were being laid for Army support, and Brigadier General Charles Billingslea, assistant commander of the 2nd Division, went to Memphis to look the marshals over. Billingslea, a tall paratrooper and a hero of the Battle of the Bulge, was not impressed with what he saw.

As his jeep drove past groups of marshals standing in seeming disorder, his military mind boggled. He was further distressed when he had trouble finding someone in command. Finally, he was taken to Oberdorfer, who was in an office in the back of a small building. Billingslea began to express dismay at what he had seen, but ex-artillery officer Oberdorfer cut him off. Rising from his chair, placing his hands on the desk and looking squarely into Billingslea's eyes, the small, husky chief of the Tax Division said: "General, there's just one thing we want to hear from you. What are your capabilities?"

(In fairness to Billingslea, the assignment in Mississippi was about the last thing he might have been expected to do for his country when he entered the military service. And the marshals were wearing ill-fitting old clothes. They didn't look like much, but they were brave, well-trained men.)

A few days later, Katzenbach led the marshals on to the campus of "Ole Miss" and surrounded the Lyceum Building to prevent interference with court orders requiring the enrollment of James Meredith, a Negro. One of the first things Katzenbach did was to open two phone lines, one to the White House and the other to the Justice Department. During that long night as the marshals staved off a howling, shooting mob and Billingslea led his men to the rescue, the President of the United States, perhaps for the first time, had direct, continuous communications with a scene of violence. When the Defense Department brought reports of developments, the President already knew them—and much more. Several days later, Katzenbach and I went to Memphis to take a small plane to Washington. A Signal Corps general was waiting at the field and asked if he could hitch a ride. Aboard the plane, the general told Katzenbach, "You guys really did it to us. Our reports to the President were always way behind yours. It's the worst thing that's ever happened in my career. Tell me, how did you do it?"

Katzenbach reached into his pocket and took out a dime. "Well, General," he said, "you take this dime and—"

The general laughed and took the ribbing good-naturedly. However, using the nearest thing at hand—in this case a pay telephone

—to open communications had been a natural step for an ex-GI. Earlier, when White led the marshals to the relief of the Freedom Riders in Alabama, Oberdorfer used a pay telephone to make contact with Bob's office.

Katzenbach, gently tough and infinitely patient, had been a navigator on a B-26 that was shot down in the Mediterranean early in the war. He spent two and a half years in Italian and German prison camps, enduring a grueling forced march over miles of ice and snow during the winter of 1944–45. He was involved in several escape attempts, but he also used his time reading books supplied by the International Red Cross that would help him complete his college education. He had left Princeton early in his junior year to enlist in the Army Air Force. When he returned in 1945, he made up the last two years in a matter of weeks by writing a senior thesis and taking final exams in all the required courses, graduating *cum laude*. Marshall had served in the Army, where his special talents for analysis played a major role in the breaking of a Japanese code. Dolan and Geoghegan had been infantrymen. Andrew F. Oehmann, who had long service in the Justice Department and was Bob's executive assistant, was a Navy lieutenant (j.g.). Clark served as a corporal in the Marine Corps. Bob left Harvard at eighteen after his brother Joe was killed over England, and volunteered, against his father's wishes. He served as a seaman aboard the U.S.S. *Joseph P. Kennedy, Jr.*, and on patrol in the Caribbean, galled at missing combat duty. Orrick and Miller served overseas in the Army. White, the legendary all-American halfback from Colorado and leading ground gainer as a professional in the National Football League, was a naval intelligence officer in the South Pacific.

There were few changes in the group while Bob remained Attorney General. In April 1962, White became a member of the Supreme Court, Seigenthaler couldn't resist when the opportunity came to become editor of the Nashville *Tennessean*, the leading newspaper in his home town. The President, on Bob's recommendation, sent Orrick to the State Department in June 1962 to attempt to untangle its administrative setup. Orrick returned to head the Anti-Trust Division after Loevinger went to the FCC a year later. John Douglas, the Lincolnesque son of Senator Paul Douglas of Illinois and another classmate of White at Yale and also a Rhodes Scholar, replaced Orrick in the Civil Division. When Katzenbach moved up to Deputy Attorney General when White left, Norbert A. Schlei, a brilliant young attorney from Los Angeles, became the Legal Counsel. He was thirty-three, a Yale Law School graduate and a former law clerk to Supreme Court Justice John M. Harlan. Seigenthaler was replaced first by James W. Symington,[5] the personable son of Senator Symington, and later by John E. Nolan, Jr., a taciturn Washington lawyer who played a key role in the release of the Bay of Pigs prisoners before joining the staff.

They participated in every major decision affecting the Department. Bob valued their judgment and included them in making decisions whether or not their specific responsibilities or legal specialties were involved. He counted on them to ask difficult questions, to be devil's advocates and to think through the consequences of proposed courses of action.

His practice was to have a meeting in his office, where the lawyers who were handling the matter to be decided would present the facts, outline the alternatives and defend their recommendations. It was characteristic of Bob that he would insist that the lawyers who were working on the case make the presentation. He not only wanted them to feel that they had been given full opportunity to present their views, but also wanted to hear their opinions directly, rather than have them filtered through their superiors.

When a decision went strongly against the wishes of the lawyers directly handling the matter, Bob would give them a second opportunity or more to argue their views directly with him.

A notable example was the out-of-court settlement in March 1963 of the dispute over ownership of the General Aniline & Film Corporation, which the government had seized in World War II on grounds that it was part of the huge, Nazi-controlled I. G. Farben chemical trust. In 1943, Interhandel, a Swiss holding company,

5. Symington was Chief of Protocol in the Johnson Administration and now is a Congressman from Missouri.

claimed that it owned 89 percent of General Aniline and brought a recovery action. The Justice Department replied that Interhandel was only a front for I. G. Farben. The case had been in litigation for twenty years—once before the International Court of Justice, twice before the U.S. Supreme Court and numerous times before the Court of Appeals—and still had not come to trial. The outlook was that the legal fight would continue for a decade or longer. Meanwhile, the continuing dispute and government control were restricting growth and diversification of the company, which had plants and research laboratories in nine states.

Bob thought the time had come to settle. The Civil Division lawyers on the case were unanimously opposed, primarily on the grounds that former Nazis well might benefit from a settlement. The lawyers had several meetings with Bob and a number of the Assistant Attorneys General and pressed their views vigorously. However, Bob decided to settle. He believed the terms were equitable;[6] that possible benefit to former Nazis, while hard to swallow, was outweighed by the advantages to the company of being free of government control and by the fact that proceeds from the government's share of the settlement would be used to pay claims of American citizens for injuries and property damage suffered at the hands of the enemy during World War II. Furthermore, there appeared little likelihood that a better settlement could be obtained by prolonging the legal battle.

Usually there was considerable disagreement among Bob's assistants over a proposed course of action. Each meeting would end with Bob requiring each man to state what he thought should be done and why. Occasionally the group would divide equally, and then Bob would comment wryly, "Thanks a lot. That makes everything easy."

It had been found in White House meetings where courses of action were being deliberated that the presence of the President

---

6. The settlement called for the government to sell its 93.5 percent interest in General Aniline and receive at least 60 percent of the proceeds, with the remainder going to Interhandel. When the stock was sold in March 1965, the government accepted a bid of $329,141,926.49—almost $100 million more than had been expected two years earlier.

could inhibit the participants. Bob mentioned this more than once. In his book on the Cuban missile crisis, *Thirteen Days,* he pointed out that respect and awe for the office of President of the United States could cause even the independent, strong-minded men who sat on the "Ex Comm" (Executive Committee of the National Security Council) to make recommendations "on the basis of what they believe the President wishes to hear." That was not the case in the Justice Department, probably because the number of advisers was smaller and they were all from the same organization. Furthermore, the aura which surrounds the President does not extend to his Cabinet officers, even when one of them is his brother. Consequently, Bob always participated in the decision-making discussions. Except for presiding, he mostly listened. His assistants knew without being told that if he had thought they were trimming their opinions to please him, they would not be invited back.

Those few lines from Shakespeare's *King Henry V* in his remarks to his men before the Battle of Agincourt, a favorite passage of Bob and President Kennedy, best described the group:

> We few, we happy few, we band of brothers.
> For he today that sheds his blood with me
> Shall be my brother. . . .
> And gentlemen . . . now a-bed,
> Shall think themselves accursed they were not here. . . .

Even after six years, I know that I cannot be objective about these men. It was one of the most rewarding experiences of my life to walk among them. I do know that I never observed any personal wrangling among them or any jockeying for Bob's favor. And I suspect that the Department had not seen their likes before.

There were a number of other steps Bob took in those early days to signal how he would run the Department. As President Kennedy, in reviewing the inaugural parade, had been shocked to see no black faces among the cadets from the Coast Guard Academy and had acted quickly to correct that, Bob was chagrined to find that of the Department's 950 lawyers only 10 were blacks. He began immediately to recruit blacks for positions throughout the Department. At his first staff meeting on February 10, he said, "The government can't overestimate the effect of cleaning up its own house. That means in hiring, in elimination of segregated offices in the South and in thorough integration of all its operations, South and North."

The order included the FBI, which had less than a dozen black special agents—including two who served as attendants in Hoover's office—out of a total of almost six thousand.[7] Later, when Hoover asserted that the FBI was having difficulty finding eligible young blacks, Bob asked each of us and U.S. Attorneys around the country to find Negroes in our home areas who could qualify. The number of black FBI agents increased. The effect was the same throughout the Department. Not only did the number of black lawyers increase tenfold or more in two years, but Negroes were appointed to key posts. Cecil Poole in San Francisco and Merle McCurdy in Cleveland became U.S. Attorneys. Luke C. Moore became the first black U.S. marshal for the District of Columbia in almost a century. For the first time, Negroes became deputy U.S. marshals in Birmingham; Phoenix; San Francisco; Los Angeles; East St. Louis, Illinois; Greensboro, North Carolina; Cleveland; Tulsa; Charleston, South Carolina; Nashville; Alexandria, Virginia; Jackson, Mississippi; Montgomery; Hartford; St. Paul; and Kansas City, Kansas.

Another thing Bob did was to become very visible throughout the Department. He frequently would appear unannounced in obscure offices where Attorneys General were not likely to go and most likely had never been before. He would open a door, extend his hand and say, "I'm Bob Kennedy." He would chat with the startled secretaries and lawyers and ask them what they were doing, if they had enough work to do, if they liked what they were doing. Lawyers in the various divisions came to his office in groups to meet informally with him until he had met every lawyer in the Department. Later, as he traveled around the country, he would visit U.S. Attorneys' offices, prisons, Immigration and Naturalization Service

---

7. A decade later, minority employment figures released by the Department of Justice showed the FBI had 51 blacks among a total of 7,910 special agents.

offices and FBI offices which had not seen an Attorney General in years, if ever. And he would spend hours, particularly in connection with organized crime, talking about current cases in detail. He seldom was interested in what had been done. He wanted to know the current status and what was going to be done.

Partly he was satisfying his insatiable curiosity, but he had a deeper concern: to let every member of the Department feel that the Attorney General—and through him the President—was interested personally in what he was doing. He also wanted to make clear that he judged people by their performance, not by their political connections. Frequently, particularly when talking to U.S. Attorneys and their assistants, he would say something like this: "We can't be concerned about politics. I don't want to screw around. I don't want someone who won't go down the line. I want you to understand that you don't owe your job to anyone.

"All your decisions must be based on facts. You'll make mistakes, but you'll have the complete support of this office as long as your decisions are made with honesty and integrity."

His curiosity extended to small details. How was the mail, which had tripled in volume since his arrival, being answered? He demanded to see samples from each division and fumed over their matter-of-factness and lack of warmth.

"If someone takes the trouble to write his government, then we can take the trouble to see that he receives a sympathetic, honest answer," he said. "Nobody should be brushed off."

Having said that and having ordered changes, as long as he was Attorney General he would check the mail periodically to see if red tape and routine had countermanded his wishes. When they had, we heard about it.

His appetite for work and information was insatiable. In the beginning he chafed in the lonely splendor of his office. "It's like being on a desert island without girls," he said. "It's the damnedest job I've ever seen. An Attorney General could sit out by a swimming pool all day and not do a damn thing!" He demanded to be kept informed about everything that was occurring in the Department, and he accomplished this by keeping his door open, having frequent staff meetings and by getting detailed written reports each night from each division head. At the first staff meeting he said: "I want to be informed. Do your homework. Don't let there be anything in your department that you don't know. Know every damn thing!"

And he would hold us to it, but as a partner, never as a taskmaster. He would not dwell on mistakes. He was not interested in explanations, only in knowing whether good judgment had been used and what corrective steps were being taken. He could be irritated but never harsh. When a mistake was his, he took responsibility cheerfully. His magnetism was such that when we made mistakes, we felt that we had let him down personally.

His concern for the morale of the Justice employees extended to how they exercised and where they ate. He built a gym on the roof and provided tables, awnings, chairs and a snack bar in the courtyard. He took a deep interest in seeing that they were recognized for their services. Lawyers, secretaries, clerks and messengers with long service in the department found themselves invited to receptions at the White House. When he went to Congress to testify before a committee, he wanted the lawyers and secretaries who had worked on his statement or the particular legislation in question to be among the spectators. He received many notes of appreciation, but none he valued more than one from Bessie M. Greene, who had operated the mimeograph room for many years. Mrs. Greene wrote:

For the first time in my life I was permitted to be a spectator at hearings before a Congressional Committee. Since you were the chief actor, and also thoughtful and courteous enough to include me in the Justice group, I want to say a special thank you!

Although I have served under ten Attorneys-General, no one before you has ever seen fit to reach this far down the ladder and include a person of my position in "The Mainstream of History." This is what sets you apart from other men. You have a heart and you use it.

I felt I was part of "history in the making" and believe me, I was highly complimented that you made me a part of it. Dorothy and Helen[8] were very

8. Dorothy Junghans and Helen Abduch were secretaries in my office whose experience, skill and untiring dedication saved me from making many a mistake and to whom I will always be grateful.

gracious and courteous to me—all the way—even finding a grandstand seat for me while they had to stand.

May God guide you in your appeal for justice and morality for all American citizens.

About a year after we came to the Department, I was talking with Byron White and he asked what I thought was Bob's most important accomplishment so far as Attorney General. I began by ticking off items—the protection of the Freedom Riders, getting all twenty-six federal law enforcement agencies to coordinate their efforts in the fight against organized crime; and so forth. White interrupted.

"Don't you know?" he said, shaking his head. "This place has always been run like a big law office. For the first time, he's given it the sense of the public man."

Chapter 7

The Cuba Crises

THE BAY OF PIGS was the turning point for the Kennedy Administration. It was a great deal more than the crushing end of the "hour of euphoria" as Arthur M. Schlesinger, Jr., called the period before the ill-fated invasion. President Kennedy was tested to the marrow before his Administration was fully prepared for a major crisis, and the whole affair—ill conceived and botched—exposed serious flaws in the White House decision-making process and in some of the men who advised the President that the invasion be carried forward.

Although as far back as October there had been unconfirmed reports in the press that a guerrilla force of Cuban exiles was being trained at a secret base in Guatemala, the attack came as a surprise to most Americans, including many persons on the White House staff. As the dimension of the disaster became apparent, shock and dismay gripped the country. The President faced not only rising doubt about his leadership at home but the death or capture of the brave Cubans he had sent to the beaches and an unpredictable chain of reaction at home and abroad.

At a press conference two days after the guerrilla brigade had been defeated, the President made a comment that would win the country's respect, cement the loyalty of his men and mark his character for all time.

"There's an old saying," he said, "that victory has a hundred fathers and defeat is an orphan. . . . I'm the responsible officer of the government and that is quite obvious."

There have been excellent, authoritative accounts written about the Bay of Pigs, including those by Sorensen and Schlesinger, who had far more firsthand insight than I did. There is Haynes Johnson's invaluable book *The Bay of Pigs*, in which the story of the gallant men of the brigade—their clandestine training, their experiences in the invasion and their ordeal in prison—was told for the first time. My vantage point was limited.

At dawn on Saturday, April 15, World War II B-26 bombers bearing the markings of Castro's air force had bombed Cuban airfields. One bullet-punctured plane made an emergency landing at Boca Chica Naval Air Station in Key West, and another, riddled from antiaircraft and small-arms fire, landed at Miami International Airport. Officials of the Immigration Service, which is a part of the Department of Justice, took the pilots into custody. As newsmen pressed for information and interviews with the pilots, Edward Ahrens, Immigration District Director in Miami, said the identity of the men was being kept secret at their request, to protect their families in Cuba. The men, Ahrens said in a statement attributed to one of them, had defected from Castro's air force after planning "for some months" to escape.

Ambassador Adlai Stevenson spoke later in the day in the United Nations in reply to charges by Raúl Roa, the Cuban Foreign Minister, that the planes had been piloted by U.S. mercenaries in a prelude to an invasion. "These two planes," said Stevenson, "to the best of our knowledge, were Castro's own air force planes, they took off from Castro's own air force fields."

The planes, of course, were the air arm of the Cuban brigade and had taken off from an airfield in Nicaragua. John Kennedy himself had authorized the mission. The statement attributed to the pilot was part of a cover story concocted by the CIA, and it was beginning to crack while Stevenson was speaking. It was to be Stevenson's most humiliating hour, for he, like so many others in the government, had not been told.

At the White House, Pierre Salinger, the Presidential press secretary, had not been told either. As reporters peppered him with questions, Salinger said the government had no firsthand information, only what the press already knew. There was no official comment at the Pentagon or the State Department, only unofficial references to the President's press conference pledge. I began to receive requests from reporters to get more information from the Immigration Service. I tried unsuccessfully to reach Ahrens and could not contact top Immigration officials in Washington. Then David Kraslow of the Miami *Herald* came to my office.

"We think this whole thing is a cover story," he said. "I've got to know. Is it?"

"I really doubt it," I replied, and then, with all the confidence in the world, added: "There's no chance that the Immigration Service would be involved in something like that and I wouldn't know about it."

Kraslow asked me to check for sure and call him. Some time later I reached Bob at home and related the conversation. There was a long pause. "Well," he said finally, "something is up down there, but I don't think a final decision has been made."

"What do I do about Kraslow?"

"Go fishing. Get lost."

The storm broke on Monday. The invading forces, fourteen hundred strong, went ashore during predawn darkness. While they fought against increasingly heavy odds, a public relations firm in New York, retained by the CIA, put out optimistic communiqués in the name of the Cuban Revolutionary Council, and around the world alarmed reaction, much of it angrily anti-American, set in.

As the crisis deepened, Bob was at the White House, and we did not see much of him during the next three days. He did return to his office late Monday afternoon, and he did not need to say that the Revolutionary Council communiqués and other reports were more than slightly inaccurate. His face was a somber mask.

"It's not going well," he said, shaking his head. "I think we've made a hell of a mistake. The worst thing is that we're caught in a lie. It's the U-2 business all over again. Do you want to know why we did it?"

Then he related what he knew, and I learned for the first time that the invasion was a CIA affair and that the plans had been war-gamed and approved by the Joint Chiefs of Staff. The main reason that the invasion had gone forward so early in the Administration, he said, was that a large number of Cuban pilots were receiving jet training in Czechoslovakia.

"They're due back around the end of the month," he said. "There are a large number of MIG's being uncrated in Cuba, and once the pilots are there to fly them, it will take the Army, Navy, Air Force and the Marines to bring Castro down and we're not about to go that route."

There were other reasons why the President had decided to put the plan in operation. But that night Bob mentioned only the return of the jet pilots, indicating, I must say in retrospect, that quite possibly it had been uppermost in the President's mind when he made his fateful decision.

I asked Bob if there was anything to be done.

"No," he said, and for several minutes he stood gloomily at a window, peering down on the homeward-bound traffic inching along Constitution Avenue.

"Well, there's one thing you can do," he said. "You can start praying for those poor fellows on the beach."

The next two days were more trying than any I can recall in the Justice Department. We wanted to help, but there was nothing to do. We wanted at least to keep up a stiff front, but that was difficult. Momentarily, the work we were doing in civil rights, antitrust and so forth did not seem to matter much. We were to face many crisis-filled days and nights in the Department, but they would be times of action, purpose and decision. Now shock gave way to deep foreboding.

Belief in the government was shaken at every level, from the President and Ambassador Stevenson on down. The combination of secrecy within the government and an elaborate but clumsy, unrealistic attempt to camouflage American involvement with the expedition irreparably damaged the government's credibility. Coming so soon after the U-2 downing, in which the truth soon caught up with another CIA "cover story," faith in the government's word withered, not only at home but around the world.

On April 23 the President named Bob to serve with CIA Director Allen Dulles and Admiral Arleigh Burke, Chief of Naval Operations, on a committee, headed by General Maxwell D. Taylor, who had been called back from private life, to investigate the whole operation. Dulles had been a major proponent of the invasion plan, and Burke, as a member of the Joint Chiefs of Staff, had approved it.

Two days later, the second warm day of spring after an unusually cold winter, Bob arrived late for one of the staff luncheons held regularly on Tuesdays and Thursdays in a dining room in the Attorney General's suite of offices. A discussion was in progress about an exceptionally bitter exchange that had taken place that morning in the Supreme Court between Chief Justice Earl Warren and Justice Felix Frankfurter.[1] He listened attentively. When it had run its course, Bob said that with his new assignment he would be absent from the Department for an indefinite period. He explained the background of the invasion and asserted that, on the basis of the information presented to the President and the approval of all the responsible officials, the President's decision was correct. "But the information was not wholly accurate," he said. "Furthermore, there were some foul-ups. The brigade went ashore with ammunition which ran out within four hours, and it was not resupplied. Castro's ability to clamp down on possible insurrectionists was underestimated. Cuba really has become a police state."

So, he said, the outlook was that the situation was going to get worse.

"The decision whether to fight a war may have to be made this

---

1. Warren had upbraided Frankfurter, accusing him of degrading the Court and lecturing to it, after Frankfurter, in dissenting from a decision overturning a murder conviction, asserted that the majority had misinterpreted its appellate function "to turn a criminal appeal into a quest for error." The decision was five to four, with Warren siding with the majority.

year," he said. "In any event, decisions similar to those made to assist the Cuban exiles will have to be made possibly many times in the next three or four years.

"The President doesn't want to blame anyone for what's happened. He takes all of that. He wants to have the process by which the Cuban decision was reached studied carefully and examined to find out why it happened and what steps can be taken to prevent it from happening again."

Bob said that he would return to the Department late each day and wanted to stay on top of what the Department was doing. However, he said, White would take over much of his work and Joe Dolan would assume some of White's duties.

"I think it's particularly fitting, Bob, that you have this assignment," White responded. "What all of us think is particularly fine about you being in the Cabinet is that you're in a strong position to help your brother."

We wished him good luck.

"Thanks," he said. "Thanks a lot." He got up to leave and then with a straight face said: "Let me just say that it will be terrible if the Department improves while I'm gone."

While serving on the committee, however, he never freed himself entirely from any major decisions that confronted the Department. He returned to his office each evening, met with us and lugged home two briefcases stuffed with departmental papers. Within a month he would be embroiled in his first major civil rights crisis—the attacks on the Freedom Riders in Alabama.

The Taylor committee finished its work in June. Its report was never made public, but many of its conclusions were documented by Schlesinger, Sorensen and Johnson and can be read between the lines of *Thirteen Days*. Changes in personnel and in the decision-making process went on apace. Taylor became the President's personal military representative, with special responsibilities in defense and intelligence, until he could be appointed Chairman of the Joint Chiefs. Allen Dulles retired as head of the CIA, ending distinguished service under eight Presidents, and was succeeded by John A. McCone.

But the most important change was that thereafter, when difficult decisions had to be made in foreign affairs, the President was never without his tough-minded, searching questioners—Bob, Sorensen, Treasury Secretary Douglas Dillon, and Under Secretary of State George Ball—as he had been at the Bay of Pigs. These men—along with Defense Secretary Robert McNamara; Secretary of State Dean Rusk; McGeorge Bundy, the President's adviser on national security affairs; Paul Nitze, Assistant Secretary of Defense; Roswell Gilpatric, Deputy Secretary of Defense; Taylor and McCone; as well as other advisers like Kenneth O'Donnell, Averell Harriman and Ambassador Llewellyn Thompson—developed such rapport and mutual respect in working together that they were able to function with increasing effectiveness, as they were to demonstrate in the ultimate test—the missile crisis. Thus, in the sense that the Bay of Pigs exposed considerable dry rot in the government early in John Kennedy's term and he acted effectively to root it out, the Bay of Pigs was something of a blessing in disguise—if there can be any positive aspect to a folly of that magnitude.

Bob drew many lessons from the Bay of Pigs, and his participation in the committee's inquiry affected him most in four ways.

1. He was ever mindful of the fact that all the leading figures in the government had favored putting the expedition ashore; that the Joint Chiefs had war-gamed the operation and found it suitable, and still its fatal weaknesses, so apparent in hindsight, had not been thoroughly debated and challenged beforehand. More than ever, he reached for advice from any person in or out of the government who he thought might contribute to solving a problem. He willingly became the means by which views within the government reached the President outside the normal channels if necessary—not to go over anyone's head, but to make sure that all points of view were heard.

2. He was dismayed that the President's orders had not been carried out to the letter. The President had ordered that no American personnel should be involved in the landing, yet the first two frogmen on the beach had been Americans. By checking and rechecking on what was being done, he sought to prevent that from

happening again, and one evidence of this was the great attention to detail and the tight controls which the President placed on the military during the missile crisis.

3. He was resentful of the continuing charges in the press and by partisan critics of the President that no responsible military commander would have approved the operation and that if air power had been used as planned, the expedition would have succeeded. The committee's inquiry had disclosed that there had not been any plan to use American military planes. The plan called only for air support from the B-26's. Their first strike had been expected to knock out Castro's air force, but it failed, and the invasion faltered because the strength of Castro's air force had been seriously underestimated, particularly with respect to his T-33 jet trainers. The truth was that the employment of American jets over the beachhead most likely would not have changed the outcome except in aiding the rescue of the members of the brigade. It would have been a direct, aggressive act on our part, quite possibly with dire consequences in Berlin and elsewhere.

The President refused to be drawn into the debate. When he was asked in a press conference about a *Time* report that Rusk had canceled air support for the brigade and that he had concurred, he said: "I said from the beginning that I would not comment or attempt to on the matter because I didn't think it was in the public interest. I'll merely state that this is the most inaccurate of all the articles that have appeared on Cuba."

But Bob would not be satisfied until someone set the record straight. On his own, he did so in interviews with *U.S. News & World Report,* which had given credence to the critics' claims, and with Kraslow. The President was displeased. He felt the interviews only added fuel to the fire.

4. As an outgrowth of the inquiry, an interdepartmental group was formed to coordinate and accelerate U.S. programs to help Central and South American governments put down Communist terrorism and insurgency. There was growing evidence that paramilitary or guerrilla operations, spawned in Cuba and supported in Moscow or Peking, would be undertaken in Latin Amer-

ica, and they would command Bob's close attention as long as he was Attorney General. He became the driving force within the Counterinsurgency Group which provided training and arms to police in Latin America and later to police in other parts of the world.

On the surface, it would appear that he made a radical change after visiting South America in 1965; that his CI Group work while Attorney General was in sharp contrast to his 1965 statement: "A revolution is coming—a revolution that will be peaceful if we are wise enough, compassionate if we care enough, successful if we are fortunate enough, but a revolution is coming whether we will it or not. We can affect its character; we cannot alter its inevitability. The question is how the revolution is to be made and guided."

But one must examine the concepts underlying the Alliance for Progress, which President Kennedy proposed in the spring of 1961, and measure Bob's actions and statements against them. The Alliance was not a design for maintaining the status quo, but a pledge of revolutionary change to be accomplished with U.S. cooperation through economic development and a comprehensive program of political and social reform.

The theory behind the establishment of the CI Group was that if civilian police forces could keep order, the progress which the Alliance pledged had more likelihood of being achieved; that there would be not only less chance for a takeover by foreign-supported Communists, but also less reason for military juntas to come to power.

In a speech in February 1964 to the first graduating class of the International Police Academy, which the CI Group was instrumental in establishing, Bob put it this way:

> This may be the generation of rising expectations throughout the world. It may be the time when millions of people are released from the chains of ignorance, poverty and disease which have bound them for centuries.
>
> But it is also the age of nails in the street and the plastic bomb: it is the age of arson, sabotage, kidnapings and murder for political purposes; it is the age of hit-run terrorist activities coordinated on a global scale.
>
> And there is an inherent contradiction between these two conditions. People cannot achieve peace and security, cannot even insure their own personal safety, except under the rule of law.

Only under a government which is an expression of their own will, administered with stability and strength, can they achieve these goals. They cannot do it in chaos.

The crucial test had come in 1963 when Communist terrorists, in seeking to foment revolution in Venezuela, vowed to kill a Caracas policeman a day and were getting away with it. The police were being outgunned and outmaneuvered and were hampered by a Venezuelan law which required them to be arrested for manslaughter if they killed anyone—terrorist or not. The Counterinsurgency Group rushed arms to the police, as well as instructors in training and tactics. An arrangement was worked out so that a policeman who killed a terrorist would be examined quickly by a civilian board of lawyers, eliminating the probability that he would languish in jail awaiting trial. The Caracas police turned the tide. As a result Venezuelans were able to elect the first constitutional successor to a constitutional president in the nation's history.

"This special effort was needed," Bob wrote in *To Seek a Newer World*, published in 1967,

even in a country with large and powerful armed forces, because of the special nature of counter insurgency. Counter insurgency is not a military problem; a military answer is the failure of counter insurgency and often the beginning of full-scale civil war. . . . There is much more to controlling insurgency than the training of police and controlling the military. Insurgency aims not at the conquest of territory but at the allegiance of men. In the Latin American countryside as in other threatened parts of the world that allegiance can be won only by positive programs; by land reform, by schools, by honest administration, by roads and clinics and labor unions and even-handed justice, and a share for all men in the decisions that shape their lives. Counter insurgency might best be described as social reform under pressure.

The Bay of Pigs inquiry also brought Bob face to face with men who had fought in the battle. The committee questioned five survivors who had escaped miraculously. Their spokesman, Roberto San Roman, had drifted for fifteen days in an open boat before being rescued. (His brother, José, was military commander of the brigade and had been taken prisoner.) From these men the committee learned that the brigade had fought with incredible bravery.

Haynes Johnson reported that San Roman came away impressed that Bob had been interested in him as a person: how had he survived his ordeal at sea; what about his family; what was he going to do?

Thereafter, San Roman was a frequent visitor to the Justice Department and Hickory Hill, and Bob worked closely with him to liberate the prisoners.

My participation in the missile crisis, as in the Bay of Pigs debacle, was largely indirect, and I can add only footnotes and vignettes to the volumes that have been written about that moment when the world stood at the brink of nuclear war.

In midafternoon on Tuesday, October 16, 1962, Bob called me to his office. He was standing by his desk, coat over one shoulder, fingering a stack of papers.

"Close the door," he said. "We've really got trouble."

It was only a little more than two weeks after the marshals had protected James Meredith at the University of Mississippi, and my first thought was that something had happened to him.

"I've been at the White House all morning because there is strong evidence that Soviet nuclear missiles are being installed in Cuba," he said in a voice tight with concern.

"What does it mean?" I asked.

"We don't know, except that there's no question that they're there and that they're going to have to be gotten out," he replied. He said that the President had been informed at breakfast and had called him at home and asked him to come to the White House. The Soviet Union had been sending large amounts of military equipment to Cuba for several months. That had been causing increasing concern, he said, but despite assertions by Senator Kenneth Keating of New York and other Republicans that offensive missiles were being installed, there had been no hard evidence until photographs from a U-2 flight Sunday had been developed.

"We've kidded ourselves, and the Russians have lied in their teeth," he said with some bitterness. "The last thing anyone expected was that they'd put offensive weapons—certainly not missiles—in Cuba. You remember when Dobrynin [Soviet Ambassador

Anatoly Dobrynin] was here last month. I told him we were concerned about the build-up, and he said he'd been instructed by
Khrushchev to assure the President they'd never place missiles—or
any offensive weapons—in Cuba. How do you like that?"

As he talked, my thoughts went back to that early September
evening when Dobrynin, smiling and affable as usual, had come to
see Bob. The Russians work at developing contacts with persons,
like Bob, who are close to a President so that they can have ex-
changes of information outside diplomatic channels—their own as
well as ours. I became involved only because one of the ways they
would contact Bob was to have a veteran correspondent for a New
York paper call me. He would say, "My friend wants to meet your
guy." Sometimes the Russians would just call directly on the telephone. The meetings were held usually in Bob's office, but occasionally he went to Dobrynin's. It became my job to meet Dobrynin or
another Soviet emissary at the Tenth Street entrance and escort him
quickly into the Attorney General's private elevator and take him
to Bob's office. These comings and goings were never detected by
the press.

Bob said that the missiles would become operative in about ten
days but that the President would have to act before they did,
possibly by the weekend. Meanwhile, it was vital that there be no
leaks so that the President would have as much time and freedom
of action as possible in deciding what to do.

"I'm going to tell Nick [Katzenbach]," he said. "I'm going to have
to be at the White House or the State Department a great deal of
the time, but I don't want any indication that anything unusual is
happening. If anybody notices I'm not around, just say I'm working
on some legislation—or anything. You can handle *that.*"

I asked what he was going to do about meetings and appointments
he'd scheduled for the rest of the week. He said he would try to keep
as many as he could. His next speech was not until October 28—
before the American Jewish Congress in the Waldorf-Astoria Hotel
in New York. I reminded him of that, and he said softly, "That's
one I hope I'm around to make."

From that moment it was impossible to think of anything else.
The knowledge that this was not one more crisis, but that nuclear

war was likely, perhaps inevitable, clouded my perception of human life and changed my perspective of the future. Washington, magnificent in clear, sunny fall weather, appeared so illusively enduring. My oldest boy, Lester, who was fourteen, and a pal of his had lunch with me in Hamel's Restaurant. I watched them devour huge hot roast beef sandwiches and then dig into pieces of ice cream pie which neither could finish. I listened to their happy, confident talk. It was difficult to witness their youthful manliness and their decency and then be forced to wonder if they would live to grow to manhood and have children of their own.

On Wednesday and Thursday when Bob returned from meetings of the Executive Committee of the National Security Council, he told Katzenbach and me about the discussions, outlining the alternative strategies of knocking the missiles out by an air blitz or forcing them out by a blockade. Meanwhile, work on the missile sites was progressing rapidly. On Thursday evening Bob said that a consensus seemed to be forming in favor of a blockade. But Friday afternoon he said that the Ex Comm members had disagreed sharply in meeting with the President Thursday night and were still divided. Time was running out, he said, so they were going to meet again at 4 P.M. and try to reach agreement on a course of action.

At 3:15 he called me to his office. He was leaning back in the big leather chair at his desk, arms folded across his chest. He looked pensively at me for a moment and said: "What would you do: bomb or blockade?"

I started asking questions. He said he thought he had figured out why the Russians were installing the missiles.

"They had nothing to lose," he said. "If we did nothing, we would be enfeebled in the eyes of the world. If we bombed, we would be the aggressors and they could do anything they wished. Or we could blockade and they could go before the United Nations and raise hell about us."

The argument for bombing, he said, was that it would knock out the missiles and the Cuban air force and get it over with in a few days. The argument against it was that eight thousand Russians and many Cubans would be killed. Russia's probable reaction would be an attack on West Berlin, and since we would not back out of Berlin without fighting, a major war probably would be at hand.

The other course, besides doing nothing—which was "unthinkable," he said—was to blockade—stop all food shipments, for example. That probably would result in a confrontation, and possibly a ship-sinking, but ultimately it would bring Cuba to its knees. The missiles still would be pointed at this country, but no one would be killed and there might be some time to salvage the peace.

"Do you want to know who is for and who is against?" he asked. He listed former Secretary of State Dean Acheson, who had joined the Ex Comm meetings, McCone, Taylor, Dillon and the Joint Chiefs of Staff as in favor of bombing. Bundy, he thought, was changing to the blockade group, which included Rusk, McNamara, Ball, Thompson, Sorensen and himself.

He kept pushing me for an answer, and I kept asking questions. Finally, I said I leaned toward bombing. If we blockaded and the Russians retaliated in Berlin and we were going to have to fight our way out, I argued, a blockade was only delaying the inevitable and the missiles would still be in Cuba. Bob looked surprised and said there was a chance that we would not have to fight in Berlin. If that were the case, I said, I'd favor a blockade. Did the Russians fully understand that we would fight for Berlin? Bob wasn't sure.

He had to return to the State Department, and we kept talking in the elevator and in the car as he drove there.

That morning, though he did not realize it, he had deeply moved his colleagues on the Ex Comm by likening our proposed air strike to Pearl Harbor in reverse and questioning whether the United States could carry the moral burden of such an act. At his office and in the car, he did not mention Pearl Harbor but stressed that the blockade was not a soft step, that it would demonstrate our determination to get the missiles out, and yet allow time for the Russians to step back.

On the steps of the State Department, he said: "Now, you have to decide."

I replied that I would go to some lengths to avoid war, that I favored the blockade. I said I thought the American people and our allies would accept that in preference to bombing Cuba just because the missiles were there. So I came down on the side of blockading, and, smiling, he pointed out that I had changed my mind.

"It's a very tough problem," he said. "When you think through each side, you can convince yourself of either. Neither course of action is pleasant or easy. It boils down to shoot now on the theory that the showdown is at hand and a blockade is only a time-consuming delay, or blockade and enter a very, very difficult winter and try to go the last mile to preserve the peace."

I watched him walk slowly up the stairs, briefcase in hand, his shoulders hunched. Near the top, he turned and waved, and I don't know why, but when I think of him now, that is the image that comes to my mind again and again: the lean figure standing in the late-afternoon sun near the top of the steps, arm outstretched, waving.

The next day, the Ex Comm was ready to meet again with the President, who, to keep up the pretense that there was no emergency, was in Chicago for a round of political appearances. Pleading a "cold," he returned to Washington at midday and late that afternoon all but decided in favor of the blockade. Troop movements and other steps were already under way within the armed forces in preparation for either course of action. Now the rest of the government machinery began to turn to prepare for Monday night when the President would tell the nation and the world.

The secret had been well kept, but reporters in Washington and around the country began to dig it out as the President returned, troops were on the move, and many top officials came and departed from the White House. Only the President's personal intercession prevented the *New York Times* and the Washington *Post,* in the interest of national security, from publishing well-informed stories in their Monday editions. What the papers did report was that secrecy shrouded the capital and that major action, possibly involving a new move against Cuba, was imminent.

On Monday the National Security Council met in midafternoon for a final session with the President before he spoke to the nation.

Bob asked Nick Katzenbach and me to go with him, and he decided to walk the five blocks from the Justice Department to the White House. It was another balmy fall afternoon, and Bob took off his coat and walked with it over his shoulder. Motorists and pedestrians waved or greeted him as we walked along Constitution Avenue and cut across the Ellipse. He waved back in a carefree manner. There was a surrealistic, ironic quality to that walk, particularly because of the weather, that became immediately apparent to us. How could the world appear so beautiful with the threat of nuclear war so immediate? We marveled that the security had held for six days, and we wondered how the Russians would react. We had no idea, of course, and as we approached the White House, Bob said that the only thing he was sure of now was that we were taking the right course.

The President was already in the Cabinet Room when we entered and he nodded to Bob. At first glance it appeared to be a routine gathering of the President and his advisers. However, greetings were sparse and there was almost no conversation going on and one almost immediately felt a sense of urgency and anticipation. But the President was calm, articulate and in full command as he began the meeting by outlining the situation. Rusk read British Prime Minister Harold Macmillan's message of support, and McCone gave the latest intelligence with the ominous news that work on the missile sites was proceeding rapidly. The President then said that the important thing was for everyone to support the final action which represented a fair consensus of the men in the room, though some disagreed.

"It is going to be a very tricky course, and we will never know whether this is the best course," the President said. He explained that he ruled out an air strike because there was no certainty that all the launching pads would be hit; moreover, there was no certain knowledge that any of the missiles were ready to be fired, and if an air strike was made, there was no assurance that in the confusion and heat of the moment one or more missiles might not be fired at the United States.

He said that between fifty and sixty missiles were believed to be in Cuba, that we knew where only thirty of them were, so there still were some that we did not know about that might be in position to fire. An air strike would make the danger of nuclear war in the next few days very great, but he added: "An air strike is tempting, and I didn't give up on it until yesterday morning."[2]

The clarity of his thoughts, his coolness and his obvious courage were reassuring. The care and deference that he took, when time was so precious, to acknowledge and deal with the beliefs of the men in the room who disagreed with him was impressive. No one in the room advocated not doing anything, but he discussed even that course, pointing out that it had some merit and that a good argument could be made for it.

"But it is important to do something," he said, because the establishment of offensive weapons outside the Soviet system represented a drastic change in Soviet policy. If we did nothing, there was great danger that the Russians would think we would do nothing in Berlin and the Soviet Foreign Minister, Andrei Gromyko, had said very plainly that there was going to be a crisis in Berlin.[3] Doing nothing, he said, also would have a serious effect on Central and South America, encouraging people to believe that the balance of power really had shifted and that Communism was destined to prevail.

The President then discussed why action had not been taken sooner. We still did not have the fourteen votes necessary for approval of the blockade (now being referred to as a "quarantine"— a less belligerent act in diplomatic terms) in the Organization of American States, he said. Had we moved prior to obtaining definite information that the Soviet build-up in Cuba had an offensive capa-

2. The President became fully committed to the blockade after meeting with Tactical Air Command Chief Walter Sweeney, Jr., and being told he could not be certain that an air strike would knock out all the missiles.

3. The previous Thursday the President had gone ahead with a long-scheduled meeting with Gromyko, who stated implacably that if the United States did not agree to a peace treaty with Germany, the U.S.S.R. would carry out its long-standing threat to sign a separate treaty with East Germany, invalidating the occupation rights in Berlin. Gromyko did not mention anything about the missiles in Cuba, asserting that his government had only supplied Cuba with "defensive" weapons. The President did not tip his hand that he knew about the missiles.

bility, there would have been no support for our moves either in the OAS or in Europe. Premature action would have rebuilt Castro's sagging prestige in Latin America, while our allies in Western Europe would have greatly criticized our acting drastically in Cuba at the risk of sacrificing West Berlin.

The President described the distinction between the Soviet missiles in Cuba and our Jupiter missiles in Turkey and Italy. Ours had been emplaced in direct response to a Soviet threat and had been done openly, he said. The Soviet action had been taken secretly and was a provocative step, aimed at upsetting the status quo, which we could not brush aside. He discussed whether the situation did not present Russia with a chance to trade off Cuba in order to get its way in West Berlin.

"There is all the difference in the world," he said. "The Soviets are going to make a big issue in Berlin anyway, and this may change their way of going about it but not the fact that they are going to do it."

Each man in the room knew what he was to do. There were no questions. Each knew the enormity of the stakes, and each knew the agonizing uncertainties that lay ahead. Their faces, grim and somber, imparted strength and purposefulness rather than worry and doubt.

"Remember," the President said in conclusion. "Quarantine is only the first move and we hope we don't have to make the others. . . ."

With the President's speech to the nation that evening there no longer was any need to keep up a noncrisis appearance. For the remainder of the week as the quarantine went into effect, Russian technicians worked around the clock to complete the missile sites and the tension mounted. Bob was at the White House virtually all the time. We saw him only fleetingly, but he kept in contact by telephone.

The government has prepared an elaborate underground complex outside Washington to enable the President, the Cabinet and skeleton staffs to continue to function in the event of nuclear attack. There is an order of evacuation, which applies to various officials depending upon the circumstances. But no wives or children, not even those of the President, can go there. They are to be evacuated elsewhere. In 1961 several members of Bob's staff, including myself, had gone to the place so that we would know what to do if that terrible eventuality came to pass. After returning we reported to Bob and urged him to make the trip. I remember saying to him: "You ought to see it, but, more important, those guys who have to stay there all the time would get a big lift if the President's brother visited them. It's a lonely duty."

Bob looked me squarely in the eye.

"You can forget about that," he said. "I'm not going. I'll never go there."

Now, as the quarantine took hold, we received our instructions in case evacuation became necessary. I talked with Bob about what he was to do, and in the same tone of voice as before—brooking no argument—he said, "I'm not going. If it comes to that, there'll be sixty million Americans killed and as many Russians or more. I'll be at Hickory Hill."

I'm sure that is exactly where he would have been if he had been forced under those terrible circumstances to make the choice between duty or family. He would never have left Ethel and the children.

Though some of the Russian ships had turned back and the Navy had boarded a Panamanian freighter under Soviet charter before allowing her to proceed to Cuba, it remained unclear how the Russians would respond. Work was continuing on the missile sites, and one of our U-2 pilots, Major Rudolf Anderson, Jr., who had made the flight which detected the missile sites, had been shot down and killed. The danger of miscalculation by either side remained great.

Our radio was on constantly, and between 9 and 10 A.M., Sunday, October 28, a special bulletin conveyed the astonishing news that the missiles would be dismantled and returned to Russia, that the President's terms had been accepted and the crisis was over. I had not really expected to hear that, but I felt no jubilation, only tremendous relief. The terrible weight had been lifted.

There was one more thing to do that day—the speech to the American Jewish Congress in New York, where Bob was to receive the Rabbi Stephen S. Wise Award for "advancing human freedom." Throughout the crisis I had been in daily contact with AJC officials. They planned to go ahead with the dinner if conditions permitted. They would understand if Bob could not appear, but they were not to be put off easily. We had left it up in the air whether he would come. Now he was exhausted and was unwinding from the tension of the thirteen days. The last thing he wanted to do was to go anywhere, put on a tuxedo and deliver a speech. But he kept the commitment. He made two concessions to himself. He asked me to arrange for a military plane to fly him to New York and back so he could go and return in the shortest amount of time and that he be allowed to speak as soon as he arrived and would not have to sit through a long program.

We flew to New York in a Navy plane. He studied his speech intermittently but spoke very little and spent most of the trip in deep thought. Mindful of the President's admonition that there be no crowing over the Russian retreat, he avoided answering the questions of reporters who were waiting when he arrived at the Waldorf. Though the AJC officials had agreed to move up Bob's speech, the program got under way, and after an hour Bob had not been introduced. He was fidgeting and obviously impatient. I whispered to an official that if they didn't put Bob on, he'd likely just leave. The word was passed, and he was asked to speak. As he was finishing he spoke about the crisis:

> The confrontation in reality is of all people who believe in human dignity and freedom with those who believe the state is supreme. It is that fact, not the drama of the particular moment, which is of real significance.
>
> In our society, laws are administered to protect and expand individual freedom, not to compel individuals to follow the logic other men impose on them. The tyranny of Communism is as old as the Pharaohs and the pyramids—that the state stands above all men and their individual aspirations. And that is why we oppose it, because by force and subversion it seeks to impose its tyranny all around the world.
>
> We will not win this struggle merely by confronting the enemy. What we do at home, in the final analysis, is just as important. Thus we all must

accelerate our efforts to banish religious prejudice, racial discrimination and any intolerance which denies to any Americans the rights guaranteed them by the Declaration of Independence and the Constitution.

That is what this crisis is all about; that is why our ships are on station in the Caribbean and why American soldiers are on duty tonight in West Berlin, South Vietnam and South Korea. They are there for the same reason the Maccabees stood their ground against Antiochus—for human dignity and freedom. . . .

The missile crisis was John Kennedy's finest hour, but it was a searing experience for the President and the men who counseled with him so effectively. Over the years, Bob's thoughts often returned to those days. After his brother died, his memories of the Ex Comm were bittersweet: how well it had functioned, how close the members had become, how open and unpretentious their discussions had been. If only it could have stayed together to focus on Vietnam. If . . .

Within a month after the crisis, Bob was enmeshed again in a Cuban problem—the release of the Bay of Pigs prisoners.

An earlier attempt to ransom them had failed miserably. On May 17, 1961, Castro proposed that the prisoners be exchanged for five hundred bulldozers. At the President's personal request, an ostensibly private committee was formed to arrange the deal. Dr. Milton S. Eisenhower, Mrs. Franklin D. Roosevelt and Walter Reuther, president of the United Auto Workers, agreed to head it, giving what was hoped would be a bipartisan complexion to the effort. Notably, a close friend of Bob's, John J. Hooker, Jr., a Nashville attorney, became executive secretary of the "Tractors for Freedom Committee."

Almost immediately the committee wallowed in bitter controversy. It was too soon after the ill-fated invasion. Public humiliation was still too raw and partisan bitterness still too strong. Despite the President's public endorsement and Bob's efforts behind the scenes, the committee could not raise enough money or support. It disbanded after six weeks. President Kennedy blamed Castro and asserted that the committee had acted in good faith. But Haynes Johnson, in his history of the brigade, said:

The prisoners suffered more from domestic politics than they did at the hands of Castro. . . . Had the political climate been less inflammatory, it is not at all unlikely that Brigade 2506 could have been released in June of 1961 for $28 million in tractors, cash and credits. Instead of freedom through tractors, however, the men were doomed to the degradation of a year and a half longer in prison. And in the end the price on their heads more than doubled.

After the collapse of the Tractors for Freedom Committee, relatives of the men formed the Cuban Families Committee for the Liberation of the Prisoners of the War, to begin a nationwide campaign to raise funds to free the brigade. But progress was slow. Meanwhile, conditions for the prisoners steadily worsened. In March 1962 they were brought before a five-man tribunal for a show trial on vague charges of treason. The trial lasted four days. Instead of reaping a harvest of guilty pleas and denunciations of the United States, however, Castro encountered a band of disciplined men who could not be broken or subverted. Only one man, whose freedom shortly afterward was "bought" by his father, praised Castro and denounced the United States. The rest, more than a thousand men, remained united in spirit, proud of what they had done and resolved not to break under blandishments or threats. They didn't.

Most of the prisoners, their relatives and the Cuban community in Florida expected that they would be executed. On the evening of the first day of the trial, Roberto San Roman and two other members of the brigade flew from Miami to Washington. When they encountered at the State Department what they felt was an unsympathetic, noncommittal response to their plea that the American Government support the prisoners, they took a taxi to the Justice Department and demanded to see the Attorney General. Bob saw them immediately.

"This man was completely different," San Roman told Haynes Johnson. "This was like talking to a Brigade man. He was very worried about the Brigade and he wanted to know everything that

I knew—if there was any possibility that they would be shot, and how the people of Miami felt about it. We talked about the families and everything. I told him that for sure some of them would get shot, maybe not all of them, but some of them, probably at least the staff, and that Miami was boiling, waiting for some kind of action from the United States."

After further discussion Bob gave his word that the government would do everything possible to prevent the prisoners from being executed. "Keep in touch—call me ten times a day if you have to," Bob told San Roman, and he sent them to see Richard Goodwin, a talented, hard-driving New Frontiersman. Goodwin had been one of President Kennedy's advisers on Latin-American affairs and now was in the State Department as Deputy Assistant Secretary for Inter-American Affairs.

Bob and Goodwin moved rapidly to persuade other Central and South American countries to put pressure on Castro to spare the prisoners. Goodwin asked President Joao Goulart of Brazil to intervene. Goulart told Castro that if the prisoners were executed, President Kennedy believed public opinion in the United States would force him to take strong action against Cuba. Meanwhile, Bob remained in continual contact with San Roman.

The tribunal found the prisoners guilty and sentenced them to thirty years at hard labor. Whether the unyielding courage and spirit of the men or Bob's and Goodwin's efforts had anything to do with the verdict probably never will be known. But to San Roman and the others working to save the prisoners, one man high in the American Government—the President's brother—had kept his word all the way.

Along with announcing the verdict, Castro declared a willingness to exchange the prisoners, but said the ransom had gone up—from $28 million to $62 million. As evidence of his good faith, he said he would permit the most seriously wounded prisoners to be released and accept payment of $2.9 million for them later. Sixty wounded men arrived in Miami on April 14, and among them was one of the brigade's most respected members, Enrique Ruiz-Williams, who like San Roman would work closely with Bob in liberating the brigade and become his close friend. Harry Williams, as he was known, was a natural leader, a man of iron integrity. He was an American-trained mining engineer and a member of a respected Cuban family. He had never been active in politics, but, resenting the corruption of the Batista regime, had helped supply Castro's rebel band in the Sierra Maestra Mountains. Because of these activities, he had felt it necessary to flee with his family to the United States in 1958 and was in Chicago when Castro came to power on January 1, 1959. He returned to Cuba, but brought his family back to the United States in the summer of 1960 when Castro nationalized the copper mines he was managing. When he and the other wounded prisoners were freed, he vowed to return to prison if negotiations for the comrades he had left behind fell through. Three days later, San Roman brought him to Washington to see Bob.

Despite all efforts, including many public appearances by Williams and other liberated prisoners and conferences with important people, money to ransom the brigade came to the Cuban Families Committee in driblets. There was less opposition in the country to a deal, but great apathy. Furthermore, because of their emotional involvement, the members of the committee and Williams and San Roman were in a poor position to bargain with Castro.

In June, Williams, discouraged and pessimistic, came to Washington to discuss the situation. Bob suggested that an outsider, not connected with the government or the cause, was needed and recommended James B. Donovan, a prominent New York lawyer and experienced negotiator. Donovan, among other things, had played a key role in negotiations which resulted in the exchange of the Soviet master spy, Colonel Rudolf Abel, for U-2 pilot Gary Powers. Donovan, without knowing that Bob had recommended him, agreed to serve without pay. The two met for the first time ten days later, when Donovan went to see Bob to receive assurances that private negotiations with Castro for the prisoners were legal and had the approval of the government at the highest level. He got those assurances and by mid-September had convinced Castro that it was idle to hope that the ransom could be raised in cash and had persuaded him to accept medicine and drugs instead. The negotiations were progressing when the missile crisis intervened and brought them to a standstill.

On Saturday, November 24, two days after Thanksgiving, I accompanied Bob to New York for a meeting which Williams and San Roman had arranged with Alvaro Sanchez, Jr., chairman of the Cuban Families Committee. Sanchez, who had been a wealthy cattleman in Cuba, had accompanied Donovan to Cuba on August 30 and had remained. His nineteen-year-old son, Eduardo, was one of the prisoners. On November 16, Sanchez had been permitted to visit the prisoners. He did not get to see much, but what he did see horrified him. The prisoners were emaciated, underweight and in rags. Some of the men were so weak that they fainted when they tried to clean their cells.

"I'm a cattleman, Mr. Attorney General, and these men look like animals who are going to die," Sanchez, speaking with emotion and earnestness, told Bob. "If you are going to rescue these men, this is the time because if you wait you will be liberating corpses."

Bob listened intently and asked a few more questions. "Yes, you are right," he said. "I think this is the moment."

On the plane back to Washington, Bob spoke with great feeling about the prisoners; the hardships they had endured; that despite starvation and inhumane treatment they had resisted all offers of food, freedom and medical care if they would denounce the United States and praise Castro.

"It's incredible," he said. "We put them there and we're going to get them out—by Christmas!" I looked at him in amazement.

"It's not possible to do it that soon," I said.

"We will," he replied.

Within a few days, after talking with his brother and conferring with Donovan, he called the Assistant Attorneys General to his office. He told them what Sanchez had reported and that the President felt that everything possible had to be done to get the men out. He briefed them on the status of Donovan's negotiations. Donovan had obtained an itemized list of the medicine, drugs and food supplies that Castro would accept, but he faced seemingly insurmountable difficulties in obtaining them quickly. Donovan needed a staff and he needed assistance in unsnarling government red tape and in convincing drug firms and other corporations that ransoming the prisoners was in the national interest. The government would have to help, but it would have to be behind the scenes, Bob said. Castro had told Donovan that he would up the ante or call the exchange off if the American Government, which never had acknowledged its part in the invasion, and not Donovan and the committee, appeared to be raising the ransom.

But the important thing was to get the men released, and we would do it by Christmas, he concluded. No one in the room, except Bob, believed that it could be done that soon. I doubt if anyone else in the government would have dared to set such a deadline when there were so many uncertainties and the chance of failure was so great. Certainly, there were few men with his ability to put together an organization so quickly and direct it so skillfully in accomplishing what he set out to do. His position as the President's brother helped, of course, but as in so many things in which he was involved, his qualities of leadership made the difference. He drove us hard, but not as hard as he drove himself. His resolve and his deep feeling about the country's moral responsibility for the men infused the group with élan and a sense of purpose that were unusual even for a Kennedy-led effort. It took a week or more, but by the tenth of December all our skepticism had given way to conviction that the men would spend Christmas with their families.

Katzenbach was assigned responsibility for coordinating the over-all policies and the participation of the various government agencies. Oberdorfer was put in charge of assisting Donovan in obtaining the supplies and getting them to Cuba, and his office became the nerve center of the operation. The government men were joined by four Washington lawyers, who, at Donovan's request, dropped their private practices for the next four weeks and rendered invaluable service. Two of them were John Nolan and John Douglas. The others were Raymond J. Rasenberger and E. Barrett Prettyman, Jr., who had been a friend of Bob's since law school.

Two major legal problems had to be cleared at the outset, and the government did so under forced draft. Industry representatives were assured by Justice that firms contributing merchandise would not be violating the antitrust laws even though they might meet to discuss costs, prices and shipping agreements. The Internal Revenue Service, in accord with long-standing policy, ruled that contributions would be tax-deductible and provided a team of attorneys to answer specific tax questions for individual companies on a twenty-four-hour basis.

The operation gathered momentum and moved ahead rapidly. On December 6 the American Red Cross, with its expertise in disaster relief, joined to receive the goods and coordinate their transportation to Miami and Cuba, providing experience and staff which the Cuban Families Committee did not have. On December 16 a $53 million letter of credit was negotiated with the Royal Bank of Canada, underwritten by the Bank of America and the Morgan Guaranty Trust Company, to meet a Castro demand that he would get cash if goods in the amount agreed upon were not delivered. The same day, Oberdorfer issued orders for the first shipments of drugs and supplies to be transported to Florida for loading aboard planes and the S.S. *African Pilot* in the Miami area.

As Donovan, Katzenbach and Oberdorfer spearheaded their task forces, Bob held a series of meetings in New York and in his office with top officials of trade organizations in the food, drug and medical supply fields to tell them of the prisoners' plight and to assure them that the Administration was supporting the operation without reservation. To each he spoke with moving eloquence and conviction.

He would begin by describing how the prisoners had sought to liberate their country and had been assisted by the American Government under plans initiated by the Eisenhower Administration and carried out by his brother. The men had fought bravely and were prisoners through no fault of their own. He stressed that none of the prisoners had defected; that they had refused to take orders from their guards but relied instead on their own officers and noncoms. They were doing this although they were starving and some would die if not liberated in a matter of weeks.

He told them about San Roman, Williams and the others he had met. To underscore their courage and their dedication to freedom, he quoted Williams as having told him: "Mr. Kennedy, I know you're doing all you can, but if you can't get them out, I'm going back."

He explained why the government could not be involved openly and that none of the goods to be shipped were of strategic value to Cuba nor would they add to Cuba's productive capacity. They would, he said, replenish Cuba's dwindling medical stocks and feed hungry children.

He tried to make it absolutely clear that the companies could not expect any favors from the government if they contributed and that they should not feel under any compulsion to do so. Obviously, he stood before the groups not only as the President's brother but as Attorney General with all the Justice Department's enforcement power. Some manufacturers may have felt indirect pressure just in meeting with him. Some may have contributed because they felt it was good politics and good business. But the impression I received at each of the meetings was that the businessmen came wary and uncertain and left convinced of the nation's obligation to the prisoners and deeply moved by their plight. The fact is that few, if any, of the more than two hundred companies that provided goods or services sought favors then or later. Some, unable to get as favorable tax rulings as they sought, took losses and made their contributions anyway. Men and women in many companies, labor unions and trade associations, as well as the Red Cross, became caught up in the spirit of the operation and pitched in as volunteers.

On December 18, Donovan and Sanchez flew to Cuba, and three days later Donovan and Castro signed a memorandum of agreement. Bob called us in a group to tell us the good news. "Okay," he said, "I've done my job. Now you get it finished by Christmas." Then, for the first time, he betrayed that he, too, had held some doubts about the deadline. "I can hardly believe it, but it looks like we might make it now," he said.

In the late afternoon of December 23, Donovan gave the order for the *African Pilot* to begin unloading, and a short time later a plane with the first 108 prisoners and Harry Williams aboard took off for Miami. (Williams arranged for himself or others of the 60 wounded prisoners to be aboard each plane to brief the men.)

After four flights had taken 426 men out, Castro demanded that the $2,925,000 which had been pledged when the wounded men were released, be paid by 3 P.M. the next afternoon or all the prisoners would not be freed. It was Sunday, and all the banks were closed. Nolan, who was in Havana with Donovan, and Williams flew to Miami and explained the situation to Bob and Katzenbach in an early-morning phone call. They would raise the money by 3 P.M., Bob said, and Nolan flew back to Cuba. Bob immediately made two phone calls. One was to Richard Cardinal Cushing, long close to the Kennedy family and a sponsor of the Families Committee, who pledged $1 million. The second was to General Lucius Clay, who was heading the Families Committee fund-raising efforts. The General and several assistants undertook to raise the other $1,925,000, and ultimately Clay signed a personal note for the sum, promising to repay it with future pledges.

Shortly before the 3 P.M. deadline, the Royal Bank of Canada notified its Havana office that the money needed only Donovan's signature to be released. In the interim, Castro had permitted two more planeloads to leave and now the last three were cleared for take-off. The last plane, bearing the leaders of the brigade, Pepe San Roman, Roberto's brother, Manuel Artime and Erneido Oliva, touched down in Miami at 9:30 P.M., Christmas Eve.

Long after the prisoners' emotional return and their hour of glory when President Kennedy came to the Orange Bowl in Miami to inspect the brigade and salute it and long after the Red Cross had delivered the last of the supplies to Castro, Bob remained in touch with many of the men. He worked to help them re-establish themselves and remained interested in their welfare. Many enlisted in the armed forces. Some worked in programs in Central and South America. None found life in exile easy, but Bob's door—as Attorney General and as Senator—was always open to them. He was particularly close to Williams, Oliva and Roberto San Roman until his death.

Chapter 8

The Most Difficult Decision

For career employees of the Justice Department, the test of each new Attorney General is how he handles the first case of great political sensitivity that comes along.

On January 5, 1961, a New York jukebox operator, Sanford J. Moore, and five associates were arrested on a federal complaint charging them with bankruptcy fraud. Except for the fact that Moore, a sturdily built man with a phlegmatic face, had been a New York City policeman from 1943 to 1946, there was nothing unusual about the case. The six were accused of disposing of assets valued at about $100,000 while their firm, Gibraltor Amusements, Ltd., which operated on Long Island, was going through bankruptcy. In difficulties of this sort, it sometimes happens that a friend or a relative of a defendant thinks he knows someone who might be "helpful." This time it was a cousin.

A few days after the arrest, Moore's cousin took him to a small, quiet office in midtown Manhattan where a prominent orthopedic surgeon, Dr. Robert M. Erdman, examined his patients and kept track of other business interests. There was somewhat of an air of mystery about the doctor, a short, slight man with thinning brown hair. He was, at forty-three, in much demand as a physician. He had a $100,000-a-year practice and was frequently used by some of the biggest insurance companies and by plaintiff's attorneys as a medical expert in negligence cases. He had a broad political acquaint-anceship, but beyond that little was known about him.

Moore recited the details of the case to Erdman and said he was considering whether to retain a prominent Washington law firm which wanted $60,000 as a retainer to handle his defense. Erdman's advice was that the fee was too high and that a New York lawyer probably would take the case for not more than $35,000. The doctor suggested that the cousin contact Elliott Kahaner, Chief Assistant U.S. Attorney in the office in Brooklyn that had responsibility for prosecution of the case.

Several days later, Moore returned to Erdman's office, and the doctor reported that he had reached an arrangement with Kahaner. For payment of $35,000, Erdman said, the charges would be dismissed against four of the defendants, but two would have to plead guilty and would receive suspended sentences. The money was to be paid in two installments—$15,000 before sentencing and $20,000 afterward. Moore asked for time to think it over.

In a few days, Moore was back in Erdman's office with a suavely attired, squat companion, Antonio Corallo, the menacing, notorious "Tony Ducks," who, among other back-alley exploits, had helped Hoffa establish the phony Teamster paper locals in New York. In Erdman's presence, Corallo said he had told Kahaner that he wanted Moore "kept on the streets." Moore, in going to Erdman and Kahaner, had "fallen into God's hands," Corallo said. Thus, with the blessing of one of the toughest, most feared men in the New York underworld, Moore decided to go ahead with the proposed fix. Erdman called Kahaner, who reported that the plan was working out well.

But Kahaner did not have direct responsibility for the case, and the Assistant U.S. Attorney who did refused to pull his punches. Shortly after Moore decided to pay the bribe, Kahaner notified Erdman that he feared he would not be able to fulfill the contract because he had discovered that Moore was associated with rack-eteers. Kahaner would need help, they concluded, and they decided

Erdman should contact a friend who was a New York State Supreme Court judge.[1] The judge's name was James Vincent Keogh.

In the fall of 1959, when John Kennedy passed the point of no return in his quest for the Democratic nomination, the task of capturing New York's huge block of 114 votes—one-seventh of the total needed for nomination—was left largely to John Bailey, the thoroughly professional leader of the Democratic machine in Connecticut, and to the shrewdness of the candidate's father, Joseph P. Kennedy, former Ambassador to Great Britain. In reconnoitering the flabby, feuding Democratic baronies in the Empire State, John Kennedy and his tightly knit group of strategists had perceived rightly that the delegates were up for grabs. They concluded that the nominal Democratic leaders in the state would keep testing the political winds until the last moment; their views hardened within the maxim that a Catholic could not win the Presidency. It seemed certain that they would feel more comfortable with Stuart Symington, Lyndon Johnson or even Adlai Stevenson again.

Through the winter and early spring, Bailey and Ambassador Kennedy made headway without arousing attention. When the leaders realized what was happening, a majority of the delegates were securely in the Kennedy fold. At Los Angeles, 104½ of New York's votes held firmly for the next President of the United States, and the Kennedys always would recognize that they owed a special debt particularly to three New Yorkers. One was Buffalo County leader Peter Crotty, who broke trail for Bailey in snaring the votes of one upstate county after another. In the metropolitan New York area, Ambassador Kennedy received invaluable help from two Irish politicians of the old school—Congressman Charles A. Buckley, the crusty boss of the Bronx, and a thin, taciturn Congressman from Brooklyn, Eugene J. Keogh, Judge Keogh's brother.

By all outward appearances, Judge Keogh was a stalwart of the Brooklyn bench. A short, dapper man with a round face, pink skin

---

1. In New York, the Supreme Court is comparable to Superior or District Courts in other states.

and Mephistophelean eyebrows, he had been a judge since 1951. His judicial salary was $34,500 a year. Brooklyn born, he was fifty-six years old, married for nineteen years and the father of two sons and two daughters. While teaching at Public School 183 in Brooklyn from 1924 to 1936, he had earned degrees from Fordham College, New York University and Fordham Law School. He entered private law practice in 1936. Mayor Fiorello La Guardia appointed him to be a trustee of the Brooklyn Public library, and on January 1, 1940, he became an assistant district attorney for Kings County (Brooklyn). The day after the Japanese attack on Pearl Harbor, he joined the Navy, achieved the rank of lieutenant commander and was commended for supervising details on flotillas during the D-day invasion of Normandy. In 1946, President Truman appointed him U.S. Attorney for the Eastern District of New York, and he served until 1950, when he resigned to run for the Supreme Court. His teaching career had left him a strict grammarian in court, but off the bench he was a pleasant personality, well liked and well regarded in Brooklyn legal and political circles. He would deny under oath that he had participated in the attempt to fix the bankruptcy case or that he had done anything improper in connection with it. He would be able to have nine judges, a rabbi, an Episcopal minister, a banker, a stockbroker, an eye surgeon, a lawyer and a social worker attest to his good character and excellent reputation, and yet, by his own testimony and that of Erdman, Moore and others, sometime in March 1961 he became enmeshed in the Moore case.

On March 30, Moore and his co-defendants, having pleaded guilty, appeared before U.S. District Court Judge Leo F. Rayfiel for sentencing. But, instead of receiving the suspended sentences which Moore thought he had paid for, he and two of his associates were sentenced to prison for three years. The next day Moore, Corallo and Kahaner met with Erdman in the doctor's office and, amid recriminations, the four mapped plans to upset Judge Rayfiel's action. But as they conspired during the weeks of April and May, two teams of Justice Department lawyers, working independently, became interested in their activities.

In Washington, John Lally, a quiet, careful career attorney in the

Criminal Division, came across Moore's tracks while examining a case involving slot machine operations in Maryland and Great Britain. Lally decided to question Moore and found him somewhat cooperative. Eventually, Moore disclosed to Lally that he had paid for a fix in the bankruptcy case, but didn't get it. He implicated Kahaner. At the same time in New York, Walter Sheridan and a young Assistant U.S. Attorney, Charles Shaffer, were reviewing the Eisenhower Administration's prosecution of a celebrated stock manipulation case involving a shell of a company called the United Dye & Chemical Corporation and a facile, unscrupulous dealer in phony stocks named Alexander L. Guterma.

The rise and fall of United Dye stock and the collapse of Guterma's financial empire exposed one of the most brazen, complex stock manipulations of the decade. There were ramifications among the Las Vegas gambling crowd as well as on Wall Street, and in 1961 there was strong feeling in several federal investigative agencies that the Eisenhower Administration, while having succeeded in sending Guterma to prison, had not gone all the way in the case. Bob had assigned Sheridan and Shaffer to find out, and during the course of their review Shaffer developed some information which led him to Dr. Erdman. Shaffer persuaded Erdman to cooperate with the government, and ultimately the doctor spilled the story about the Moore case. He implicated Corallo and Judge Keogh.

Lally, Shaffer and Sheridan brought their findings to the attention of the chief of the Criminal Division, Assistant Attorney General Herbert J. Miller, Jr. Miller notified Bob, and it was decided that Lally and Shaffer should concentrate on the Moore case and take it before a grand jury in New York for further investigation. And so it was that for the next five months Bob lived fretfully and uncomfortably with the closely held knowledge that Gene Keogh's brother faced possible indictment, disgrace and ruination.

A minimum number of officials in the Department were made aware of the investigation, and in speaking and writing they referred to it only as "the New York Case." By August, Shaffer and Lally had made impressive progress, but because of their different temperaments—one intense and aggressive, the other careful and soft-spoken—they encountered increasing difficulty in working together. Miller decided it was time to put a more experienced hand in charge when the two were unable to resolve a dispute except by calling Miller, who had gone to Oregon to make a speech. Shaffer was assigned to another case, and William G. Hundley, assistant chief of the Organized Crime and Racketeering Section—a ten-year veteran whose round, boyish face exuded cheerfulness and competence—took over.

"Look at it dispassionately and objectively" was the only guidance Bob offered when Hundley met briefly with him before leaving for New York. Bob and Miller both made clear to Hundley that he would have a free hand in the investigation. But, unbeknown to Hundley, the grand jurors were steaming. Shaffer, a tiger, had been taken off the case. More than one juror had jumped to the conclusion that the government's fortitude and resolve were weakening. When Hundley entered the grand jury room for the first time, one of the jurors remarked so he could hear it: "Oh, here's the man from Washington who is going to fix the case!"

Hundley spent the next few days allaying the jurors' suspicions. He quickly picked up the threads of the case and by early October was ready to recommend that indictments be sought against Moore, Erdman, Corallo, Kahaner and Judge Keogh. On October 9, Miller met with Bob to present the evidence in detail. As was Bob's custom whenever a major decision had to be made, he asked a number of his assistants, including Byron White, Nicholas Katzenbach, Burke Marshall and Louis Oberdorfer, to be present. Seigenthaler and I also attended, as did several top men of the FBI.

Miller's summary of the evidence and testimony showed that about the time Erdman decided to contact Judge Keogh, Moore delivered the first installment of the payoff—$15,000—to the doctor. Kahaner assertedly came by and picked up an envelope containing $7,500. Erdman told the grand jury that he delivered another envelope the same afternoon to Judge Keogh. He could not remember how much was in the envelope, but Moore testified that Erdman told him that he had divided the $15,000 equally between Kahaner and the judge.

The record showed that on March 28 Erdman notified Moore that the balance of the payoff—$20,000—would have to be handed over before sentencing, two days hence, instead of after, as agreed. The two testified that Moore put $2,500 in an envelope, which was handed to Kahaner in a restaurant; that Erdman gave the remainder to Judge Keogh, who, in Erdman's presence, called Judge Rayfiel and asked to see him.

There was no question that Moore had raised $35,000 for the fix. The FBI had verified it through bank records which showed that Moore obtained $25,000 from a man in England and $10,000 through Corallo's good offices.

Judge Rayfiel testified before the grand jury that Judge Keogh had contacted him about the Moore case. He remembered telling Judge Keogh that in view of Moore's background and the nature of the crime no consideration could be given him. Furthermore, Judge Rayfiel said he had been told by another judge that Moore was claiming he had the case fixed.

According to Erdman, about 2:30 P.M. on March 29 he received a call from Judge Keogh, who told him that his friends were bad and that they were going to jail. When Erdman gave this news to Moore, Moore denied that he was connected with racketeers. Erdman said he then called Keogh and protested that Moore was being sentenced because of his associates rather than his crime. Judge Keogh assertedly replied that Erdman should see Judge Rayfiel and that he would make an appointment for him at 9:30 o'clock the following morning.

Judge Rayfiel told the grand jury that Judge Keogh called him on the morning of March 30 and asked him to see Erdman. He said he agreed to do so, and a short time later Erdman came to his chambers. Judge Rayfiel said that he told Erdman that Moore could not receive any leniency, whereupon the doctor left. Erdman, picking up the story in his testimony said that after leaving Judge Rayfiel he went directly to Judge Keogh's office accompanied by Moore's attorney. Erdman said he told Judge Keogh, "I can't do anything, he won't do anything," and that the judge replied, "You'll have to talk to him again."

No further attempt was made to contact Judge Rayfiel, but immediately after the sentencing and in the days following Erdman said he was in repeated contact with Judge Keogh. And there was strong evidence of Judge Keogh's direct intercession after Kahaner suggested that Judge Rayfiel might reduce the sentences if Moore could reach a settlement with the trustee in bankruptcy. According to four witnesses, Judge Keogh summoned the attorney for the trustee to his chambers, introduced him to Erdman, vouched for Erdman and participated in a discussion which resulted in agreement on a tentative settlement of $50,000.

As Bob and the rest of us listened intently, Miller then summarized Judge Keogh's testimony before the grand jury. The judge, appearing voluntarily, had categorically denied ever receiving any money from Erdman or anyone else for the purpose of attempting to influence Judge Rayfiel.

Judge Keogh told the grand jury that his friendship with Erdman commenced around 1956 when he went to the doctor for treatment of a back ailment. He said he first heard of Moore on March 29, 1961, when Erdman brought Moore to his chambers, identified him as a lifelong friend and asked Judge Keogh if he would inquire of Judge Rayfiel whether leniency could be shown Moore.

Judge Keogh said he called Judge Rayfiel and they had lunch on the twenty-ninth, but when he inquired whether any consideration could be given Moore, Judge Rayfiel cut him off. Judge Rayfiel said Moore had a bad reputation and he had heard that Moore was bragging that there was a fix in the case. The following morning, Judge Keogh said, Moore's attorney and Erdman were waiting when he arrived in his chambers. Erdman asked if he thought Judge Rayfiel would see him, and Judge Keogh called and made an immediate appointment for Erdman.

After the sentencing, Judge Keogh said he had no further connection with the case until May, when Erdman told him that he, Erdman, was going to make himself liable for a settlement in the bankruptcy if they could get the trustee to agree on a figure. The judge said he called the attorney for the trustee, but beyond bringing the attorney and Erdman together, he really had nothing more to do with the negotiations.

Judge Keogh testified that he borrowed $4,000 from Erdman during 1960 and 1961 to help pay for renovation of his summer home at Great Barrington, Massachusetts. However, he had not given the doctor a note or any other sign of indebtedness. He admitted that in 1959 Erdman had purchased a new $3,700 automobile for him. He said he considered it a gift. He also admitted that Erdman put new storm windows on his home for him and that he never had paid the doctor for any medical care over the years.

Erdman had testified that, in addition to the $4,000, he had given approximately $16,000 of his own money to Judge Keogh during the years of their acquaintance.

That was the sum and substance of it. Miller, Hundley and Lally believed that proof of Erdman's, Moore's and Kahaner's involvement was unquestionable. The case against Corallo was weaker because it depended on Erdman and Moore and Moore was reluctant to testify against the formidable Tony Ducks. Erdman already had been threatened, and he and his family were under twenty-four-hour federal protection.

As to Judge Keogh, the weight of the evidence indicated he had been involved, Miller told us, but the case was by no means airtight. There had been only one witness to the payment of fix money— Erdman. The doctor's version of the facts was supported by Judge Keogh's undue interest in the case, the fact that he contacted Judge Rayfiel, his involvement in the bankruptcy settlement, his acceptance of gifts from Erdman and his personal financial involvement with the doctor.

On the other hand, Miller pointed out, while what Judge Keogh had done was unethical, it was not unlawful unless he had accepted some of the bribe. Erdman would be vulnerable as a witness because it could be shown that he was undergoing psychiatric treatment and there seemed no motive for him to have "helped" Moore except that fixing cases apparently gave him a sense of power. But, Miller said, unless the FBI could establish that Erdman had kept the payoff money that didn't go to Kahaner, it would be difficult to try the case without making Keogh a defendant. He pointed out that Erdman would testify that he gave part of the payoff to the judge, and it would be difficult to explain to a jury that the government believed

Erdman was telling the truth about Kahaner, but not about Judge Keogh.

Still, it was a close, difficult decision, and as the group, seated in a semicircle around Bob's huge desk, questioned Miller and debated, Bob listened carefully, but said little.

There was in Erdman's favor the fact that he had completely implicated himself, even though he had been told from the beginning that he would be indicted along with the others. He was the only one of the suspects who had not changed his story before the grand jury, although he had added to it, particularly with respect to Corallo. In contrast, Judge Keogh had given conflicting testimony to the grand jury, and his explanation for the loans, the car, the storm windows and the free medical care seemed less than plausible. The one disinterested witness in the case—the lawyer for the trustee in bankruptcy—supported Erdman's version of his meetings with Judge Keogh: that Judge Keogh had taken more of a role in arranging a settlement than he would admit.

Now, after nearly two hours, Bob, pointing his finger, asked each man for his opinion and his reasoning behind it. The group came down strongly on the side of asking the grand jury to indict Judge Keogh along with the others. But Bob was hesitant. There still was an area of doubt that Erdman was telling the truth, he pointed out, and the FBI had not completed its financial investigations of Erdman, Kahaner and the judge.

"The problem is," Bob said, "that if the judge is indicted, even if he is acquitted, his usefulness as a judge will be over. The indictment alone will destroy him. I'd hate to have that on my conscience."

He directed Hundley and Lally to continue the investigation until they had done everything that could be done to resolve any reasonable doubt that the judge was involved. But that evening the debate carried over to the White House, where the President was giving his annual reception for the judiciary. As the guests thronged through the first-floor rooms, Bob, White, Miller and Hundley withdrew halfway up the front staircase to continue talking about the case. Each of the four later remembered a fragment of the discussion—that it became quite heated when White argued that Judge Keogh should be included in the indictment, that Bob's connection with the Keoghs was not sufficient reason for him to be any more sure than he normally would be in reaching a decision. "Bob, I hope you make sure you treat this fellow like everyone else," White said. Bob, mistakenly thinking White was inferring that he was dragging his feet, replied angrily and then, despite Hundley's and Miller's attempts to cool the discussion, turned and walked away. He never discussed the incident with White again, and still insisted on having every thread of evidence checked and rechecked.

Hundley and Lally went to Judge Keogh's lawyer, laid out all the allegations against the judge and gave the lawyer the opportunity to disprove them, if he could. The lawyer turned over to Hundley the judge's checkbooks and canceled checks. Despite the intensive investigation, the FBI never was able to trace the money after it left Erdman's hands. At one point, Bob called Hundley and said, "It's your case. I don't want you to think I'm interfering, but I'd feel better if you'd give the judge a lie detector test."

At first the FBI refused. John F. Malone, special agent in charge of the FBI office in New York, didn't think it was a good idea. J. Edgar Hoover backed Malone. However, when Hundley explained that the Attorney General wanted the test given, Malone decided to go ahead, and Hoover was said to have remarked: "Sherlock Holmeses must have their fun." The FBI agent who was to give the test was briefed thoroughly on the contradictions between Erdman's allegations and Judge Keogh's explanations. The judge willingly submitted to the test. He again asserted his innocence, but the FBI reported that the results were "inconclusive," and Hoover was reported to have said, "See, that shows I was right."

The weight of the evidence was against the judge, but Bob kept looking for the clincher and it eluded him. Adding to his discomfort, the investigation became public knowledge when details began to surface in New York in mid-October. On October 19 the afternoon papers carried stories about the investigation, and the next morning the New York *Herald Tribune* implicated a "Congressman" in the case. The front-page headline read:

A JUDGE AND
CONGRESSMAN
IN "FIX" QUIZ

The story, by Milton Lewis, began:

A special Federal grand jury is investigating a Brooklyn Supreme Court Justice, a Brooklyn Congressman and a former assistant Federal Brooklyn prosecutor. They are suspected of having split an alleged $25,000 payoff to fix a Federal criminal case. . . .

A top Washington source said last night he doubted that the Congressman was involved.

The inference, of course, was that the Congressman was Eugene Keogh, but there was no evidence in the case against Keogh or any other Congressman. It would have been wrong for us to discuss any details of a matter pending before a grand jury, but when Lewis called, we indicated as strongly as we could, without saying so flatly, that the Justice Department did not have any evidence that Eugene Keogh was involved. Dr. Erdman and others may have jumped to the conclusion that Judge Keogh would ask his brother for help. Erdman so testified later at the trial. However, the FBI questioned Eugene Keogh, and Erdman's suspicions never checked out.

During this period, it seemed to me, the *Herald Tribune* was being edited flamboyantly and not too carefully in the attempt to stimulate circulation, and that, coupled with its traditionally strong Republican leanings, seemed to cause the paper to go out of its way to knock the Kennedy Administration.[2] Even looking back in calm hindsight there seems no other reasonable explanation for implicating the Congressman, for the next day the paper com-

2. The paper's most careless attack on the Administration came the following spring in connection with the Billy Sol Estes case. A *Herald Tribune* reporter obtained Estes' financial records and found an entry showing $146,000 had been withdrawn from bank accounts for "the Washington project" the day before Estes made a trip to Washington. The paper inferred that Estes had used the money to bribe high officials in the Administration. The FBI later proved that the money had been withdrawn to make a payment on a housing project in Washington State.

pounded its error with the following front-page headline and story:

"FIX" FIGURE
CALLED FRIEND
OF KENNEDYS
by Milton Lewis

The Brooklyn Congressman under suspicion in the widely-reported attempted fix of a Federal criminal case is friendly with President Kennedy and the President's father, Joseph P. Kennedy.

That was the only paragraph that supported the headline. The rest of the article repeated essential elements of the previous day's story and added a few details about the case. President Kennedy, who later canceled the White House subscription to the *Herald Tribune* during the Estes controversy but kept right on reading it, was furious. It was a Saturday morning, and in one of the few times that he called me directly, he reached me at home about 8 A.M. He wanted to know how the story could have been written. I told him what I knew, relating the conversation with Lewis. Satisfied that the Department had not furnished any basis for the story and that we had tried to convey the truth to Lewis, his tone of voice softened. "All right," the President said. "What are you going to do about it?"

I told him I would call Robert J. Donovan, chief of the *Herald Tribune*'s Washington bureau and try to persuade the paper to retract the story. "I hope you can," he said. "Let me know what happens. This story is an outrage, and I don't want it to stand."

Then I heard from Bob, who also was incensed, and I called Donovan directly. Donovan was one of the most respected newsmen in Washington, and when I told him that Congressman Keogh absolutely was not involved and that the story was not only inaccurate but a great injustice, he quickly conferred with his editors. Not long afterward, Lewis called and I repeated what I told Donovan. He, and later Donovan, told me the paper would run a retraction the next morning. The story appeared on the front page as follows:

NOT ANY CONGRESSMAN
INVOLVED IN THE "FIX"
by Milton Lewis

The New York Herald Tribune learned on high authority last night that a Brooklyn Congressman is not involved in the $25,000 attempted fix of a Federal criminal case.

The Herald Tribune reported on Saturday that the Congressman, a friend of President Kennedy and the President's father, Joseph P. Kennedy, was under suspicion. It was emphasized by key Washington official sources that no congressman is implicated in any way.

(The Herald Tribune, of course is happy to set the record straight.—The Editors.)[3]

The special Federal grand jury investigating the scandal is expected to act in the near future.

Despite the retraction, the stories troubled Bob greatly and deepened his concern. Still, he did not lose his sense of humor. Up to this time, every investigation in the Department with political overtones had involved Democrats, including several who had strongly supported President Kennedy. On November 10, Miller, in his daily report, stated that he had requested the FBI to investigate allegations that a Republican district chairman in Georgia and several other local GOP officials had sold jobs in the Post Office for up to $5,000. Bob sent the report back to Miller, the one Republican among his top assistants, with a handwritten notation:

Don't tell me, Jack, even Republicans don't behave. I would never have thought (based on reports I get from you).

On December 5, in the early evening, Miller and Hundley went to Bob's office. Bob had been ailing all day and had gone home with a strep throat. Miller and Hundley talked with Bob's secretary, Angela Novello, and then from phones in Bob's office they talked to Bob at Hickory Hill. They told him the FBI had checked every investigative lead as far as possible. Every person who had relative knowledge had been questioned and taken before the grand jury. They said they had reviewed all the testimony and evidence, and there was no question but that there was "a triable law suit" against the judge. They recommended going ahead.

"All right, all right," said Bob in a weak voice. "Go ahead." Then

---

3. Congressman Keogh sued the *Herald Tribune* for libel and, after protracted skirmishing, won an out-of-court settlement in 1968.

Bob called Congressman Keogh and told him his brother would be indicted.

Two days later the grand jury returned indictments against Judge Keogh, Kahaner, Corallo, Moore and Erdman, charging them with conspiracy to obstruct justice. Because Erdman and Moore agreed to testify for the government, they were not tried with Judge Keogh, Kahaner and Corallo. The three went on trial on May 14, 1962, and were found guilty by a jury of nine men and three women a month later. Hundley, assisted by Lally, presented the government's case. The three were each given sentences of two years in prison, which they began serving in October and November 1963 after their appeals were turned down. Judge Keogh and Kahaner were released on parole the following June after being in prison just short of eight months. Corallo was required to serve his full term.[4] For assisting the government, Moore's three-year sentence in the bankruptcy case was reduced to one year. Erdman pleaded guilty and was given a one-year suspended sentence, fined $5,000 and placed on probation for five years.

Bob regarded the decision to prosecute Judge Keogh as the most difficult he had to make as Attorney General. Certainly it tortured him more than any other, although there were other cases in which persons closer to the Kennedys than Congressman Keogh were indicted or suffered deep distress because of the Department's investigative work. A notable and particularly pitiful instance involved the conviction of James M. Landis for failure to file income tax returns. Landis, former dean of the Harvard Law School, was sixty-three years old and in failing health. He had been an adviser to Presidents Roosevelt, Truman and Kennedy. He helped draft the

4. Corallo's only previous conviction was for a narcotics violation in 1941, for which he served six months in a workhouse. Between that time and the verdict in the Keogh case he became known as "Tony Ducks" because he repeatedly beat the rap while being tried or investigated for crimes ranging from robbery and labor racketeering to extortion and murder. His conviction in the Keogh case apparently broke his magic. Released from prison in 1965, he was convicted in 1968 and sentenced to three years in prison, this time for conspiring with five other men to arrange for a $40,000 kickback to a New York City Commissioner in the award of an $840,000 contract to clean and repair a reservoir.

Securities Act of 1933 and succeeded Ambassador Kennedy as Chairman of the Securities and Exchange Commission in 1935. He had drafted reports and speeches for Bob as well as for President Kennedy and had been a trusted friend for many years. But in his case and in the others the evidence was more clear-cut than it was against Judge Keogh. Obviously, a part of Bob's torment was caused by the obligation he felt to Congressman Keogh, Landis, and others who had been instrumental in President Kennedy's nomination and election. But I am sure it was the small unresolvable area of doubt with respect to Judge Keogh's involvement and the irreparable damage that an indictment would cause to the judge's career rather than personal loyalties or political considerations that caused Bob to agonize so long.

There was another question that he had to resolve as well, and that was whether ordinary standards for asking a grand jury to return an indictment should be applied to public officials. While working for Congressional committees Bob had become increasingly concerned with the frequency with which the corruption of public officials figured in matters under investigation. He tended by nature to be severe in his judgment of persons who deserted their trust. But now, as he faced for the first time as Attorney General a case involving a public official, he debated whether or not he should require more evidence than normally in seeking an indictment or less because the public trust was involved. Finally, he decided to treat all suspects alike, and in the last analysis that is what was done with Judge Keogh.

I do not think Bob was aware how closely the career lawyers in the Department, particularly in the Criminal Division, were watching to see how he handled the case or that it would have influenced his decision if he had been. He believed deeply that a civilized society depends upon honest, impartial administration of its laws. But he never demonstrated his allegiance to the law more clearly than in the Keogh case, and in so doing won the Department's respect. Hundley and other career attorneys and many other persons in the Department became Kennedy men and women from that point on.

After Bob's death, in talking with Congressman Keogh, I told him how hard the decision had been for Bob. The Congressman had never wavered in his belief that his brother was innocent, and he said he had undergone enormous criticism from within his family and his circle of friends for not using his influence with the President or Bob to prevent his brother from being indicted.

"But I knew," he said, "that a call from me or any intercession on my part would only have made matters worse. Besides, I knew that everything that could be done would be done and that if there was nothing that could be done, nothing would be done."

Chapter 9

The Freedom Riders

In the ten days preceding May 24, 1961, there had been three incidents of enormous violence as the Freedom Riders pressed on with their test of segregation in bus terminals in the South. A force of six hundred deputy U.S. marshals was in Montgomery, Alabama, and the city was under martial law. On that day, two buses with twenty-five black and two white Freedom Riders aboard—heavily guarded by Alabama and Mississippi National Guardsmen and highway patrolmen—had arrived safely in Jackson, Mississippi, from Montgomery. But now the twenty-seven Freedom Riders were in a Jackson jail for attempting to use segregated restrooms upon their arrival. At 9:15 that evening Bob, in Washington, talked by telephone with the Rev. Martin Luther King, Jr., in Montgomery. Bob, who had been trying to protect the right of the Freedom Riders to travel interstate and to cool passions on both sides, was concerned for their safety. But Dr. King protested that the convoy of soldiers and patrolmen had made the ride meaningless. Bob wanted to get the Freedom Riders out of the Jackson jail, but Dr. King said they would stay in as "part of the philosophy of this movement."

"It's a matter of conscience and morality," Dr. King said. "They must use their lives and their bodies to right a wrong. Our con-

155 • *The Freedom Riders*

science tells us that the law is wrong and we must resist, but we have a moral obligation to accept the penalty."

"That is not going to have the slightest effect on what the government is going to do in this field or any other," Bob replied. "The fact that they stay in jail is not going to have the slightest effect on me."

"Perhaps it would help if students came down here by the hundreds—by the hundreds of thousands," Dr. King said.

"The country belongs to you as much as to me," Bob said sharply. "You can determine what's best just as well as I can, but don't make statements that sound like a threat. That's not the way to deal with us."

There was a pause.

"It's difficult to understand the position of oppressed people," Dr. King said. "Ours is a way out—creative, moral and nonviolent. It is not tied to black supremacy or Communism, but to the plight of the oppressed. It can save the soul of America. You must understand that we've made no gains without pressure and I hope that pressure will always be moral, legal and peaceful."

"But," Bob argued, "the problem won't be settled in Jackson, Mississippi, but by strong federal action."

"I'm deeply appreciative of what the Administration is doing," Dr. King said. "I see a ray of hope, but I am different than my father. I feel the need of being free now!"

"Well, it all depends on what you and the people in jail decide," Bob said. "If they want to get out, we can get them out."

"They'll stay," said Dr. King, ending the conversation.

On April 10, 1968—a week after Dr. King was assassinated in Memphis—Bob, campaigning in the Indiana primary, talked to an audience in Fort Wayne about the meaning of the civil rights leader's death:

It could be the beginning of a final successful effort to make one nation of all our people—equal in justice and in opportunity, or it could foretell a continuing civil strife which threatens to transform our cities into armed camps and our streets into passageways for violence and fear. . . .
This generation did not create most of the conditions and convictions

which have led us to this day, but this generation has the responsibility to resolve them. Leaders can explain and propose, but this problem will not yield to any man—even the President of the United States. It will yield only to the moral energy and belief of a free people. . . .

There is no sure way to suppress men filled with anger who feel they have nothing to lose. That is an important lesson of the modern age. . . .

There are twenty million American Negroes—a population larger than that of South Vietnam. Most of them are peaceful and still retain faith in this democracy. We cannot now—or ever—set them apart or ring them with guards, deny their just expectations or refuse them membership in our society without risking a conflict which force and violence can never fully resolve.

After all, the claims of most Negroes are simple claims: a job which pays enough to support a family, a decent education for every child, a place to live and a place to play and—perhaps most important of all—a sense, not of being loved, but that they are a part of this country, welcomed to share in its ideals, its purposes, its politics and in all the manifold enterprises of our society. In all this there is nothing more than all of us want. . . .

So there is our problem. Among us are millions who wish to be a part of this society—to share its abundance, its opportunity and its purposes. We can deny this wish or work to make it come true. If we chose denial, then we chose spreading conflict, which will surely erode the well-being and liberty of every citizen and, in a profound way, diminish the idea of America. If we choose fulfillment, it will take work but we will choose to improve the well-being of all our people; choose to end fear and heal wounds; and we will choose peace—the only peace that can last—peace with justice.

The difference between his rather hard-nosed replies to Dr. King in 1961 and his sensitive remarks in Fort Wayne in 1968 accurately measures how greatly his attitude toward the black struggle for equal rights changed in seven years.

In 1961 he recognized that the country had been too slow and too intractable in redressing the Negroes' historic grievances, and he had acted within the government to accelerate the pace. But, like most whites in the North and West, he thought in the clichés of the times. He did not then regard the incipient black rebellion as the gravest threat to American society. There still seemed to be time for steady, rational progress that would satisfy the Negroes' demands and peacefully accommodate within the democratic process their hardening insistence on freedom "now." Bob was confident that resolute leadership by the federal government and the good sense of the American people would overcome the centuries of prejudice and white insensitivity to the human aspirations of those who were not white. He thought about the problem then in terms of leadership, tactics and the law. He urged Dr. King and other Negro leaders to concentrate on registering black voters instead of demonstrating. The surest way to improve conditions in the South was to get the vote and exercise it, he thought in 1961.

During the 1960 campaign when President Kennedy talked about the plight of Negroes, he often referred to a set of statistics. "The Negro baby born in America today," he would say, "regardless of the section of the nation in which he is born, has about one-half as much chance of completing high school as a white baby born in the same place on the same day, one-third as much chance of completing college, one-third as much chance of becoming a professional man, twice as much chance of becoming unemployed, about one-seventh as much chance of earning $10,000 a year, a life expectancy which is seven years shorter, and the prospects of earning only half as much."

These statistics concerned Bob and affronted his sense of justice and fair play, but it was not until he became Attorney General that they began to take on flesh and blood. His road to full recognition of what was behind the black rebellion and its crucial implications for the future of the nation, however, lay not only in discharging his official duties but in frequent walks through ghetto neighborhoods, in many visits to ghetto schools, particularly in Washington, and in countless conversations—some of them acrimonious confrontations—with black leaders.

The hard battles in Congress to enact new civil rights laws, the Justice Department's efforts to help Negroes gain some of their rights in hundreds of Southern towns and cities, the Freedom Riders and the major battles over school integration at the University of Mississippi, University of Alabama and in Birmingham and the violence, first in the South and later in the North, made him more aware of the need for forthright, moral leadership and strong official action to deal fairly with blacks. If the articles of freedom as spelled out in the Declaration of Independence and the Bill of Rights were to have any validity, it made no sense to him to follow a different course despite the practical difficulties and the political dangers.

What he saw in the ghettos and his face-to-face encounters with blacks, particularly the children, spurred him to act in many ways, small and large, far beyond his official responsibilities. If Washington officialdom was content to let a swimming pool in Dunbar High School remain closed for lack of repairs for eight years, he wasn't. He raised the money from interfaith sources and saw that the pool was reopened, restoring a badly needed recreational facility to a run-down, impoverished neighborhood and signaling to ghetto dwellers that the brother of the President, and hence the President himself, cared about improving the quality of their lives. If the white officials of Prince Edward County, Virginia, would deny education to fifteen hundred black children for four full years while the white children went to "private" schools supported mostly with public funds, he would see that schools were established for the black children and that they would have some of the finest teachers in the country. If the problems of decay, debilitation, hunger, violence and unemployment seemed unsolvable despite the much-vaunted War on Poverty and other government programs, that was an outlook he could not accept. In 1965 he would go into Bedford-Stuyvesant in Brooklyn, into the second largest Negro ghetto in the nation, and seek to create jobs, rehabilitate homes and revive hope by establishing two corporations—one black to provide a means for local decision and control, and one white to bring in outside resources as needed.

Long before 1968 his brother's words about "the Negro baby born in American today" were more than rhetoric and shocking statistics to him. By 1968 his was a white voice, unlike any other in the land, calling to the American people to live up fully to their historic commitment to equality and the rights of free men.

On May 6, 1961, two days after seven black and six white members of the Congress of Racial Equality (CORE) left Washington in a bus for the "Freedom Ride" through the South, Bob flew to Athens, Georgia, to deliver a Law Day speech at the University of Georgia. It is important now to look back on that speech. Given without apology or threats, it provided the first full insight into how the Kennedy Administration would enforce the civil rights laws, and it was the first time a top-ranking federal official had gone into the Deep South to deliver a major civil rights address. It also was Bob's first major speech as Attorney General, and it was one of the most memorable and one of the best he ever gave. Finally, it typified a mark of his public style, that when he had something controversial to say, he would say it straight out before an audience of the people most directly affected.

The president of the Student Advisory Council of the University of Georgia Law School, Jay Cox, a young Georgian with a game leg and a winning personality, had come to Washington in March to deliver the invitation. On January 11 racial rioting had forced Georgia officials to suspend, for "their own safety," Charlayne Hunter and Hamilton Holmes, the first two blacks to be enrolled at the university. Miss Hunter and Holmes had been reinstated under terms of a federal court order, but Cox reported that tension had not eased completely and that the two were being subjected to abuse almost daily as they attended classes.

Cox warned that there was some risk that an appearance by Bob might make conditions worse. However, Cox predicted that it would have the opposite effect: that speaking at the school so soon after the violence of January would be a gesture which many people in Georgia would appreciate and it could help the university put the incident behind it. Bob consulted with a number of Southern politicians and Southern friends, including Ralph McGill, publisher of the Atlanta *Constitution*. While some thought such a speech would be unwise since Bob was the federal official most directly responsible for enforcing the civil rights laws, most urged him to go for the same reasons that Cox had advanced. Thus the opportunity possibly to help in a troubled situation and the challenge of going South to articulate the Administration's civil rights policies looked attractive, but he accepted for a third reason, too—one quite typical of him: he took an immediate liking to Cox.[1]

The speech was five weeks in preparation. John Seigenthaler with his Southern background did a major part of the drafting after Bob outlined the points he wanted to cover. John Bartlow Martin, the writer and President Kennedy's Ambassador to the Dominican Republic, submitted another draft. McGill, James Landis, Sylvan Meyer, then editor of the Gainesville, Georgia, *Times,* Burke Marshall, Nicholas Katzenbach and others contributed ideas and comments. The speech was revised and rewritten seven times. Bob painstakingly edited each new draft, correcting sentences and rewriting whole paragraphs in his small, cramped handwriting which sometimes only Angela Novello could decipher. The final version contained more of his language than anyone else's for he had honed each sentence to convey his thoughts precisely.

We flew in the *Caroline* to Athens, arriving on a warm spring morning that had a hint of the sultriness of summer. The night before, Athens police had arrested five persons for painting "Kennedy Go Home" and "Yankee Go Home" on downtown sidewalks, but Cox and a few fellow law students formed the only welcoming committee at the airport and the town was quiet as we drove to the university. En route, one of the students asked Bob why he had decided to speak on civil rights. "It would have been hypocritical of me to come here and not do so," he replied.

An almost all-white audience of eighteen hundred—students, their parents and friends, professors and dignitaries—awaited him. Charlayne Hunter, with press credentials from the Atlanta *Daily World,* was the only black in attendance. The atmosphere was hushed and tense as Bob was introduced, but he eased it somewhat with a joke. Alluding to awards that had just been given out to honor students, Bob said that as a law student at the University of Virginia he, too, had received a prize—"for having the fifth best sense of humor." Then he went directly to his prepared text, which began and ended with references to Georgia. At the outset, he emphasized his ties with Georgia and the South, saying, among

---

1. After receiving his law degree, Cox became an attorney in the Civil Division.

other things, that he had been advised when speaking in Georgia to claim Georgia kinfolk if possible. "I have no relatives here and no direct ties to Georgia, except one," he said. "This state gave my brother the biggest percentage majority of any state in the Union, and in this last election that was even better than kinfolk."

Then, he spoke about the meaning of Law Day, saying:

We know that we cannot live together without rules which tell us what is right and what is wrong, what is permitted and what is prohibited. We know that it is law which enables men to live together, that creates order out of chaos. We know that the law is the glue that holds civilization together.

And we know that if one man's rights are denied the rights of all are endangered. In our country the courts have a most important role in safeguarding these rights. The decisions of the courts, however much we might disagree with them, in the final analysis must be followed and respected. If we disagree with a court decision and thereafter irresponsibly assail the court and defy its rulings, we challenge the foundations of our society.

Then he alluded to the Bay of Pigs and the committee of inquiry on which he was serving. It had become clear, he said, that "we must come forward with the answer to how a nation, devoted to freedom and individual rights and respect for the law, can stand effectively against an implacable enemy who plays by different rules and knows only the law of the jungle. . . . As we turn to meet our enemy, to look him full in the face, we cannot afford feet of clay or an arm of glass."

Thus it was important, he said, to consider three major areas of "difficulty" which sap the nation's strength, and he mentioned briefly organized crime and price-fixing, collusion and fraud in business.

"The third area is the one that affects us all the most directly—civil rights," he continued. "Southerners . . . don't like hypocrisy. So . . . I must tell you candidly what our policies are going to be in the field of civil rights and why."

He referred to an action the Justice Department had filed a few weeks earlier in federal court to force reopening of the schools in Prince Edward County:

It is now being said that the Department of Justice is attempting to close all public schools in Virginia because of the Prince Edward situation. That is not true, nor is the Prince Edward suit a threat against local control.

We are maintaining the orders of the courts. We are doing nothing more nor less. And if any one of you were in my position, you would do likewise for it would be required by your oath of office. You might not want to do it, you might not like to do it, but you would do it. For I cannot believe that anyone can support a principle which prevents more than a thousand of our children in one county from attending public school—especially when this step was taken to circumvent the orders of the court.

Our position is clear. We are upholding the law. . . . In this case—in all cases—I say to you today that if the orders of the court are circumvented, the Department of Justice will act. We will not stand by or be aloof. We will move.

He emphasized carefully that he considered civil rights a problem for every part of the country, not just the South; that he needed to look no further than the Department of Justice for evidence of discrimination, and added:

My firm belief is that if we are to make progress in this area—if we are to be truly great as a nation, then we must make sure that nobody is denied an opportunity because of race, creed or color. We pledge, by example, to take action in our own backyard—the Department of Justice—we pledge to move to protect the integrity of the courts in the administration of justice. In all this, we ask your help; we need your assistance.

Then he spelled out what would be a major element in the Kennedys' approach toward civil rights enforcement—one that was often misunderstood in the North as well as in the South:

We are trying to achieve amicable, voluntary solutions without going to court. These discussions have ranged from voting and school cases to incidents of arrest which might lead to violence.

We have sought to be helpful to avert violence and to get voluntary compliance. When our investigations indicate there has been a violation of law, we have asked responsible officials to take steps themselves to correct the situation. In some instances this has happened. When it has not, we have had to take legal action.

He said it was important to avoid violence and incidents such as occurred in Little Rock, Arkansas, in 1957 when President Eisenhower had to send paratroopers to prevent interference with court orders ending segregation in a high school.

We cannot afford them. It is not only that such incidents do incalculable harm to the children involved and to the relations among people. It is not only that such convulsions seriously undermine respect for law and order, and cause serious economic and moral damage. Such incidents hurt our country in the eyes of the world. . . .

For on this generation of Americans falls the full burden of proving to the world that we really mean it when we say all men are created free and are equal before the law. All of us might wish at times that we lived in a more tranquil world, but we don't. And if our times are difficult and perplexing, so are they challenging and filled with opportunity.

To the South, perhaps more than any other section of the country, has been given the opportunity and the challenge and the responsibility of demonstrating America at its greatest—at its full potential of liberty under law.

Then he closed with a clear statement of the Administration's civil rights policies in language which Anthony Lewis of the *New York Times* reported was "firm and his voice was even firmer":

You may ask, will we enforce the Civil Rights statutes?
The answer is: "Yes we will."
We also will enforce the antitrust laws, the antiracketeering laws, the laws against kidnaping and robbing Federal banks, and transporting stolen automobiles across state lines, the illicit traffic in narcotics and all the rest.
We can and will do no less.
I hold a constitutional office of the United States Government and I shall perform the duty I have sworn to undertake—to enforce the law, in every field of law and every region.
We will not threaten, we will try to help. We will not persecute, we will prosecute.
We will not make or interpret the laws. We shall enforce them—vigorously, without regional bias or political slant.
All this we intend to do. But all the high rhetoric on Law Day about the noble mansions of the law, all the high-sounding speeches about liberty and justice, are meaningless unless people—you and I—breathe meaning and force into it. For our liberties depend upon our respect for the law.
On December 13, 1889, Henry W. Grady of Georgia said these words to an audience in my home state of Massachusetts:

"This hour little needs the loyalty that is loyal to one section and yet holds the other in enduring suspicion and estrangement. Give us the broad and perfect loyalty that loves and trusts Georgia alike with Massachusetts —that knows no South, no North, no East, no West, but endears with equal and patriotic love every foot of our soil, every State of our Union.

"A mighty duty, sir, and a mighty inspiration impels everyone of us tonight to lose in patriotic consecration whatever estranges, whatever divides. We, sir, are Americans—and we stand for human liberty!"

Ten days later Mr. Grady was dead, but his words live today. We stand for human liberty.

The road ahead is full of difficulties and discomforts. But as for me, I welcome the challenge, I welcome the opportunity and I pledge my best effort—all I have in material things and physical strength and spirit—to see that freedom shall advance and that our children will grow old under the rule of law.

Except for laughter at the beginning, the audience had not given a sound or sign to indicate how the speech was being received. Now Bob was finished. He sat down. For fifteen or twenty agonizingly long seconds there was silence. Then applause spread through the hall. It continued for almost a minute, with many people standing as they clapped. Bob stood up twice to bow self-consciously. What caused the surprising ovation was difficult to discern. Certainly his frankness and his manner were well received. Dr. Thomas A. Hopkins, chairman of the Department of Speech at Mount Mercy College in Pittsburgh, who made a study of Bob's speeches for his book *Rights for Americans*, commented:

Whether it was due to simple courtesy, or whether it was evoked by the Henry W. Grady quotation ("a stroke of genius" wrote a University of Georgia professor, delivered as it was in Athens, Grady's hometown), or whether it was a tribute to Kennedy's candor in giving that speech in the South ("rather than in New York," as another Georgia faculty member wrote later), or whether it was an acknowledgement of the law of the land, no one can say with certainty. That it was not given as a sign of complete espousal of the speaker's stand may more closely approximate the truth.

Except for the *New York Times*, which ran Anthony Lewis' account on the front page and a partial text inside, the speech did not receive the attention it deserved. Considering not only the place that it was given, but the time—only four months after Bob had taken office—it was a remarkable speech for what it revealed then and what it reveals now.

Except for the question of whether more civil rights laws were needed, the speech accurately blueprinted the course of civil rights enforcement that the Kennedys followed and the philosophy that would guide them. It was all there—for George Wallace, Ross Barnett, Bull Connor or anyone else to see: court orders would be upheld; the law would be enforced.

But the speech also reflected that new, creative initiatives were being undertaken; that the federal government would seek compliance through negotiation; that subpoenaing records and filing complaints would be the last step; that the Justice Department would act only after local officials either could not or would not do so. This approach was a result of the developing relationship between Bob and Burke Marshall, each giving so much to the other: Bob, the public man, understanding at the outset that with an attitude of frankness and a willingness to communicate constantly with Negro leaders and Southern officials, the Justice Department could be far more effective than it had been in meeting its responsibilities to end discrimination and head off violence; and Marshall, the gifted innovator and negotiator, implementing Bob's policies with an unshakable conviction that laws, if enforced, could change the hearts of men, General Eisenhower's contrary philosophy notwithstanding.

Further, the speech disclosed that though Bob was new to the civil rights problem, he had grasped its magnitude and instinctively understood its deeper meanings for the country. We can see now his words reflecting the transformation that was taking place in his mind, and certainly that of the President, as they came to grips with the problem; a change that would lead them irrevocably to put their strong moral commitment to equal rights ahead of the short-term political hazards. And we can look back now to his actions between May 6, 1961, and June 6, 1968, and know that he meant every word of what he said that morning in Athens, right to the very last sentence: ". . . and I pledge my best effort—all I have in material things and physical strength and spirit—to see that freedom shall advance and that our children will grow old under the rule of law."

After the speech Bob flew to Chicago to participate in a colorful Polish-American community celebration of the 170th anniversary of

Poland's adoption of a constitution. Meanwhile, the Freedom Riders proceeded southward through Richmond, Petersburg and Lynchburg, Virginia, bound for New Orleans. In just eight days they would provide the first hard test at home of the new Administration's mettle.

It was not the most propitious time. The Administration was coming off the ropes after the belting it took at the Bay of Pigs. Just ahead for President Kennedy was a trip to France and England and a sobering meeting in Vienna with Chairman Khrushchev, who, believing the tide of events was moving his way, was in a bellicose mood. As the President looked forward to the meeting, he wanted not only to get as much insight as he could on Khrushchev and Soviet policies, but to impress Khrushchev with America's strength and determination so that there would be less chance of a dangerous misjudgment on either side. Thus within the Administration there was hope that, in the wake of the Bay of Pigs, there would be no domestic upheaval before the President left that would further undermine in any way his posture as the leader of a strong, united people. But Americans have a basic right to travel freely within their country as long as they do so peacefully, and the Freedom Riders were on their way.

As they passed through Charlotte, North Carolina, a black member of the group was arrested for trespassing when he refused to leave a barbershop in a bus station. In Rock Hill, South Carolina, three members of the group were assaulted, but police quelled the fracas. Two of the riders were arrested in Winnsboro, South Carolina. They reached Atlanta, and on May 14 divided into two groups to make the trip to Birmingham, one going by Greyhound bus and the other aboard a Trailways bus.

The departure of the riders from Washington and the incidents in Charlotte and Rock Hill had been reported on inside pages in the *New York Times* and some other papers. Otherwise, the ride attracted almost no attention. Later, in the heat of controversy, some Southern officials and some Southern newspapers asserted that the government had encouraged the Freedom Riders, and specifically that Bob had sent them into the South. The charge was totally untrue.

In late April CORE sent a copy of a press release about the trip to the Justice Department, and it was routed to Marshall's desk. Marshall did not bring it to the attention of Bob or Byron White. Then Marshall came down with the mumps, and Bob was preoccupied with the Bay of Pigs inquiry and his speech at the University of Georgia.

Six miles out of Anniston, Alabama, a gang of Ku Klux Klansmen, carrying clubs, chains and blackjacks, attacked the Greyhound bus and burned it, injuring twelve persons. Another gang, including members of the KKK, attacked the Trailways bus when it pulled into Birmingham. It was at this point that Bob first became aware of the Freedom Riders. Marshall reached him at home to tell him about the violence.

The FBI, however, had been tipped off by an informant in the Klan that the buses might be attacked and had alerted the Birmingham and Anniston police. It did not report this information to Marshall or anyone else in his division or to the Attorney General's office. The FBI did tell the police which buses the Freedom Riders would be aboard, but no officers were on hand to restrain the Klansmen. In Birmingham the mob beat the passengers for ten minutes, injuring three seriously enough to require hospitalization, though the terminal was near the police station. Police Commissioner Eugene (Bull) Connor's explanation revealed the twisted sense of law enforcement that would be a major factor in turning Birmingham into a caldron of racial violence during 1962–63. The police were short-handed because it was Mother's Day, Connor said sardonically.

As Bob, Marshall and White assessed reports of the incidents, they made a judgment at the outset that would underlie all their actions as the crisis developed: there was no reason or point in attempting to persuade the riders to abandon their project. In the first place, the riders had the right to travel between the states, and the government had a clear responsibility to guarantee their safe passage if local authorities could not or would not do so. In the second place, it was clear that, despite the attacks and lack of protection, civil rights groups would rally behind the Freedom Riders and would be bent on completing the ride all the way to New Orleans; that if the original riders dropped out, others would take their places. With that in mind, as well as the hope of avoiding an ugly domestic incident just before the President left for Europe, Bob and his associates thought the best course of action would be for local or state authorities to guarantee the riders' safety and get the ride completed as quickly as possible.

On Monday, Bob telephoned Governor John Patterson of Alabama. They were on a first-name basis, for Patterson, though a hard-line segregationist elected with Klan support, had been the first Southern Governor to back John Kennedy for President. He had stood fast, despite differences with JFK on racial matters and even though his delegation at the Los Angeles convention went for Lyndon Johnson. Bob asked Patterson to provide protection for the buses, and Patterson agreed. But in the afternoon he changed his mind. He issued a statement saying he would not be responsible for the Freedom Riders' safety.

Then Patterson disappeared, undercutting an intensive effort by the Administration to convince Alabama authorities that it was in their own interest—as well as in the national interest—to accept responsibility for the safety of citizens traveling interstate and permit the Freedom Ride to proceed without further violence. Bob tried repeatedly on Tuesday, Wednesday and Thursday to talk again with Patterson, but was told the Governor was out of town and not available to take a phone call.

In the Governor's absence, the situation deteriorated slowly. However, outside of Alabama, the White House and the Justice Department, there was no feeling in the country that a crisis was at hand. The communications media had reported the violence, but then gave very little attention to the situation, underestimating the dimensions of the problem and its implications. Thus, when Bob, White and Marshall had breakfast at the White House on Tuesday and Wednesday to explain the situation to the President and discuss what they might do, there was virtually no pressure on the White House to intervene and very little on Justice.

But the specter of another Little Rock—the use of troops against

American citizens, with all the unpleasant consequences that would accrue at home and abroad—was forming as a distinct possibility. This was something President Kennedy had strongly believed he would be able to avoid during his term. The use of troops was personally distasteful to him, and it would be added embarrassment when he faced Khrushchev. Furthermore, he had been critical of the Eisenhower Administration at Little Rock, asserting that planning and stronger, more affirmative action by the President could have ended defiance of the court orders before the dispute reached the point that troops had to be sent in.

Thus, while Bob and Marshall talked with anyone they thought might be helpful, White with his two chief assistants, Joseph Dolan and William Geoghegan, and Louis Oberdorfer, William Orrick and others began considering what steps, short of sending troops, the government might take if Patterson continued to remain incommunicado and it became necessary to intervene. After Little Rock, Attorney General Rogers had started to provide an alternative by giving riot training to the U.S. marshals and their deputies. However, only about a hundred deputies had received the training, and many of the others were middle-aged and ill prepared for strenuous duty. Now the World War II experience of White and his aides began to pay off. They improvised a plan to augment the marshals with men from the well-trained Border Patrol of the Immigration Service, guards from the Bureau of Prisons and from the Treasury Department's large number of alcohol and tobacco tax agents stationed in the South. This had the virtue of being a nonmilitary-appearing force, which could possibly forestall the need for uniformed soldiers with rifles and fixed bayonets. With quiet haste, White and his planners formalized steps to assemble the men, move them to Alabama, house and feed them and organize them into a force capable of dealing with disorder.

Meanwhile, Bob issued several statements calling on both sides to exercise restraint. In one he said: "In order to insure that innocent people are not injured, maimed or even killed, I would call upon all people who have paramount interest in the future of our country to exercise restraint and judgment over their activities in the next few weeks or next few days." In another, he said: "What is needed now is a cooling-off period"—an unfortunate phrase, for it angered Negro leaders, who replied that Negroes had been "cooling off" for one hundred years.

The original Freedom Riders, battered and frightened, abandoned the ride and flew to New Orleans, but others, including students from Fisk University in Nashville, began arriving in Birmingham to carry on. Police arrested some of the would-be riders and took others into protective custody, and on Friday, as the situation became more explosive, President Kennedy placed a call to Patterson. But even to the President of the United States the Governor of Alabama was said to be "out of town and still unreachable." The President did reach Lieutenant Governor Albert Boutwell, however, and several hours later an intermediary for Patterson called to say the Governor would meet with a personal representative of the President.

Within an hour, John Seigenthaler was flying to Montgomery, and he met with the Governor for two hours that evening. Near the end of their negotiations, Seigenthaler called Bob. In Patterson's presence, Seigenthaler said he had been assured that Alabama did not need or expect assistance from the federal government; that it had, in Patterson's words, "the means, ability and the will to keep the peace without outside help"; that the Governor had the will and the force to protect everyone in the state, whether residents or visitors, and that he would provide that protection on the highways and elsewhere.

Based on Patterson's assurances and further conversations between Bob and Floyd Mann, chief of the Alabama Highway Patrol, twenty-one students—eighteen blacks and three whites—boarded a bus in Birmingham the following morning bound for New Orleans. After a delay until someone could be found who would drive the bus (Bob engaged in a long and hotly worded conversation with George E. Cruit, a Greyhound representative in Birmingham, and a driver was located), it headed south toward Montgomery, guarded by Mann's troopers. On that Saturday morning the FBI informed the Montgomery police that the bus would be arriving. When it was about fourteen miles from the capital, Mann so informed Montgomery Police Commissioner Lester B. Sullivan. Despite the warnings, no policemen were on duty at the Montgomery bus terminal, but a crowd of about a thousand persons was.

John Doar, Marshall's chief assistant in the Civil Rights Division, whose name and calm, commanding presence would become a legend in civil rights enforcement throughout the South, was in the U.S. Attorney's office overlooking the scene. He had placed a call to Bob's office before the bus was due to arrive and now he reported:

"The bus is in. The people are just standing there watching. . . . Now the passengers are coming off. They're standing on a corner of the platform.

"Oh, there are fists, punching. A bunch of men led by a guy with a bleeding face are beating them. There are no cops. It's terrible. It's terrible. There's not a cop in sight. People are yelling 'Get 'em, get 'em.' It's awful. . . .

"The cops are there now."

Two white girls aboard the bus, Susan Hermann and Susan Wilbur, found themselves isolated and began walking away from the station. Some of the mob followed them. Women slapped at them with purses and cursed them. The girls asked a man in a car to help them. "You deserve what you get," he said. "I hope they beat you up good." Then another man in a car came up and said: "Come on, I'll help you. I'm a federal man." The mob converged on the car. The man was struck from behind and left lying on the sidewalk. He was John Seigenthaler. The girls escaped.

Seigenthaler lay on the pavement unconscious for twenty-five minutes before police took him to a hospital. Later, Commissioner Sullivan explained that an ambulance was not called for Seigenthaler because "every white ambulance in town reported their vehicles had broken down."

It was long after the violence had broken out that police reached the scene in sufficient force to restore order. People with no apparent connection with the Freedom Riders were beaten. A boy's leg was broken and another boy had inflammable liquid poured on him and was set on fire.

As Doar was giving his blow-by-blow account, Bob tried to reach Patterson. Again he was told the Governor was out of town and that no one knew where he was or when he would return. When a report of the attack on Seigenthaler reached the office, Bob had already ordered White to get his force moving. James McShane, then U.S. marshal for the District of Columbia, and twenty of his deputies, left shortly afterward by plane, and other marshals, border patrolmen, prison guards and revenue agents began heading for Montgomery by air or in their own cars. By the next morning, four hundred men, commanded by White, had assembled at Maxwell Air Force Base just outside Montgomery.

Two other steps were taken that Saturday afternoon. Doar went into U.S. District Court in Montgomery and obtained an injunction enjoining the Ku Klux Klan and the National States' Rights Party from interfering with interstate travel by bus. Additional teams of FBI agents were sent into the area to investigate the mob action at Montgomery.

With the arrival of the marshals, Patterson reappeared, protesting vehemently that the action was unconstitutional and that the marshals were not needed, but developments the next day would demonstrate that they were.

Dr. King flew into Montgomery that day and went to the home of the Reverend Ralph Abernathy to prepare for a rally that evening at the First Baptist Church. During the afternoon White went alone to a meeting with Patterson which was held with newsmen present and a number of Alabama officials on hand. Patterson threatened that the federal men might be arrested if they broke local laws. White replied that the marshals were there to enforce federal law and would do so. A memorable exchange followed when Patterson asked if White was willing to make all information the government had on CORE available to Alabama authorities.

"No," White replied.

"Will you make available all the information you have about the Freedom Riders who came in yesterday?"

"No."

"You know where some of these Freedom Riders are, don't you?"

"Yes, in the hospital."

"Do you know where the others are?"

"No, I don't."

"If you knew where some of these people are, would you inform us?"

"I will never know where these people are."

During the day the marshals using Border Patrol radio cars patrolled bus and railroad terminals, along interstate bus routes and near Negro churches. In the evening about fifteen hundred Negroes jammed every foot of space in the First Baptist Church to hear Dr. King and to cheer the Freedom Riders. As the program got under way, one of the radio cars reported that a crowd of whites was gathering in the park across the street and that no police were doing anything about it. White immediately dispatched the marshals by every means of transportation at hand—cars, small postal delivery trucks and a prison truck.

About a hundred marshals, wearing business suits with identifying arm bands and equipped with night sticks, tear gas grenades and side arms, hastily formed a skirmish line when the mob burned a car and then, howling its anger, advanced toward the church throwing rocks and bottles. The marshals went into action with their night sticks and then hurled tear gas grenades. The mob retreated and retaliated with a barrage of rocks. Again the mob advanced, and at a crucial moment Floyd Mann led a squad of troopers to the marshals' aid and helped drive the mob back. When reports of the skirmish reached Patterson, he declared martial law and the mob was forced to disperse when troops under command of Adjutant General Henry Graham, a National Guard Major General, reached the scene. Tear gas seeped into the hot, stifling church, adding to the discomfort and apprehension of the Negroes, who prayed and sang over the sounds of the battle, some coming close to panic before the mob was driven off.

It was a dreadful racial incident, the culmination of a week of mounting tension and terror and official foot-dragging by Patterson and the Montgomery police. In any assessment, however, one thing was beyond debate: had the marshals not held off the mob which was bent on burning the church, many people would have been injured and many probably have lost their lives.

I have gone into detail about the Freedom Riders not only because they provided Bob with his first major test as Attorney General, but also because the Justice Department's actions established the pattern for future civil rights enforcement. Thereafter, Bob, Marshall, Doar and others, improvising, leading, urging peaceful solutions, but determined to uphold the law, moved into the middle of hundreds of potential confrontations, heading off many before violence broke out. Most were small and received almost no notice. Others made news around the world.

Bob did not succeed during the Freedom Rides in preventing further violence after Anniston and Birmingham. He did succeed in averting another Little Rock, but even so President Kennedy carried the burden of Alabama, as well as the burden of Cuba, to his meeting with Khrushchev. However, the load was somewhat lighter because the Administration's actions had left no doubt in the world where the President stood in the struggle for equal rights. It also was clear that Bob had met his first test with courage and decisiveness, demonstrating at the first opportunity after the Georgia speech that the federal government would "move," that the law would be enforced.

It was the decade's first confrontation testing the federal government's resolve to protect federal rights in the face of Southern intransigence and Southern ingenuity in depriving Negroes of those rights. As Burke Marshall later pointed out in his book *Federalism and Civil Rights,* the white people and authorities of Alabama tried to deal with the federal right of the Freedom Riders to travel in their state, with which they disagreed, by abdicating responsibility for the maintenance of law and order. "The expectation," Marshall wrote, "was that the matter would be resolved, as Reconstruction was finally resolved, and as the entrance of a Negro girl into the University of Alabama in 1956 had been resolved, by terror and violence which the Federal government would not stop."

But the government did step in and stop it—at the church—and unquestionably that action stiffened the resolve of some Southern lawmen and elected officials to put law and order ahead of their personal beliefs. The retreat of the mob at the church ended violent opposition to the Freedom Riders. The trouble was that it did not diminish Southern opposition to the federally protected right of passengers using interstate bus lines to be free from racial discrimination in bus terminals. Mississippi authorities, for example, protected the Freedom Riders on the highway from Montgomery to Jackson and then arrested them when they ignored discriminatory signs in the bus terminal. Hundreds more Freedom Riders underwent harassment and arrest through the summer as the court system dealt slowly with the problem.

The moment of decision at the church was not the psychological turning point in the civil rights struggle that Dr. King thought it would be, but sympathy for the riders and disgust with mob violence added considerable momentum to the movement. And it was at long last the beginning of the end for segregated facilities in bus, rail and air terminals throughout the South. At Dr. King's suggestion, Bob instituted action before the Interstate Commerce Commission, which issued strong regulations requiring desegregation of terminals used in interstate bus travel—although it should not have been necessary. By the end of the year Marshall could report substantial progress in ending discrimination in interstate travel of all kinds.

From the moment that General Graham arrived at the church the evening of May 14, the federal presence in Montgomery began to diminish, although during the night Bob ordered two hundred more federal men to Maxwell Air Force Base as a precaution. As order was being restored, White was in frequent contact with Mann and Graham, and Bob talked with them by phone. It was decided that the marshals would be withdrawn to Maxwell and that the National Guard would assume responsibility for the safety of the Negroes in the church. In the early morning hours, when the city was quiet, they returned to their homes protected by Graham's men.

Though the city of Montgomery, for all practical purposes, had been secured, the potential for further violence continued to be high for the next few days as more Freedom Riders headed for Alabama. White Southerners bitterly resented the federal intervention, and, under Dr. King's leadership, the Freedom Riders were more determined than ever to travel through Mississippi to New Orleans. The marshals worked closely with Graham's and Mann's men, but the key decision, taken after lengthy behind-the-scenes negotiations and much soul-searching in the White House and the Justice Department, was that the marshals would not accompany the riders when they left Montgomery for Jackson, Mississippi. Bob was determined to protect the future safety of interstate bus travelers and to uphold the right of blacks to assemble peacefully, but the federal government, as a practical matter, could not protect many groups of demonstrators traveling in the South without a massive commitment of troops. Thus the negotiations with Alabama and Mississippi officials were undertaken, and when the evidence was that they fully intended to maintain law and order, Bob wanted nothing better than to give them the chance. Even so, as the two buses traveled from Montgomery to Jackson under elaborate security, Bob received minute-by-minute reports of their progress, and the government was prepared to move in troops if violence broke out. The day after the Montgomery-to-Jackson ride was completed, despite Dr. King's protests that the heavy guard had made the ride meaningless, White and all but one hundred marshals were withdrawn from Alabama.

The Freedom Riders' saga left members of Bob's staff with a new sense of *esprit de corps,* heightened respect for Bob's leadership and confidence in the Department's ability to act effectively under heavy pressure. The experience gained in quickly assembling the force of marshals and getting them to Alabama, in the complex negotiations that were carried on and in averting another Little Rock—these formed the basis for future operations, not only in civil rights enforcement, but in ransoming the Bay of Pigs prisoners, in combating crime and in aiding the Washington public schools.

Finally, two incidents that occurred on the night the mob tried to burn the church are worthy of mention—one that seemed so important then and seems so inconsequential now and another that provides an insight into the kind of man Bob was.

On that Sunday, Bob came to his office about noon. He had been playing with his children and was dressed in slacks, an open shirt and a blue and white sweater that buttoned down the front. About 1 A.M., after order had been restored in Montgomery and the tension was easing, a United Press photographer, who had been waiting in the hall since early evening, asked if he could take a picture of Bob. It seemed like a good idea. It would show a somewhat haggard but working Attorney General and would make the point that he had been at his desk for thirteen harrowing hours.

It was a bad idea. The picture showed Bob, shirt open, feet on the desk, telephone in hand, and it was used widely in newspapers and on television. Hundreds of persons wrote to him, chiding him for dressing carelessly. Many said the photograph degraded the high office he held. It seemed that a large number of Americans wanted dignity as well as performance, and he took their criticism to heart. Thereafter, except when engaged in some strenuous sport like skiing or shooting a rapids or when he was relaxing with his children, he tried to avoid being photographed unless he was wearing a business suit.

Not long after the photographer left the office, Dr. King called from the church as Bob was talking with a *Time* reporter, Harold B. Meyers. Dr. King was extremely upset and accused Bob of abandoning the blacks to the mercy of the Alabama National Guard. Bob held the phone away from his ear, and Meyers, sitting about fifteen feet away, could clearly hear Dr. King's deep, angry voice.

"My people are concerned for their personal safety," Dr. King said. "They're frightened about what will happen to them tonight. You shouldn't have withdrawn the marshals. Patterson's National Guard won't protect us."

Bob explained in a tired, even voice that he had talked with both Floyd Mann and General Graham and that he had confidence in them. He tried to calm Dr. King and assure him that he and all the others would be kept in the church only until it was safe for the Guardsmen to escort them to their homes. But Dr. King would not believe it and said bitterly that he felt he had been betrayed.

"Now, Reverend," Bob said without changing his tone, "don't tell me that. You know just as well as I do that if it hadn't been for the United States marshals you'd be as dead as Kelsey's nuts right now!"

Neither man spoke for ten or twelve seconds. "All right," Dr. King said finally. "All right."

A few minutes later, Bob's phone rang again, and when he answered, Governor Patterson, as upset as Dr. King, unleashed a torrent of accusations. Again Bob held the phone from his ear and Meyers could hear Patterson's strident, acerbic voice. He blamed Bob for sending the Freedom Riders into Alabama and held him responsible for the violence.

"Now, John," Bob interrupted in the same tone of voice he had used with Dr. King, "you can say that on television. You can tell that to the people of Alabama, John, but don't tell me that. Don't tell me that, John."

Patterson repeated the accusations and said the National Guard would protect the Negroes in the church, but could not guarantee protection to Dr. King.

"I don't believe that, John," Bob replied. "Have General Graham call me. I want him to say it to me. I want to hear a general of the United States Army say he can't protect Martin Luther King."

Patterson backed down and allowed that it was he, not Graham, who thought Dr. King could not be protected. Then Patterson shouted that the presence of the marshals had created a "very serious political situation." "You're destroying us politically," he said shrilly.

"John," Bob replied, "it's more important that these people in the church survive physically than for us to survive politically."

Chapter 10

Three Encounters

At the end of 1961, Bob submitted a report to the President taking stock of the Justice Department's civil rights records for the year. The purpose of the report, of course, was to inform the public, not the President. It was drafted to demonstrate that the Administration was being vigorous in enforcing the law and was making significant progress in reducing discrimination. To attract the maximum attention, it was made public as a White House release during the usual Christmas-week news lull, a device which every Administration employs.

At the outset, the report sought to meet a charge that galled the President and Bob: that the Kennedys were heavy-handedly imposing their will on the South, violating the Constitution as Governor Patterson had charged and as many Southerners were convinced, all leading to a pervasive, growing belief in the South that the federal government was the "enemy":

First, it should be understood, that it is the Department's basic policy to seek effective guarantees and action from local officials and civic leaders voluntarily and without court action. This has been done quietly and without publicity. Informal conversations to this end have been conducted wherever our investigations have disclosed evidences of civil rights violations. We know you feel strongly that these matters should be resolved at the local and state level and the Federal government should intervene only if all other efforts have failed.

On numerous occasions, I am happy to report, local action has been taken voluntarily. In all such instances we have taken steps thereafter to keep currently informed on developments. It has been only where local officials have not taken effective steps to correct a situation or where there has been an attempt to evade court orders that the Department has taken formal legal action as authorized by the Congress.

Despite the violence that had exploded against the Freedom Riders and the intransigence that the Department was encountering among Southern school administrators and voting registrars, and despite signs of growing Negro impatience, the report did not recommend that Congress be asked to enact any new civil rights laws. There was no recognition of the hardships and discrimination that blacks lived with in the North. It was essentially a hopeful document. In a final paragraph, which Bob added, he said:

> I can report to you that the law enforcement officers and civic leaders in the vast majority of communities have met their obligations. The experiences of the past year have strengthened my belief that despite the efforts of a small minority, the people in the United States are law-abiding people who wish to live by the law, do not want to circumvent court decisions, and are opposed to actions which will result in violence. I am confident, therefore, that this year's progress will continue, and that it will be carried forward with the effort and approval of the vast majority of the American people.

Bob did not add the paragraph for effect, nor was it simply rhetorical. It accurately reflected his views at the time: that strong positive leadership by the President, persistent federal action to protect federally guaranteed rights, and continuing dialogue with Southern officials and civil rights leaders would isolate violence and gradually but steadily lift the burden of discrimination from the backs of Negroes with civility and justice. The men around Bob shared this view, although Marshall, perhaps, saw the inflexibility of white supremacy in its true perspective sooner than the rest.

The trouble, as the passage of a few years would show, was that temporary solutions and the heady atmosphere of the New Frontier obscured our view of the depth of the problem. Despite the enlightened Southerners among us, we lacked a sense of Southern history. Particularly lacking, I can see now, was full understanding of the destructive effect of the federal government's long record after Reconstruction of vacillation and finally abandonment of the Negro to the wiles of white supremacy. There, we did not reckon fully with the ingrained stubbornness of Southern leaders and their adeptness at forestalling federal action to help Negroes. Nor did we fully confront what all must have known instinctively; that the beliefs, fears and customs of discrimination were embedded into the nation's mind and soul much more deeply against Negroes than against any other minority.

The year 1961 did not seem a time to cast shadows. For the first time since Reconstruction, the federal government was making a positive, intensive effort to eliminate official discrimination in the South. It was the start of a new decade, with a new President, whose own election signaled a new advance in religious tolerance which seemed to point the way the country was going. Only six days after Montgomery, in a Voice of America message transmitted around the world, Bob said that race relations were improving and predicted that a Negro could be elected President before the year 2000. Bob recalled that when his grandfather immigrated to Boston, "the Irish were not wanted there. Now an Irish Catholic is President of the United States. There is no question about it. In the next forty years, a Negro can achieve the same position my brother has."

As Bob spoke, interpreters simultaneously translated his remarks in thirty-seven languages. There were some who would say he made his prediction only to offset the bad publicity the violence in Alabama had given the country, but he believed what he said. His hopeful statements of 1961 would be tempered by a growing understanding of the deeper problem as he came up against the refusal of Mississippi authorities to obey a court order to admit James H. Meredith to the University of Mississippi; as he faced the hard-line demagoguery of George Wallace; as he visited Negro schools and tenements; as he sought out Negro leaders and felt the fury of violence as it erupted in the Northern ghettos. Still, he would remain hopeful, and his faith in the conscience of the American people and in their sense of justice remained constant. Minutes before he was shot, while speaking extemporaneously to his followers in the Ambassador Hotel, he said:

I think we can end the divisions within the United States. What I think is quite clear is that we can work together in the last analysis and that what has been going on within the United States . . . the divisions, the violence, the disenchantment with our society; the divisions, whether it's between blacks and whites, between the poor and the more affluent or between age groups or on the war in Vietnam is that we can start to work together. We are a great country, an unselfish country and a compassionate country. I intend to make that the basis for running.

In a twelve-month period between September 15, 1962, and September 15, 1963, Bob's faith was tested and sorely tried repeatedly. It began with the Meredith case and culminated sorrowfully with a deadly church bombing which killed four Negro girls attending Sunday school in Birmingham. In between there were confrontations with Wallace over the court-ordered admission of two Negro students to the University of Alabama and court-ordered desegregation of the Birmingham public schools; the assassination of Mississippi civil rights leader Medgar Evers; the massive March on Washington for Jobs and Freedom; and violence in Birmingham and many other Southern cities and towns as Negroes demonstrated against discrimination in public facilities, triggering the President's request for new civil rights legislation.

It was a period of almost continual crisis, in which Bob occupied the pivotal role in the government. Between May 1 and June 30, 1963, he not only dealt with the violence in Birmingham and with Wallace at Tuscaloosa, but directed the drafting of legislation; helped write the messages that supported it; worked on the President's moral-crisis speech of June 11; organized a series of meetings in the White House and elsewhere in which President Kennedy, Vice President Johnson and Bob urged leaders of religious, labor, business, legal and women's groups to work for voluntary elimination of racial discrimination, particularly in places of public accommodation;[1] and held innumerable meetings with Senators and Con-

---

1. Within three weeks, a survey of 566 communities in Southern and border states

gressmen, as well as with the press, to explain the need for the legislation and the need for local leadership to improve relations between the races.

On the day John Kennedy was inaugurated, James Meredith, twenty-nine, a veteran of nine years in the Air Force and one of ten children of a "good" Negro farmer in the central Mississippi town of Kosciusko, took the first step on what would be a lonely, torturous path. After months of debate and self-doubt, he mailed a letter to the University of Mississippi asking for an application for admission. He met with refusal, then another and another.

In June 1961 the National Association for the Advancement of Colored People lawyers filed suit for Meredith in Federal District Court in Mississippi claiming that Meredith had been refused enrollment solely because of his race. At Justice, Marshall asked for a copy of the complaint and began keeping a file on the case. But it was not until the case reached the Supreme Court in August 1962 that the Justice Department took an active hand. District Court Judge Sydney C. Mize had twice decided against Meredith, ruling that he had not been denied admission because of his race. In June 1962 the Court of Appeals for the Fifth Circuit reversed Judge Mize, declaring with biting language that the university was segregated and that Meredith had been turned down "solely because he was a Negro." Then followed a strange duel in which a member of the Fifth Circuit from Mississippi, Judge Ben Cameron, who had not been on the panel that decided the case, issued an unprecedented order blocking the decision. The court vacated the order, but Cameron retaliated by staying the ruling again. Twice more the court and Cameron jockeyed with the ruling, and after Cameron issued his fourth stay, the NAACP appealed to Supreme Court Justice Hugo Black. It was Black who brought the Justice Department into the case, asking for a memorandum on the Department's thinking on Cameron's power to issue his successive stays and whether Jus-

---

showed that the meetings had caused at least one type of privately owned public facility to desegregate voluntarily in many areas. The statistics were: theaters in 109 communities; restaurants in 141; hotels-motels in 163; and lunch counters in 204.

tice Black had the power, while the Court was in summer recess, to intervene.

The Department's answers were that Cameron's orders were fallacious and that he had issued them "to frustrate the decision of his own court"; that Justice Black had the power to set the orders aside; and that he should do so. Justice Black did, ordering the university on September 10 to enroll Meredith immediately. A few days later, Judge Mize bowed to the order, but Ross Barnett, Mississippi's courtly, segregationist Governor, didn't. Wrapped in the mystique of the Confederacy's "lost cause," Barnett called for defiance to "the evil and illegal forces of tyranny," and requested all Mississippi officials to stand with him, ready to go to jail, if necessary, to keep Meredith out of the hallowed school.

With Barnett's inflaming cry of "Never!" Mississippi began a series of frenzied, last-ditch maneuvers to block Meredith; maneuvers that would unleash a torrent of segregationist emotion and hostility, that would end in violence, tragedy and futility. In the White House and in the Justice Department, Barnett's defiance and the prospect of violence seemed unreal. There the issue was not whether a black man would enroll at "Ole Miss," as Mississippians fondly called the university, but whether the orders of the federal courts were to be obeyed and the integrity of the judicial system was to be upheld. It was, after all, 1962—five years after Little Rock, sixteen months after Montgomery. One was slow to accept the fact that there were Senators, governors, Congressmen and mayors, as well as prominent laymen, who believed and advocated that open defiance of a Supreme Court order was not as bad as allowing one Negro to study at a university.

At the Justice Department, in anticipation of Justice Black's decision, preparations were begun to assemble the deputy marshals, border patrolmen and prison guards who had performed so effectively in Alabama. But, as in Alabama, the President and Bob were intent on getting peaceful compliance. They began cautiously hopeful that they could, anxious not to use troops and determined not to make a martyr of Barnett or any other Mississippi official. They did not succeed in their first two objectives, and Barnett missed martyrdom only because he grew fearful of the violent passions he had encouraged, and, in the crunch, secretly made a deal that brought Meredith to Ole Miss.

Ross Barnett was a product of his background and his times. His roots were deep in the rutted, impoverished clay hills of central Mississippi, an area that became in the 1930's the archetype of William Faulkner's Mississippi: a poor and impotent country wrapped in the past and fearfully suspicious of the future. Barnett, like Meredith, was one of ten children. He had pulled himself up to become a lawyer and, with a kindly personality and a homespun courtroom manner, had developed a highly successful practice. Coming from a strongly Fundamentalist area, Barnett believed in the Bible and just as sincerely in the supremacy of the white race. He had been elected Governor in 1959 with the strong backing of the Citizens' Councils, groups which had come into being after the Supreme Court school decision in 1954 as a bulwark against integration. After the 1960 Democratic Convention, Barnett had quickly disavowed the Kennedy-Johnson ticket and had led the state's electors in November to cast their votes for Senator Harry Byrd of Virginia. Now, at sixty-four years of age, Barnett, caught in the swirling, rising tide of hatred and resistance that he had done so much to let loose, faced the federal government and the Kennedys.

Bob made his first contact with Barnett on September 15, two days after Judge Mize issued his final order. Before placing the phone call, Bob, talking with Marshall and Katzenbach, decided to proceed on the assumption that Colonel T. B. Birdsong, head of the Mississippi Highway Patrol, and other Mississippi authorities would protect Meredith from harm as they had protected the first two busloads of Freedom Riders to travel from Montgomery to Jackson. When Barnett came on the line, Bob briskly outlined a plan to bring Meredith to the university for registration on September 20. A few marshals would accompany Meredith. He would be refused. The Justice Department would go to court, which would order university officials to enroll Meredith, and it would be done. "That will take about a year," Barnett said. Bob did not respond, and all that they seemed to agree upon was that violence should be avoided.

Walter Lord, in his detailed book on the Meredith case, *The Past That Would Not Die,* observed: "To Kennedy the Governor had been told exactly what he was going to do; now he could move on to a quick, orderly solution. To Ross Barnett everything was just beginning."

But the events of September 20 showed Washington that a "quick, orderly solution" was out of the question. After much telephoning between Bob and Barnett and between Marshall and Mississippi Attorney General Joe Patterson and Tom Watkins, a Jackson lawyer who was one of Barnett's advisers, Meredith arrived at Ole Miss to register. He was accompanied by St. John Barrett, third-in-command in the Civil Division; Chief Marshal McShane; and Charles Chamblee, a courageous border patrolman who had been at Montgomery. Barnett, assuming the duties of the university registrar, met them. While two thousand students milled outside yelling, "We want Ross, we want Ross," the Governor read a long proclamation, turning down Meredith's application. "Take it and abide by it," he said, handing the proclamation to Meredith, who remained silent.

"Do you realize you are placing yourself in contempt of court?" asked St. John Barrett.

"Are you telling me this or does it take a judge?" Barnett queried back.

A line of highway patrolmen restrained the students as Meredith, Barrett and McShane got into their car and, with Chamblee driving, headed back to Memphis. Word spread through the state that "Ross had won." But the Department was prepared to take the issue to a judge and that evening filed an order in Judge Mize's court requiring Chancellor John D. Williams, Liberal Arts Dean Arthur B. Lewis and Registrar Robert B. Ellis to show cause the next day why they should not be held in contempt of court. It was the first legal move in a strategy to gain compliance with the court orders by pressing rapidly for Meredith's admission and applying pressure on the people around Barnett. The hope was that Mississippi would change course before Barnett was cornered—when things got to the point where he would be held in contempt of court if he continued his defiance. The last thing the President and Bob wanted was to give Barnett the chance he seemed at the moment to covet

—achieving martyrdom in a federal prison.

However, the next day, a Friday, Judge Mize absolved the three university officials of contempt, asserting that they had been relieved of their duties when the university trustees had voted to give Barnett "full power, authority, right and discretion" in dealing with Meredith. Again the Department moved swiftly, appealing the decision that evening to the Fifth Circuit in New Orleans, which ordered the three officials and the trustees to appear the following Monday.

During the weekend there was intense activity in Washington and in the Governor's mansion in Jackson to prepare for the court hearing. Bob telephoned Barnett several times. Now FBI agents and newsmen were reporting from Mississippi that emotion was running dangerously high, and Bob repeatedly expressed his concern to Barnett that violence would break out. "This matter must not be resolved in the street," he said, and he urged Barnett to issue a statement, as had been done during the Freedom Ride, that the state would not tolerate violence. But Barnett, while asserting that he was as opposed to violence as anyone, begged off and complained bitterly about the speed with which the court was requiring the university officials and trustees to appear before it.

Bob issued a statement urging Mississippi to comply with the court's orders. It contained what seemed to be a telling argument. Barnett was basing his resistance on the doctrine of interposition, that state officials had the right to interpose state sovereignty between the federal government and the people. It had been raised by John C. Calhoun in South Carolina in 1832, and Arthur M. Schlesinger, Jr., who had come over from the White House to help, remembered that the Mississippi legislature of that time had rebuffed Calhoun. Schlesinger could not put his finger on the text of the legislature's action and finally said, "My father will know." We called Arthur M. Schlesinger, Sr., in Cambridge, and the kindly Harvard historian replied that we'd find it in the *Resolves of the Mississippi Legislature* and accurately provided the approximate date. Thus Bob's statement pointed out that 130 years earlier Mississippi had turned down interposition as "a heresy, fatal to the existence of the Union . . . contrary to the letter and spirit of the Constitution and in direct conflict with the welfare, safety and independence of every state."

There was another bit of irony that weekend, for exactly a century earlier Abraham Lincoln had issued the Emancipation Proclamation that freed the slaves. The centennial was observed in many parts of the nation, and at ceremonies at the Lincoln Memorial in Washington President Kennedy called on the nation to regard the day "not as an end, but a beginning."

Neither the President's appeal nor the reminder of the judgment of that long-forgotten Mississippi legislature had any effect on Barnett. At Justice, as plans moved ahead to prepare for the court hearing and to muster the force of deputy marshals, a number of other possible steps were discussed and discarded. One was for the President to invite Barnett to meet with him in the White House, as during the Little Rock crisis President Eisenhower had met with Arkansas Governor Orval Faubus at Newport, Rhode Island, where the President was vacationing. But the Eisenhower-Faubus meeting had only enhanced Faubus' posture and expended the President's personal prestige. It did not cause Faubus to back down; troops eventually had to be used, and there seemed little likelihood that a Kennedy-Barnett meeting would have any better result.

Another proposal was to have Vice President Johnson fly to Mississippi and personally escort Meredith to the university to register. The prospect of Mr. Johnson, with his Southern background, standing up with Meredith at first appeared to have merit. But when the idea was broached to one of Barnett's advisers, the word came back that even in the face of Mr. Johnson's prestige Barnett would not back down, that Barnett was intent on forcing a final showdown. Thus it appeared probable that the Vice President would be humiliated publicly, the court orders would again be defied and so that plan was abandoned.[2]

2. Mr. Johnson while Vice President seldom, if ever, participated in any of the strategy discussions during the major civil rights crises. Rightly or wrongly, Bob felt his presence would complicate the discussions rather than further them. Mr. Johnson, with his sense of the Vice President's place and his massive pride, did not offer any advice or volunteer to sit in on the discussions. However, the suggestion that he could be of considerable help in civil rights matters was advanced several times in the columns of William H. White, who often reflected Mr. Johnson's thinking.

Another suggestion was that it might have a sobering effect on Barnett if it were let known that an Army division had been alerted for duty in Mississippi. No division had been alerted, and Bob said he wanted to see what the Court of Appeals ordered before making any decision. "Sending troops in is a hell of a thing for the country," he commented. In the end, he decided to continue tightening the pressure on Barnett a notch at a time.

While waiting for the Fifth Circuit's decision on whether to hold the university officials and trustees in contempt, Bob disclosed that he'd been talking with Senator James Eastland. Eastland had telephoned from his home in Mississippi and told Bob, "The Governor thinks you can back down a little," and then in a weak voice added, "I think so, too." Bob said he told Eastland, "You don't really believe that, Senator. You've been in the Senate too long to believe that." Eastland didn't answer, but said that he would be in Washington the next day and would have more to say to Bob then.

That evening the court held unanimously that the trustees had violated the court's orders, noting that Ellis had registered all other students on the day Meredith was rejected by Barnett. The trustees, under threat of being held in contempt of court, quickly agreed to register Meredith by 4 P.M. the next day in Jackson. Marshall called and, after describing what had happened in the hearing, said, "That brings us to our problem, doesn't it?" Bob replied that it did. Marshall was of the opinion that there would be no difficulty getting Meredith registered. "If you had heard the trustees pledge themselves to the court, you'd know they won't fiddle-faddle around," Marshall said. But he pointed out that the trustees and the university officials would not be in contempt if Barnett interposed again and turned Meredith away. The problem would be in protecting Meredith. Now it became paramount to know what Barnett would do. Bob said he would call the Governor while Marshall tried to talk with Attorney General Patterson, who had already issued a statement saying Mississippi had been dealt a "staggering blow. . . . The constitutional rights of over 5,000 students at the university have been ignored to gratify the pretended constitutional rights of one."

A short time later, Bob reached Barnett, who said he was "shocked" at the trustees' "surrender." Bob explained to Barnett what the situation was, reminding the Governor several times that he was a citizen of the United States as well as a citizen of Mississippi, but Barnett replied that "I consider the Mississippi courts as high as any other court and a lot more capable. . . . Our courts have acted too, and our legislature has acted too. I'm going to obey the laws of Mississippi!" Bob could not pin down Barnett on what protection would be given Meredith the next day, and the conversation ended with Barnett stating he would give his decision the next morning by phone or telegram.

With Bob unable to get assurances from Barnett that Mississippi would protect Meredith, Katzenbach raised the question whether it would not be advisable to start moving more marshals to Memphis. However, Bob said he did not want to do that without knowing what was going to happen and that if Mississippi would not protect Meredith, he would postpone having Meredith try to register for twenty-four hours.

When Barnett phoned the next morning, the conversation was almost a repeat of the night before except that the Governor, expressing his abhorrence of violence, promised that highway patrolmen would maintain order when Meredith made his second attempt to register. However, the conversations convinced Bob that there was no longer any use in keeping Barnett's name out of the legal proceedings. Accordingly, before Meredith left New Orleans to fly to Jackson, Marshall obtained an injunction from the Court of Appeals ordering Barnett not to interfere with Meredith's enrollment.

This time, to raise the level of the federal presence one degree higher, John Doar, Marshall's chief assistant, accompanied Meredith along with McShane. The plan was that Registrar Ellis would meet Meredith at the Federal Building and process his application. However, a state legislative committee issued a subpoena calling for Ellis to appear before it that afternoon; in effect, the registrar was taken into protective custody to prevent him from meeting with Meredith. When that happened, Meredith, Doar and McShane drove to a fifteen-story state office building, made their way through a booing, hissing crowd and were met by Colonel Birdsong and led to the tenth-floor offices of the trustees. There, standing in the doorway, Barnett refused to accept copies of the court's orders and read another proclamation "finally denying" Meredith's admission. Outside, the crowd listening at loudspeakers and transistor radios burst into cheering.

"Do you refuse to let us through that door?" Doar asked.

"Yes, sir," said Barnett, "I do so politely."

"And we leave politely," said Doar.

But as they emerged from the building, the crowd shouted "Communists" and "Go home, nigger" and moved forward menacingly. Highway patrolmen formed a path to allow the three men to reach their car and drive away safely.

The next moves were already being discussed in Bob's office. He decided to seek an order from the Fifth Circuit requiring Barnett to show cause why he should not be held in contempt and to send Meredith to Oxford the next morning to try to attend classes. When Bob called Barnett and informed him of the plans, the Governor was taken aback. He was shocked and surprised that Meredith would make another effort to attend Ole Miss. He complained that he could not be "running all over the State of Mississippi" to keep Meredith out.

"Why don't you try it for six months and see how it goes?" Bob asked.

"It's best for him not to go to Ole Miss," Barnett said.

"But he likes Ole Miss," Bob replied.

A few minutes later, Bob called Barnett again to inform him that Meredith would appear on the campus at 10 A.M. Once again Barnett pleaded that the best course would be to keep Meredith away, but Bob said that if Barnett were in his position, he would be doing the same thing; he had taken an oath on the Bible to uphold the laws of the United States and would have to do so. Barnett replied that Bob should tell the American people to tell the Supreme Court that its 1954 school segregation decision was not the law of the land. Bob repeated that Meredith would be on the campus at 10 A.M.

Bob was going that evening to the opening of Irving Berlin's musical *Mr. President,* and as he was changing into a tuxedo in his back office, Doar called from Memphis. Bob and Marshall briefed Doar and McShane on the plans for the next day. Then Meredith came on the line, and Bob spoke to him for the first time.

"It's going to be a long, hard and difficult struggle, but in the end we're going to be successful," Bob said.

"I hope so," Meredith said.

"Not hope," Bob cut in. "We will be successful, but much is going to be required of you and it is going to be a difficult time." Bob asked Meredith if he understood that his return to the university the next morning would signify that nothing was going to make him quit and that it would keep the pressure on Barnett. Meredith said he did. "Good luck," said Bob.

By now the unrealistic impression had spread throughout Mississippi that "Old Ross" had won. However, the rising potential for violence and the ultimate futility of the state's course were beginning to gravely concern Watkins and others of the Governor's more stable advisers, as well as leading businessmen who feared for the state's economy and alumni who believed that the most important thing was to prevent damage to Ole Miss. During the night Marshall talked with Watkins, and the next morning Watkins suggested that the marshals escorting Meredith should attempt to push Barnett aside gently, that the mildest show of force might give the Governor the out that Meredith had been brought on the campus by federal force.

Low clouds prevented Barnett from flying from Jackson to Oxford the next morning. However, at 9:30 A.M., right on schedule, Meredith, Doar and McShane landed at Oxford's small airport and were escorted by highway patrolmen to the campus. There, four hundred yards from the gates of school, drawn up in a line, were twenty unarmed patrolmen led by Lieutenant Governor Paul Johnson, and backed by a line of county sheriffs. Johnson read another proclamation denying Meredith entry. Doar then tried to talk Johnson into letting Meredith in.

"We want to take him in," said Doar.

"I heard you," said Johnson.

Then McShane moved to try Watkins' plan, telling Johnson, "Governor, I think it's my duty to try to go through and get Mr. Meredith in there."

"You are not going in."

"I'm sorry, Governor, that I have to do this, but I'm going in," McShane said, placing his hand lightly on Johnson's arm. If Johnson was a party to Watkins' plan, he didn't indicate it. "You are not going in," he repeated. McShane then tried to walk around Johnson, but the line of patrolmen held fast. Convinced that the show of "force" was not going to cause Johnson to change his mind, McShane stepped back and, with Doar, escorted a solemn-faced Meredith back to a car and they returned to the airport. "Well," said Meredith, shrugging, "at least I'm getting a lot of flying time."

From this point on, events moved rapidly toward an inevitable conclusion. Each rejection of Meredith, forcing federal officers to retreat, had emboldened many in Mississippi to believe that Barnett's course would win out. Barnett had all but joined Mississippi's pantheon of its most sainted heroes. Voices calling for resistance "regardless of the cost in human life" were being heard in mounting crescendo in the legislature and elsewhere. But Barnett was not prepared to take the final step and was looking desperately for a way out. Now aware that emotions were rising out of control, facing an appearance before the Fifth Circuit in two days and really unwilling to go to jail, Barnett plainly was a frightened man as he talked with Bob.

The morning after Lieutenant Governor Johnson barred Meredith, Watkins called Bob and outlined a new plan: Barnett needed a show of federal force and would stand aside if the marshals accompanying Meredith would draw their revolvers. It was a dangerous plan, but Bob grasped at it.

The plan was on, then off, then on again as Bob and Barnett haggled over refinements in what was to be done. Barnett and Johnson would be flanked by unarmed state patrolmen. About thirty marshals would accompany Meredith, but only McShane would draw his revolver, which would not be loaded. Barnett pleaded that all the marshals would have to draw their revolvers so that it would appear that he had backed down to avoid bloodshed and in the face of overwhelming odds. Bob countered with the suggestion that as McShane drew his revolver the other marshals would slap their holsters. No, Barnett said, it would not be real enough, and so it finally was agreed that all the marshals would draw, Barnett and Johnson would step aside, Meredith would be enrolled and the Highway Patrol would keep the peace.

During these discussions, Bob had a number of telephone conversations with Senator Eastland, who was now acting as an intermediary in attempting to arrange the grand "showdown." Eastland was wary. He felt that Barnett had "gone too far" and that the plan for Barnett to back down after being confronted by marshals with drawn revolvers was "play-acting" and "silly." Eastland several times told Bob that he realized the government would have to use troops if the issue could not be resolved any other way.

After these conversations Bob was more dubious than ever that the plan would work but remained hopeful for, as he told Eastland, "If the plan fails, the next step is irrevocable and we all know what that is. I don't want to have to do it."

Thirteen Border Patrol cars bearing Meredith and his escort headed south from Memphis for Oxford. At Ole Miss, a crowd of students and townspeople waited tensely. Some carried clubs. A force of several hundred sheriffs, their deputies and town marshals had gathered in Oxford to "stand with Ross." None of them, nor anyone in the crowd, nor the highway patrolmen knew that Barnett had decided to let Meredith in. Johnson toured the area and using a loudspeaker warned: "Someone could very easily get killed. I want to ask all students to return to their homes." But nobody moved.

All the patrolmen and sheriffs had been disarmed on the Governor's order. But as rumors spread through the crowd, Judge Russel D. Moore, the Governor's liaison officer on the campus, heard that a "goon squad" was escorting Meredith and gave orders for the patrolmen to wear helmets and carry gas masks and night sticks.

A Border Patrol plane flew over Meredith's convoy and maintained radio contact with it as it moved into Mississippi, through

Pleasant Hill, Hernando, Senatobia—with word of each point of progress being received with mixed emotions in the Attorney General's office where Bob, Katzenbach and Marshall waited. During this time, Bob had several conversations with Barnett. At 3:35 Oxford time (5:35 in Washington) Bob called Barnett to be reassured that Meredith could be protected when he arrived. Barnett replied that he was using "reasonable diligence," that he was doing everything he could. It was not very reassuring and Bob, Marshall and Katzenbach debated whether to call the whole thing off.

Within the hour, Barnett called back. He was worried, he said, and felt unable to control the crowd. A hundred people might be killed, he said, and that would "ruin all of us." It would be "embarrassing."

"I don't know if it would be embarrassing," Bob said. "That would not be the feeling." Bob said he would turn Meredith back, quickly ended the conversation and gave orders for the convoy to return to Memphis. It was passing through the little town of Como, thirty miles from Oxford. Bob took the setback coolly, showing neither disappointment nor relief. He called the President, who was in Wheeling, West Virginia, for a political dinner. Then he gave orders for the marshals to begin gathering in Memphis and called Defense Secretary McNamara to alert the Army that it probably would be needed.

But the next morning, Friday, he arrived at his office in a somber mood. An almost sleepless night had brought doubts about the sureness of his actions and the sickening realization that the chances for a peaceful solution were all but gone. He met with General Maxwell Taylor, Chairman of the Joint Chiefs of Staff, and top Army officials including Secretary Cyrus R. Vance, General Earle G. Wheeler, Chief of Staff, and a tough, plain-speaking ex-tank commander, Major General Creighton W. Abrams, director of operations. They decided to have two military police battalions, a battle group from the 2nd Infantry at Fort Benning and support troops ready for action in Mississippi and to alert other units that might be needed.

A few doors down the hall, Assistant Attorney General Norbert

Schlei began drafting a proclamation for the President, calling upon Mississippi to cease its policy of defiance, and an Executive Order directing McNamara to take all "appropriate steps" to enforce the court order including calling up the Mississippi National Guard. Assistant Attorney General Louis Oberdorfer, the Tax Division chief, flew to Memphis to take command of the marshals. And in New Orleans the Fifth Circuit found Barnett guilty of contempt and gave him until 11 A.M. Tuesday to admit Meredith or face a $10,000-a-day fine and possible arrest. The court thus set a deadline, but it doubled the problem. The possibility that Barnett would be arrested created a likelihood that fanatics would form a human wall to attempt to keep federal officers from taking the Governor into custody.

From St. Petersburg, Florida, to Los Angeles, bands of hard-eyed men met to offer their support to Barnett and some made final plans to take guns and head for Mississippi. How many were heeding a call from former Major General Edwin A. Walker would never be determined, but the night before, the man who had commanded the federal troops at Little Rock and had lectured to high school students there on obedience to the law—now obsessed that a dark conspiracy was destroying the nation—had proclaimed from Dallas:

> It is time to move. We have talked, listened and been pushed around far too much by the anti-Christ Supreme Court. Rise to a stand beside Governor Barnett at Jackson, Mississippi. Now is the time to be heard: 10,000 strong from every state in the Union. . . . Bring your flags, your tents and your skillets. It is time. Now or never . . . The last time in such a situation I was on the wrong side. . . . This time I am out of uniform and I am on the right side and I will be there.

Walker had resigned from the Army in 1961 after being reprimanded for trying to indoctrinate his troops with ultrarightist political views. Now, wittingly or unwittingly, he let his prestige and his words become a rallying point for all the Ku Klux Klansmen, Citizens' Council members, National States' Rights Party die-hards and others whose hatred of Negroes, fears and frustrations had been brought to the boiling point by the two weeks of neo-Confederate oratory and resistance. Bob read a wire service report of Walker's statement and handed it wearily to Marshall. "Well, Burke, what are you going to do about this?" he said. Marshall shook his head. There was nothing to do.

Just before noon Saturday, Watkins called. Barnett was not going to cooperate, he said, and the situation looked hopeless. Bob put down the phone and said, "We'd better get moving with the military." He called the President, who told him to come to the White House. Bob then called General Taylor to ask him to join them. As he waited for Taylor to come on the line, he shook his head in resignation. "Maybe we waited too long," he said.

"No," I replied. "The results would have been the same, and the record is clear that everything has been done to avoid this step." Bob did not reply.

Bob had planned to fly that afternoon to speak at the dedication of the University of San Francisco Law School's new Kendrick Hall. The trip would have to be canceled, but before he left for the White House, I showed him a new draft of language in the speech criticizing the American Bar Association as well as lawyers in Mississippi for failing to speak out against Barnett's defiance. It said:

One of my great disappointments in our present efforts to deal with the situation in Mississippi as lawyers has been the absence of any expression of support from the many distinguished lawyers of that state. I realize in that difficult social situation that to defend the fundamental principles of respect for the law and compliance with federal court orders would be unpopular and require great courage. I also understand that many of them may not agree with the decision in *Brown* vs. *The Board of Education,* but whether they agree or not, they still have their obligations as lawyers and they have remained silent. However, I might also note that there have been no pronouncements in this matter by the American Bar Association.

"There's nothing wrong with saying it," Bob said. "Let's get the speech out. I wouldn't have believed it could have happened in this country, but maybe now we can understand how Hitler took over Germany."

The Administration did have one move left. Up to this point, the President's personal prestige and his power of persuasion had not been committed. He had not talked with Barnett nor been involved directly in any of the negotiations. Now this last card had to be played, and twice during the afternoon the President called Barnett.

"Here's my problem, Governor," the President began. "I don't know Mr. Meredith and I didn't put him there. But under the Constitution I have to carry out the law. I want your help. . . . I don't want a lot of people down there to be hurt or killed."

All the help that Barnett could offer was that Watkins could fly to Washington and discuss a new plan. But in the second conversation Barnett suggested that perhaps Meredith could be brought secretly to Jackson on Monday and registered while Barnett diverted attention by going to Ole Miss. The Governor was vague when pressed for a promise to maintain law and order, and so the plan was received by the President, Bob and Marshall with skepticism. Still, it offered a shred of hope. As they debated, the TV networks made ready for a Presidential address at 8 P.M. And at the Pentagon and Justice, in Memphis and on a half-dozen military bases men prepared for a long night of action.

At 7 P.M., Barnett called the President and did not equivocate on the matter of whether the Highway Patrol would keep order if Meredith would go to Jackson while Barnett was manning the line in Oxford. The patrol could and it would, he said. Having appeared to have been tricked, Barnett said he would accept it and see that Meredith got safely on the campus the next day. With these assurances the President agreed reluctantly even though the deception would be transparent, even though the chances of avoiding violence were dropping steadily and even though there was no longer any basis to put much stock in Barnett's promises. Still, the slim chance that major violence and the use of troops might be avoided seemed worth the risk. The request for TV time was canceled, and the President held up on issuing his proclamation and Executive Order. Bob and Marshall returned to the Justice Department, and shortly before 10 P.M. Bob headed for home. Minutes after he left, Barnett called to say he could not go through with the arrangements.

It was only 8 o'clock in Jackson, and the Governor then went to Memorial Stadium, where the Rebels of Ole Miss were playing Kentucky. At half time, with over forty thousand fans cheering worshipfully and waving Confederate flags, Barnett stepped to a microphone at mid-field. There was a moment of electric suspense as the crowd fell silent. "I love Mississippi!" The crowd cheered shrilly. "I love her people!" Bedlam. "I love our customs!" Hysteria. But that was all Barnett had to say.

It was a few minutes after midnight in the White House when President Kennedy, with only Norbert Schlei present, sat at a table in the Indian Treaty Room and signed Proclamation 3497 ordering persons obstructing justice in Mississippi to "cease and desist therefrom and to disperse and retire peaceably forthwith." Then he signed the Executive Order putting the Mississippi National Guard on federal service.

On Sunday morning Mississippi basked in the high tide of resistance, and many of its leaders and citizens prepared to go to Oxford to repel the "invaders." In Washington the New Frontiersmen went grimly ahead with their plans. In both places the expectation was that the confrontation would come on Monday and that it would be extremely unpleasant. General Walker had arrived in Jackson. Ominous reports flooded into Bob's office of armed men heading for the university. Criticism mounted from the NAACP and many other people in the North that the government had wasted an inordinate amount of time enforcing the court orders. Bob, Marshall and Katzenbach wrestled with whether to put Meredith on the campus on Sunday and to do it somehow with Barnett's help to avoid the need later to arrest him. Troops began arriving in Memphis. The marshals were alerted to be ready to fly to Oxford by noon. Meredith, who had spent the night in New Orleans, was flown to Memphis. The President reserved network time to address the nation at 7:30 P.M.

At 10:45 A.M. Barnett called Bob and pleaded with him to "postpone this matter." Bob said he couldn't.

"Then you had better have enough troops to be dead sure that peace and order will be preserved," said Barnett.

Then Barnett offered a new subterfuge. A large Army force should escort Meredith to the campus. Barnett would meet them, standing in front of a line of unarmed highway patrolmen who would be backed by a line of unarmed sheriff's deputies and a third line of students and citizens. Barnett said he would read a proclamation barring Meredith, then the soldiers should draw their weapons, and then he would give up and call on the people to preserve law and order. The plan was riddled with unacceptable risks, including the distinct possibility that with one misstep the Appomattox-like melodrama would dissolve into armed conflict between state and federal forces. Bob rejected it out of hand.

Then, still determined to avoid using troops and having to arrest Barnett, Bob countered with the suggestion that the marshals occupy the campus on Sunday and that Meredith be flown in on Monday by helicopter. Barnett hesitated, and Bob, for the first time in their many conversations, lost his cool. Angrily, he threatened that if Barnett did not go along, the President would disclose in his televised speech that night that the Governor had made a deal "with the President of the United States" and then had broken his word. The President would tell all the details, Bob said.

"That won't do at all," Barnett replied.

"You broke your word to him."

"You don't mean the President is going to say that tonight?"

"He is."

Barnett sounded utterly deflated. He pleaded over and over that the President not tell the nation of the secret dealings. Then he capitulated. "Why don't you fly him in this afternoon?" he said.

Quickly the details were worked out. Barnett would be notified thirty minutes before Meredith and the marshals left Memphis. Barnett would order the Highway Patrol to assist in preventing violence. Barnett then would announce that the federal government had sneaked Meredith onto the campus and that he was ceasing resistance in the face of overwhelming force, but would continue to fight in the courts.

Katzenbach, Schlei, Dean Markham, a friend of Bob's since college, and I were to fly immediately to Oxford and meet the marshals. As we were about to leave, Schlei's assistant, the ubiquitous Harold Reis, poked his head into Bob's office. True to the promise he made the night of the *Santa María* incident, he had come to his office early in the morning to be available but had not been asked to do anything. Now he was hungry. "I'm going home for lunch," he said.

Bob looked up. "Harold, you can help," he said. "Can you go, too?"

"Yes," said Reis, and he was halfway to Andrews Air Force Base in Schlei's convertible before he had any notion of where he was going.

Within five hours, Katzenbach, accompanied by Colonel Birdsong, led several truckloads of marshals onto the campus, which was almost deserted. University officials met him. While they did not oppose Meredith's coming on the campus Sunday, they did object to registering him on the Sabbath on the grounds that the churches would be critical. The marshals were placed around the stately, columned Lyceum Building where Meredith would register the next morning. With the delay in registering Meredith, there seemed no other place to put them. The plan was to secure the building so Meredith would be able to enter. A small number of students gathered and bantered with the marshals. A line of highway patrolmen stood between the marshals and the crowd.

Katzenbach drove back to the airport and met Meredith and Doar. They escorted Meredith to Baxter Hall, a dormitory about a mile from the Lyceum where he would spend the night guarded by twenty-four marshals. It was dusk when Katzenbach returned to the Lyceum. The crowd had grown to about a thousand persons, mostly students, but its tenor had changed. Organized cheers— "2–4–1–3, we hate Kennedy!" and "Go to Cuba, nigger lovers"— taunted the marshals. As it became dark, the crowd doubled in size; its threats became meaner and increasingly more obscene. First pebbles, then rocks began landing on the marshals. Students flipped lighted cigarettes onto the canvas tops of Army trucks parked in front of the Lyceum. Nearby, a news photographer from Texas and his wife were beaten. Some of the highway patrolmen tried to keep order and some didn't.

Inside the Lyceum, Katzenbach haggled with Barnett's representatives, who wanted to withdraw the patrolmen. Outside, the crowd was getting larger and losing control, and heavier and heavier barrages of rocks and bottles crashed on the Lyceum steps. At 7:25 the FBI monitored a radio signal ordering the Highway Patrol to withdraw. Who gave it was never determined. A few patrolmen stayed, but most departed, leaving the gates of the campus unguarded and the marshals to fend off the crowd.

From a phone in the Lyceum, I described the scene to Bob, who was in the Cabinet Room, and told him that Chief Marshal McShane had ordered the marshals to put on their gas masks and have their gas guns at the ready. "I hope it won't have to come to that," Bob said. "Why don't you get Colonel Birdsong and let me talk to him?"

A Mississippi state senator who had been inside threatening to withdraw the patrol was now trying to quiet the crowd. Rebel yells and cheers drowned his voice. Rocks pelted down on the marshals. I found Birdsong and told him the Attorney General wanted to speak with him. We walked up the steps of the Lyceum and just as Birdsong reached the phone, the sound of tear gas grenades going off—"Thump! Thump! Thump!"—delivered its own message. Katzenbach hurried in and took the line, "Bob, I'm very sorry to report we've had to fire tear gas. We had no choice."

It was 7:58 Mississippi time. The President had delayed his address until 10 P.M. EST, in the belief that the campus would be safely secured. He began to speak just before Bob could tell him what had happened. He asked for obedience to the law, praised the valor of Mississippians in combat and, appealing to the students, said: "The eyes of the nation and of all the world are upon you and upon all of us, and the honor of your university and state are in the balance."

But the fight was on. The crowd—now a mob—retreated and surged back throwing hunks of wood, stones and chunks of concrete. About three hundred marshals encircled the Lyceum. The 250 at the front and two sides took the brunt of the attacks. At about 9 o'clock the marshals came under sporadic shotgun fire and three were felled. One, Graham Same of Memphis, suffered a wound in the neck, and as he was carried into the Lyceum, he looked as if he would not last long. We had neglected to bring any first-aid equipment. Frantic efforts to get a town doctor to come finally brought one, Dr. L. G. Hopkins, an Ole Miss alumnus, who worked without respite through the night.

As the fury of the fight mounted, many of the students drifted to the sidelines, their places to be taken by hate-filled men, some who had driven long distances and brought their shotguns and rifles to "stand with Ross." Three times, the marshals were almost out of tear gas, but Chamblee, the cool border patrolman from New Orleans, made three perilous trips to the airport and returned with more gas in the nick of time.

At 10 o'clock, as rifle and shotgun fire intensified, Katzenbach sadly told Bob he'd better send the Army. With the exception of fifty-five men of the Oxford company of the National Guard—who arrived about forty-five minutes later under the command of Captain Murray Falkner, the novelist's nephew—it would take the Army contingents at Memphis four and a half hours to reach the scene and disperse the mob. During that time, the marshals defended the Lyceum tenaciously and at times desperately. The mob, howling and menacing, sent an unoccupied car with the accelerator tied down, out of the night into the line of marshals and drove a bulldozer and a commandeered fire engine at them. More than one-third of the marshals—160 in all—were injured; 28 were wounded by gunfire. An identification wallet stopped a bullet from penetrating the heart of Deputy Marshal Joseph O. Denson of Brooklyn. Many in the mob suffered injuries, and a French newsman, Paul Guihard, and a bystander, Ray Gunter, an Oxford repairman, were killed. Nevertheless, at 8 A.M. the next morning Meredith walked up the steps of the Lyceum, and Registrar Robert Byron Ellis, with an air of resignation and studied courtesy, enrolled him.

There would be recriminations and post-mortems and the years to reflect for all who participated in that unfortunate incident. To me now, three things stand out. First, it was all so necessary, and yet so unnecessary. No political or cultural reasons, even those so deeply rooted as segregation has been in the South, justified what happened. The federal government should not have been required in the year 1962 to send some twenty thousand troops to see that one Negro was enrolled as a student in a university. Other Negroes followed Meredith to Ole Miss and the university was not the worse off for it. Furthermore, the end was inevitable. Once the specific issue of Meredith's right to enroll in September had been decided by the Court of Appeals and the Supreme Court, the government was bound to see that the court orders were obeyed and that they were made effective. To have delayed, to have agreed with Barnett's appeals to postpone Meredith's entrance, would have allowed the courts to be frustrated by contemptuous action. Time was of the essence.

All the marshals carried revolvers but never used them. Several times during the battle they asked for permission to return the fire. Katzenbach relayed the requests to the White House, but the President and Bob each time said "No" unless it was necessary to save Meredith. Baxter Hall was never attacked, and the marshals at the Lyceum, though embattled and furious at seeing their comrades shot down, held their fire. They were loyal men, well trained in their respective fields, but they had been assembled hurriedly and there had not been time to organize them into well-disciplined units —yet they obeyed. One would remember them in the racial riots and wild campus demonstrations of the latter half of the 1960's and at Kent State and at Jackson State universities in 1970, when lawmen, with far, far less provocation and injury than the marshals endured, gunned people down. And when politicians defended such action, one would remember John and Robert Kennedy, the responsibility they shouldered that night and their restraint and judgment.

Sometime during the height of the riot when I reported to Bob, he asked, "How's it going down there?" "Pretty rough," I replied. "It's getting like the Alamo." There was a pause, and then Bob said wryly, "Well, you know what happened to those guys, don't you?" The exchange has been included in many accounts of the incident and in articles about Bob as a classic example of the easy relations he had with his staff. The way I look at it, we were beleaguered and blood-spattered and he knew it and worried for our safety. And yet when I think of Oxford, this is what I remember first: the light remark that raised our morale and helped us through the night.

The first time Bob spoke in public after the riot, he spoke of the action of individuals rather than deploring the violence or giving the Administration any credit for having upheld the orders of the court. The speech was on the following Saturday night in Milwaukee, at a dinner for the Democratic candidate for Governor of Wisconsin. Bob said:

We live in a time when the individual's opportunity to meet his responsibilities appears circumscribed by impersonal powers beyond his influence. On the surface the individual in American society is pressed on all sides by the mightiest materialistic forces in man's history. The power of atomic weapons seems to dwarf the heroism of any individual soldier and City Hall looms too big to fight in a hundred walks of life.

But even today there is so much that a single person can do with faith and courage, and we have had a number of outstanding examples just this week. . . . James Meredith brought to a head and lent his name to another chapter in the mightiest internal struggle of our time.

At the same time . . . there were 500 United States marshals, most of them from the Southern states, who remained true to their orders and instructions and stood with great bravery to prevent interference with federal court orders.

A troop of armored cavalry—men from Oxford, Mississippi—were the first soldiers to come to the aid of the marshals. Some of these young men had graduated only last June from the University of Mississippi. As one of them said: "We don't like being here but we don't like that mob shooting at you either."

The belief that one person could make a difference and that every person, regardless of the odds, had a responsibility to work at the national, state or local level to advance individual and social freedom was one of the most constant threads that ran through his public statements. He perhaps expressed it most eloquently at the University of Capetown in South Africa in 1966 when he warned that the first of all dangers to a free and peaceful world is the sense of futility:

the belief that there is nothing one man or one woman can do against the enormous array of the world's ills—against misery and ignorance, injustice and violence. . . . Few will have the greatness to bend history itself, but each of us can work to change a small portion of events, and in the total of all those acts will be written the history of this generation. . . . Each time a man stands up for an ideal, or acts to improve the lot of others, or strikes out against injustice, he sends forth a tiny ripple of hope, and crossing each other from a million different centers of energy and daring, those ripples build a current that can sweep down the mightiest walls of oppression and resistance.

He hewed to this philosophy in his approach to each problem. An adviser who dwelt too long on what courses of action should not be taken invited the curt interruption: "Don't tell me what I can't do, tell me what I can do." He would innovate, he would take chances and he would pursue with energy and hope each opportunity for a reasonable solution, however uncertain the outcome or however slim the prospects were for success, as he did in rescuing the Bay of Pigs prisoners, or in advising President Kennedy during the missile crisis or in dealing with Governor Barnett. People who worked with him drew on his intrepidness and his refusal to give way to gloom or despair.

Bob and all the key government participants in the Mississippi crisis had conducted a two-day critique of their actions and had concluded that they made mistakes which contributed to the outbreak of violence. A crucial miscalculation, for example, had been an assumption that Colonel Birdsong, head of the Mississippi Highway Patrol, would order his men to prevent violence, regardless of the political consequences, as Floyd Mann, chief of the Alabama Highway Patrol, had done when he led his men to the aid of the marshals at Montgomery. But Birdsong's authority had been undermined by the Mississippi politicians, and he was ineffective, whatever his intentions, when the storm broke. The critique made it evident that investigation beforehand would have disclosed that Birdsong was not a Floyd Mann, and thus less reliance would have been placed on getting support from his men.

The critique also made clear that Meredith was brought to Ole Miss in such haste that the organization of the marshals was disrupted, reducing their ability to control the mob. In the hurry to get to Oxford, the marshals' squads were broken up and equipment that might have been helpful in crowd control, like bullhorns, was left behind.

Some writers who investigated the whole incident thought that violence might have been prevented if there had been better rapport with Barnett. The most knowledgeable, Walter Lord, wrote in *The Past That Would Not Die:* "To the crisp New Frontiersmen, used to quick decisions, the Governor's initial courtliness sounded like accommodation. To a good Mississippian, on the other hand, it might be difficult to conceive of wrapping up a deal with a single phone call."

It is possible, of course, that if Bob or anyone else high in the Administration had met face to face with Barnett, the disastrous confrontation might have been averted, but neither Bob nor Marshall believed it. By the time the Justice Department became involved in the case, Mississippi's fantasy of resistance had reached such emotional fervor that a conflict between state and federal forces—civil war—was a definite possibility. That was avoided. There was a riot, but while the Mississippi highway patrolmen did not help the marshals much, at least they did not join the mob. Bob and Marshall thought in retrospect that the negotiations with Barnett had accomplished that, but nothing more, and with Barnett's state of mind, the pressures that were working on him and the hatred and defiance that gripped the state, it was no small accomplishment.

In the spring of 1963, Bob sought to meet with George Wallace. Five black students had applied for admission to the University of Alabama, and the university was prepared to admit those who qualified. However, Wallace had won the governorship the year before vowing he would stand in the door of any Alabama school to prevent integration and had concluded a flamboyant inaugural speech with these words: "In the name of the greatest people that have ever trod on this earth, I draw the line in the dust and toss the gauntlet before the feet of tyranny. And I say: Segregation now! Segregation tomorrow! Segregation forever!"

Wallace refused to answer phone calls from Bob, but the meeting was arranged through intermediaries. To give it an appearance of casualness, Bob arranged several meetings and speeches in other Southern states. But the atmosphere in Montgomery on that warm April morning was anything but casual as Bob, Burke Marshall, and I, along with Ed Reid, an Alabama political stalwart who had a hand in arranging the meeting, walked up the steps of the columned capitol that had served as the first capitol of the Confederacy. Before Bob arrived, police dispersed pickets carrying signs reading "KOSHER TEAM KENNEDY KASTRO KHRUSCHEV" and "CHRISTIANS WAKE UP 'COME OUT FROM AMONGST THEM AND BE YE SEPARATE.'" State troopers ringed the capitol. A wreath had been placed on the iron star marking the spot where Jefferson Davis had taken the oath as President of the Confederacy. A stern, middle-aged member of the United Daughters of the Confederacy, dressed in white, stood guard, arms folded, to make sure that the foot of the Attorney General of the United States did not tread on that spot.

Inside, Bob, Marshall and Reid found Wallace in his office with his feisty finance director, Seymore Trammell. Wallace said he would record the conversation as a precaution, and for the better part of an hour they debated warily like boxers sparring for an opening.

"I have a responsibility that goes beyond integration and segregation, to enforce the law of the land and to ensure court orders are obeyed," Bob began. ". . . If you were in my position, you would do no less.". . .

"You just can't have any peace in Alabama with an integrated school system," Wallace replied.

"You think it would be so horrifying to have a Negro attend the University of Alabama, Governor?"

"Well, I think it's horrifying for the federal courts and the central government to rewrite all the law and force upon the people that which they don't want, yes. . . . I will never myself submit voluntarily to any integration of any school system in Alabama."

The opening exchange set the tenor of the conversation. They could agree that the issue should be settled in the courts and that there should not be violence, but on nothing else.

"Of course, I understand your position and I—I'm sure you understand mine, and it looks like we may wind up in court," Wallace said at one point.

"As long as we wind up in court, I'll be happy, Governor," said Bob. "That's all I ask. . . . I just don't want it to get into the streets. I don't want to have another Oxford, Mississippi; that's all I ask."

"I don't want another Mississippi myself," Wallace replied, "but you folks are the ones that will control the matter, because you have control of the troops."

"We have a responsibility to ensure that the orders of the court are followed, and all the force behind the federal government must be used for that purpose."

Wallace sensed an opening.

"I know that," he said. "I know you're going to use all the force of the federal government. In fact, what you're telling me today is that, if necessary, you're going to bring troops into Alabama."

"No," Bob answered quickly. "I didn't say that."

"You didn't? Well, you said all the force of the federal government."

"To make sure that the orders of the court are obeyed."

"But all the force includes troops, doesn't it?"

"Well, I would hope that it would stay in the courts and be litigated."

"But it does involve troops if the law is not obeyed?"

"I'm planning and hoping that the law will be obeyed," Bob said anxiously.

"But you gonna use all the power of the federal government, which involves troops—" Wallace persisted.

"I had hoped that wasn't necessary," Bob broke in. "Maybe somebody wants us to use troops, but—uh—we're not anxious to."

"I can assure you," said Wallace, "I do not want to use troops. I can assure you there's no effort on my part to make a show of resistance and be overcome."

But it was evident to Bob that that was exactly what Wallace did want. The conversation drifted on.

Near the end, as they talked about what each would say to the press, they debated again whether Bob had threatened to use troops. This time, Trammell, a short, sandy-haired man with a combative air, took up the cudgels.

"Well, you're going to send in the Army? The Navy? The Air Force and the Marines, aren't you?" he demanded.

Bob, now weary and nearly out of patience, snapped back, "I don't plan to. You seem to want me to say that I'm going to use troops. . . . You're pushing it so much, I sort of get that opinion. In any case, so we understand each other, we haven't the use of any force prepared. . . . I don't want to have any inferences about that."

"Just that one statement in there that you would use whatever powers the central government had to carry out the court order," Trammell insisted.

"Well, that's the implication," Bob said. "I mean you can decide whether the federal government is going to use troops, that's your decision."

Wallace pressed the argument. Bob held his ground, and the conference ended. Wallace told reporters that the talk had not changed his determination to block desegregation by standing in the schoolhouse door. Meeting separately with newsmen, Bob expressed hope that Alabama political, business and school leaders would assume responsibility for complying with court orders without mob violence. Privately, however, Bob was dumbfounded by Wallace's attitude. It was the closest I ever saw him come to throwing up his hands in despair.

Bob and Marshall walked a few blocks to the offices of the Montgomery *Advertiser* to call on the editor, Grover C. Hall, Jr., a confidant of Wallace's. Bob related the details of his conversations with Wallace. Hall, a chatty, unpredictable man, listened with amusement. His father had won the Pulitzer prize in 1928 for editorials opposing the Ku Klux Klan, and while he was as much opposed to school integration as most white Southerners, he respected his father's accomplishments and stood for compliance with court orders. He said he had told Wallace that it would be folly to stand in the doorway, but was sure Wallace would do it. Bob and Marshall, still somewhat numb from their encounter with Wallace wonderland, expressed incredulity that, with the example of Mississippi still so fresh, any Governor would court violence by advocating resistance to the bitter end. Weren't there any pressures that would cause Wallace to change his mind? they asked. How about the influence of Hall and other leaders, particularly the leading businessmen? No, Hall said, smiling. Wallace had enough influence with the Klan to prevent violence, but he would stand in the doorway.

Dejected, Bob and Marshall were deep in thought and hardly exchanged a word as they rode to the airport. "Well, I suppose I can understand Wallace's position politically," Bob finally said. "But that Trammell is something. He really wants trouble."

Though the chances that Wallace could be moved appeared nil, Bob refused to accept the possibility that the situation was hopeless. After he returned to Washington, the Justice Department redoubled its efforts with Alabama businessmen, labor leaders, editors, clergymen and educators to bring pressure on Wallace to stay away from the university and to see that violence did not break out. Every person in the Department who had an influential friend in Alabama participated in the effort. Banks in New York which had financial connections in Alabama and businesses like U.S. Steel which had important branches in the state were contacted.

President Kennedy, rather than waiting until the eleventh hour as in Mississippi, committed his personal prestige in mid-May when he went to Muscle Shoals, Alabama, to speak at an observance marking the thirtieth anniversary of the Tennessee Valley Authority and then toured the Redstone Arsenal at nearby Huntsville. At Muscle Shoals, Wallace heard the President say:

From time to time, statements are made labeling the federal government an outside, an intruder, an adversary. In any free federation of states, of course differences will arise and difficulties will persist. But the people of this area know that the United States Government is not a stranger or an enemy. . . . For without the national government, without the people of the United States working as a people, there would be no TVA.

On the Presidential helicopter on the flight to Huntsville, Wallace conferred briefly with the President. But after the President departed, Wallace called a press conference and made it clear that, while their conversation had been "courteous and friendly," his mind had not been changed.

Meanwhile, university officials, under terms of the court order, had found three black applicants eligible for admission for the summer term starting June 10—Vivian J. Malone, twenty, of Mobile, and Jimmy A. Hood, twenty, of East Gadsden, at the main campus at Tuscaloosa and David M. McGlathery, twenty-seven, at the university extension center at Huntsville, his home town.

After the President's brief conversation with Wallace there were no further talks between the Kennedys and the Governor. The Kennedys had no intention of sliding into a tragicomic charade as they had with Barnett. Wallace was much shrewder than Barnett and had a script for his own melodrama—to fulfill the campaign "covenant made with you the people of this state," as he put it. He intended to turn away Miss Malone and Hood when they came to enroll, force the federal troops to occupy the campus and, if he could manage it, force them to arrest him. "The action that I am going to take involves even my personal freedom, but I intend to carry it out, regardless of what risk I take," he said after U.S. District Court Judge Seybourn H. Lynne issued an injunction, requested by the Justice Department, ordering Wallace not to interfere physically with the enrollment of the black students.

Just as determinedly, the Kennedys sought to devise strategy that would rob Wallace of his moment of glory—that would accomplish enforcement of the court orders without putting the Governor into a position where he would have to be arrested. They wanted desperately to avoid another riot. This time there would not be an agonizing, five-hour delay if troops were needed. Soldiers would be sitting in helicopters at Fort Benning, Georgia, 160 miles away, ready to move. And the talks with Alabama leaders went on unabated to create a climate of public opinion against violence. To what degree this effort was successful could not be assessed with precision, but the fact is that as June 11 approached—the day the students were to enroll—Wallace was under heavy pressure in Alabama to maintain order and to discourage Klansmen and members of the National States' Rights Party who wanted to converge on Tuscaloosa. There were other factors, of course. The officials of the university and the people of Tuscaloosa were trying to prevent their city from becoming another Oxford. They had three strong-willed city commissioners, a stern lawman, W. N. Marable, as chief of police, and a courageous editor, Buford Boone of the Tuscaloosa *News*.

Furthermore, while the confrontation at the university was in the making, dreadful violence had rocked Birmingham continuously for several weeks as Negroes, with many schoolchildren in their ranks and led by Dr. Martin Luther King, marched to protest discrimination in employment and places that served the public. They were routed repeatedly with fire hoses, police dogs, night sticks and mass arrests. On May 7, Burke Marshall negotiated an uneasy truce, which was broken five days later when the home and hotel of a Negro leader were bombed.[3] President Kennedy had to dispatch three thousand troops to an air base near Birmingham to forestall a move by Wallace to send a state force of highway patrolmen, liquor agents, game wardens and deputy sheriffs into Birmingham to take over law enforcement and sabotage the agreement Marshall had worked out. Thus, with tension in Birmingham high and the nation's conscience deeply stirred, prominent Alabamians in every walk of life were anxious that the university not be a scene of further violence.

When Wallace went to Tuscaloosa to take his stand and Deputy Attorney General Nicholas Katzenbach arrived to lead the federal forces, Wallace had his force of troopers, deputy sheriffs, liquor agents and game wardens and several companies of the National Guard ready to seal off the campus. Chief Marable was adamantly

---

3. News photographs of Negroes being knocked down by streams of water from high-pressure hoses, of Negroes being attacked by police dogs and of a policeman sitting on a woman demonstrator aroused sympathy for the Negroes' cause throughout the nation. The violence also convinced the President and Bob that stronger federal civil rights laws were needed. When Marshall returned to Washington from Birmingham on May 17, after the truce went back into effect, he flew with Bob to Asheville, North Carolina, where Bob was to speak to the North Carolina Cold War Seminar. Aboard the plane they worked out the essential elements of the Civil Rights Bill which was submitted to Congress a few weeks later and became law when President Johnson signed it on July 2, 1964.

escorting agitators out of town. However, neither Wallace nor Katzenbach knew exactly what the other was going to do when Miss Malone and Hood arrived to register.

University officials reported to Katzenbach that they could not find out about Wallace's plans, not even whether his security patrols would attempt to impede the students' entry on the campus. All that they knew was that State Patrol Chief Al Lingo had had a line painted in front of the entrance to Foster Auditorium, where the students were to register, and that Wallace had taken over an office just inside the doorway and had installed two air conditioners. With no precise knowledge of the moves Wallace planned to make, Bob had not decided exactly what the federal moves should be.

Two plans were being considered when Katzenbach arrived in Tuscaloosa thirty-six hours before the students were to register. One was to let Miss Malone and Hood go unescorted to the auditorium. It had the advantage of forcing Wallace to confront two attractive young Negroes with no federal officers anywhere in sight. But it had the disadvantage of exposing them to possible attack, while only delaying the confrontation with federal officers that Wallace wanted. The second plan called for Katzenbach to escort the students. After Wallace blocked them, Katzenbach would say that going through the door was not important, that the government would consider the students enrolled and that they would begin classes in the morning. This would have the effect of minimizing the stand in the doorway and force Wallace to make further moves to block the students. Katzenbach then would make clear that whether troops would have to go on the campus would be Wallace's choice.

During the evening and several times the following day Bob and Marshall in Washington discussed the plans by telephone with Katzenbach and his aides. The first plan was discarded as being too risky, and the second plan was adopted. But about 5 A.M. on the morning of the confrontation, Bob and Marshall decided on a new plan that would deny Wallace a starring role. At 6 A.M. they awakened Katzenbach and informed him that the 31st Division National Guardsmen from the Tuscaloosa area, whom Wallace had called up for duty, would be federalized at 7:30. They would then go on the campus, secure it and prevent Wallace from entering. Katzenbach objected.

"It's better than last night's plan, but not as good as bringing the students on campus without troops and staying there," he said. "Besides, I think we should let Wallace have his show."

"Well, Nick, we don't have much time," said Bob. "What do you propose?" Katzenbach wasn't sure what to do, but as they continued to talk, they worked out a new plan: The students would drive on the campus with Katzenbach but remain in their cars while Katzenbach walked to the entrance of the auditorium. If Wallace blocked the doorway, as he was expected to do, Katzenbach would then drive the students to their dormitories. They would be on campus and they would stay there. Then the National Guard would be federalized if Wallace persisted in his resistance.

"All right," said Bob. "That's it. Wallace will get to read his proclamation or whatever he is going to do, but he won't bar anyone. Be sure you make that clear."

The scheduled time for the students to arrive was 10 o'clock. At 9:53 Wallace arrived, accompanied by uniformed state troopers wearing helmets, side arms and night sticks. He told newsmen there would be no violence and went into the auditorium. The students and Katzenbach, accompanied by marshals in civilian clothes, arrived in two cars at 10:48. Bill Jones, the Governor's press secretary, quickly placed a lectern in front of the auditorium door. While the students remained in the car, Katzenbach, flanked by Macon Weaver, the U.S. Attorney for the district, and Peyton Norville, the district's U.S. marshal,[4] walked between lines of lawmen and newsmen several hundred feet to the doorway, where Wallace stood with his hand raised. It was a morning of wilting heat; the temperature near 100 degrees.

"I have a proclamation from the President of the United States ordering you to cease and desist from unlawful obstructions," Kat-

---

4. Neither Weaver nor Norville was in sympathy with the court order, but both deemed it their duty to accompany Katzenbach. They were not asked to do so. They volunteered.

zenbach began. After an interruption from Wallace, who said Katzenbach need not "make a speech," Katzenbach continued:

"I'm asking you for an unequivocal assurance that you will not bar entry of these students and you will step aside peacefully and do your constitutional duty. . . . Do I have your assurance?"

Then Wallace briskly began reading a proclamation castigating the "central government," justifying his stand and propounding an explicit exposition of states' rights.

As he spoke, I stood between two Tuscaloosa city commissioners on the edge of the crowd. One of the commissioners, George Ryan, swore softly, "Damn him. Damn him." "Yes," I said, "he keeps referring to the central government like it was the Kremlin." "I know," replied Ryan. "We didn't want this, but you should have seen what he did to us when we went to Montgomery to ask him not to come. He told us there'd be no road money for our county if we opposed him. He treated us like dogs." Ryan asked me what was going to happen. I told him that the National Guard from Tuscaloosa would be federalized. "You mean you're not sending in Negro soldiers like you did at Oxford?" "No," I said. "Just boys from your own home town." "Thank you," said Ryan. "Thank you —and thank Mr. Kennedy, will you?"

Katzenbach, towering over the Governor, listened patiently, arms folded.

". . . The unwelcomed, unwarranted and force-induced intrusion upon the campus of the University of Alabama today of the might of the central government offers frightful example of the suppression of the rights, privileges and sovereignty of this state," Wallace said.

". . . The illegal and unwarranted action of the central government on this day contrary to the laws, customs and traditions of this state is calculated to disturb the peace. I stand before you today in place of thousands of other Alabamians whose presence would have confronted you had I been derelict and neglected to fulfill the responsibilities of my office. It is the right of every citizen, however humble he may be, through his chosen officials of representative government to stand courageously against whatever he believes to be the exercise of power beyond the constitutional rights conferred upon our federal government. . . .

"Now, therefore, I, George C. Wallace, as Governor . . . do hereby denounce and forbid this illegal and unwarranted action by the central government."

Katzenbach replied that he was not interested in a show. "I don't know what the purpose of the show is. I am interested in the orders of the courts being enforced. . . . The consequences of this stand must rest with you. . . . Two students who simply seek an education on this campus are presently on this campus. They have a right to be here, protected by that court order, and they have a right to register. It is a simple problem scarcely worth this kind of attention."

Katzenbach asked the Governor to reconsider his actions, but the Governor remained silent and unmoved. Katzenbach returned to his car. Miss Malone and Hood were taken to their dormitories. Four hours later, Brigadier General Henry V. Graham led the Dixie Division Guardsmen onto the campus, and Wallace, smartly returning the General's salute, scolded the federal government briefly and withdrew. The next day he did not bother to go to Huntsville, where McGlathery was enrolled without incident.

Bob thought Wallace had been made to look ridiculous; that it would be understood around the country that Wallace had only been posturing; that Katzenbach's rhetoric had been a match for the Governor's. The Governor's reaction was: "I stood eyeball to eyeball with them and they turned back." Who was right? With the enrollment of Miss Malone and Hood, Alabama became the last state in the Union to have school integration. Within a few years more than three hundred black students were attending classes at the university, and their presence went virtually unnoticed. Wallace, despite his pledge to stand in the schoolhouse door, which implied that blacks would not be allowed to enroll, did not succeed in preventing the color line from being broken. But perhaps that was understood by many of his followers, for as Marshall Frady noted in his book *Wallace:*

It had been little more than a ceremony of futility—and, as a historical moment, a rather pedestrian production. But no other Southern governor had managed to strike even that dramatic a pose of defiance, and it has never been required of Southern popular heroes that they be successful. Indeed, Southerners tend to love their heroes more for their losses.

But Frady also pointed out that the incident gave Wallace a brief, dramatic moment of national attention which brought him many invitations to speak outside the South and led him to forage for votes in Wisconsin, Indiana and Maryland in the 1964 Presidential primary elections. There, Frady noted, "it was also clear that Wallace had invoked, had discovered a dark, silent, brooding mass of people whom no one—the newspapers, the political leaders, the intellectuals—no one but Wallace had suspected were there."

Bob never believed that the narrow hardness of Wallace's views, his appeal to the deepest reaches of white supremacy and bigotry would find a wide base of support among the American people. In the spring of 1963 he believed that the violence in Birmingham and Wallace's intransigence, following so soon after the shameful scene at Oxford, had made it evident that the time was long past when the nation could tolerate denial of voting rights to black people or "White Only" signs in places that served the public, or that there should be separate schools for blacks and whites. He believed that a growing majority of Americans would come to see clearly that unless there was much faster progress in redressing the blacks' grievances there would be more and more violence, deepening hatred and dividing the races until America's historic promise of justice and equal opportunity would be lost to the next generation. But, in addition to what happened in Alabama and elsewhere in the South that hectic spring, there were rumbles from the volcano of resentment and frustration that was building toward eruption in the Northern and Western ghettos. Bob first heard them when he exchanged angry words with a group of Negroes assembled by James Baldwin. It was an unsettling meeting and one that was to have a considerable, though confusing effect.

The suggestion that Bob should meet Baldwin was made by the militant black comedian Dick Gregory through Burke Marshall, and Bob, having read a penetrating article in *The New Yorker*, "The Fire Next Time," which Baldwin later published as a book, invited Baldwin to have breakfast with him at Hickory Hill.

Baldwin, an exotic, gifted writer, had vividly described the "incessant and gratuitous humiliation and danger" black men, women and children encountered every day of their lives; the Negro's past "of rope, fire, torture, castration, infanticide, rape; death and humiliation; fear by day and night, fear as deep as the marrow of the bone; doubt that he was worthy of life, since everyone around him denied it; sorrow for his women, for his kinfolk, for his children, who needed his protection, and whom he could not protect; rage, hatred, and murder, hatred for white men so deep that it often turned against him and his own and made all love, all trust, all joy impossible."

Baldwin's main point, outlined in concise, pungent language, was that the American dream was decaying and could only be salvaged through the total liberation of the Negroes:

What it comes down to is that if we, who can scarcely be considered a white nation, persist in thinking of ourselves as one, we condemn ourselves . . . to sterility and decay, whereas if we could accept ourselves *as we are*, we might bring new life to the Western achievements, and transform them. The price of this transformation is the unconditional freedom of the Negro; it is not too much to say that he, who has been so long rejected, must now be embraced, at no matter what psychic or social risk. He is *the* key figure in his country, and the American future is precisely as bright or as dark as his.

At the end—and it was this that Bob particularly wanted to discuss—Baldwin concluded:

Everything now, we must assume, is in our hands; we have no right to assume otherwise. If we—and now I mean the relatively conscious whites and the relatively conscious blacks, who must, like lovers, insist on, or create, the consciousness of the others—do not falter in our duty now, we may be able, handful that we are, to end the racial nightmare, and achieve our country, and change the history of the world. If we do not now dare everything, the fulfillment of that prophecy, recreated from the Bible in song by a slave, is upon us: *God gave Noah the rainbow sign. No more water, the fire next time!*"

Baldwin's plane was delayed, and Bob had only time for a brief conversation. It was amiable. Bob wanted to know what Baldwin thought the government should be doing and suggested that they meet the next day in New York and that Baldwin invite other blacks to participate.

The meeting was to be in Ambassador Kennedy's apartment overlooking Central Park, and Bob, accompanied by Marshall, went expecting to have a serious discussion about possible government action with a group of blacks who understood and appreciated the efforts he and his brother were making to end discrimination. Among those whom Baldwin had invited were Professor Kenneth B. Clark, a distinguished psychologist, the writer Lorraine Hansberry and Lena Horne and Harry Belafonte. Bob and Belafonte had been friends for several years. But the meeting began on a painful, acrimonious note and got steadily worse.

Jerome Smith, a twenty-four-year-old CORE chairman in New Orleans who had been beaten and jailed during the Freedom Rides, opened with the comment: "Mr. Kennedy, I want you to understand I don't care anything about you or your brother." Smith then assailed Bob for failing to give black demonstrators in the South more protection and said that being in the same room with Robert Kennedy made him feel like vomiting. Bob tried to answer Smith, but was interrupted repeatedly.

"Just let me say something," Bob demanded.

"Okay," said Smith, "but this time say something that means something. So far you haven't said a thing!"

Bob tried to recount what the Administration had accomplished; that a civil rights bill was before the Congress and a new, much stronger bill would be submitted shortly. But the others, like Smith, did not want to hear about what had been done. They, too, wanted to pour out their pent-up feelings of rage and indignation. Bob responded with impatience, particularly when one young Negro said he would not fight for the United States. "How can you say that?" Bob snapped. But the young man could and repeated it. After more than three hours, the meeting ended with feelings inflamed and nothing settled.

Bob and Marshall were shocked. The next day they related what had happened with disgust and hostility. "They didn't want to talk about doing anything, they don't know the facts," Bob said. "They just wanted to shout." He spoke bitterly about Belafonte and several others who came up to him after the meeting was over and praised him. Belafonte had said, "Of course you've done more for civil rights than any other Attorney General."

"Why didn't you say this to the others?" Bob said he asked the singer.

"I couldn't say this to the others," Bob said Belafonte replied. "It would affect my relationship with them. If I were to defend you, they would conclude I had gone over to the other side."

After a day or two, Bob's attitude about the meeting began to shift. He had never heard an American citizen say he would not defend the country and it troubled him. Instead of repeating, as he had, "Imagine anyone saying that," he said, "I guess if I were in his shoes, if I had gone through what he's gone through, I might feel differently about this country."

Later, Baldwin and Clark and others would credit the meeting with having caused a major shift in Bob's thinking. At that time it did seem terribly important. In retrospect its principal value seems to have been symbolic: blacks felt that for the first time the true feelings of militant Northern blacks had been communicated directly to someone high in the government. However, by the time the meeting was held, the Justice Department had intervened in Birmingham and all the elements of the new Civil Rights Bill had been decided upon. Indeed, the reason Bob and Marshall were in New York that day was to meet with representatives of major chain stores which operated lunch counters in the South to persuade them to desegregate immediately, without waiting for enactment of the bill. So, nothing changed specifically because of the meeting.

Yet the impact of all that was happening added an increasingly moral tone to Bob's public statements on civil rights, as it did unquestionably to the President's statements.

Bob had coined the phrase that the purpose of the new Civil Rights Bill was to get racial strife "out of the streets and into the courts," but now the matter of *right*, of grievances that had to be redressed somehow in the hearts of white Americans as well as by the law and government tactics, took ascendancy in his and the President's thinking. When Bob appeared before the House Judiciary Committee two weeks after the confrontation with Wallace to testify on behalf of the new Civil Rights Bill, he said:

I am here today to testify in support of a bill that will go a long way toward redeeming the pledges upon which this Republic was founded— pledges that all are created equal, that they are endowed equally with unalienable rights and are entitled to equal opportunity in the pursuit of their daily lives. In this generation, we have seen an extraordinary change in America—a new surge of idealism in our life—a new and profound insistence on reality in our democratic order. Much has been done. But quite obviously much more must be done—both because the American people are clearly demanding it and because, by any moral standard *it is right.*

Then he documented his moral tone with hard facts, carefully researched evidence of discrimination, justifying and explaining each section of the bill.

As he worked for its enactment, he also was the driving force within the government in arranging meetings for the President and the Vice President with all elements of leadership in the South and North to prepare for constructive action after the bill became law. He believed that the racial crisis of the 1960's was due in no small part to the fact that after the Supreme Court school desegregation decision in 1954 there had been no clear, strong appeal for compliance from President Eisenhower or any Southern leaders. The void had been filled by extremists who advocated "massive resistance." Thus he believed it was urgent for leaders North and South to speak up for massive compliance with court orders and the law.

The Kennedy political antenna was too sensitive for either the President or Bob to underestimate the political danger that their new urgency in civil rights entailed. The phrase "white backlash" already was creeping into the language, and national polls showed that while a majority of whites favored the new Civil Rights Bill, a majority also believed that the Kennedys were pushing "too fast" in behalf of Negroes. Bob read the signs in his anti–civil rights mail, which began to come in greater volume from the North as well as from the South and in tone steadily more caustic and unreasoning. He heard it in the streets. Just after Tuscaloosa, when he was walking in Manhattan, a construction worker standing on a girder of a new building several stories above the street shouted: "Hey, Bobby, don't forget about the Irish and the Italians!"

But there were other signs—the New York meeting with the militants was just one—that the resentful and the desperate blacks in the North were losing patience and were less inclined to peaceful protest than their counterparts in the South. And the North seemed strangely insensitive. In the meetings to ease the crisis in Birmingham and to drum up support for the Civil Rights Bill, Bob invariably told Northern leaders—businessmen, editors and publishers and civic officials—that they soon would face in their own communities racial problems more difficult than Birmingham had endured. Almost to a man, they would deny that any such problems could arise in the North.

Thus, with most Southern officials unwilling to end discrimination in even so basic a right as voting and with Northern leaders deceiving themselves about discrimination in jobs, housing and education, it seemed obvious that black protests would spread and become more violent and that the federal government had no moral choice but to take the initiative.

"How can we say," Bob asked the Senate Judiciary Committee, "to a Negro in Jackson: 'When war comes you will be an American citizen, but in the meantime you're a citizen of Mississippi and we can't help you'?"

And so the course was set, and during a discussion with Bob about the political disadvantage of the all-out fight they were going to make for the Civil Rights Bill, the President remarked:

"Well, if we're going to go down, let's go down on a matter of principle."

Chapter 11

Laughter and Concern

DESPITE THE PASSING YEARS, Bob's appearance and mannerisms remain vivid in my memory—the perceptive blue eyes, the tousled brown hair, the large forearms and his hands, trembling during a speech; the sloping shoulders and the hunched, leaning walk; the angular nose; the quizzical look and his broad, crinkling smile; the vulnerability that a child could penetrate, but an adult could not. Each of us who knew him well has special memories of him—his courage, loyalty, compassion and his extraordinary energy and capacity for growth—and from them we salvage something lasting in the face of his tragic death.

He could communicate with a child with a look or a touch on the head. Children seemed to refresh his spirit—his own children or a child in a hollow in Appalachia or a solemn tot in a Navajo hogan. No matter how difficult a problem he was working on or how serious the crisis, he made time to be with his family. Often if he had missed being home for several evenings, Ethel and the children would come to his office and have dinner with him. If there was a meeting at his home and Michael burst in crying because David had pummeled him or Kerry wandered in with a picture she'd crayoned, the meeting would stop. Bob would gently remind Michael that "Kennedys don't cry," cheer him and send him on his way with a pat on his rear end, or he would praise Kerry's artistic talent, exhibit her drawing to all in the room and then the meeting would continue.

I asked my children to write about how they remembered Bob. Gary, fourteen, wrote:

> I remember one night when he was at our house. I went to say good-night to him and he shook my hand and said, "Good-night, Gary," in such a warm and friendly way that to this day it has stuck in my mind. I could not and never will understand how people could call him ruthless. Whenever I saw him he was always so gentle and cheerful. On the trip down the Colorado River, I remember him going down a very dangerous rapid on a rubber mattress on which he could have lost his life. I'm sure many people think it foolish to risk your life on such an unimportant thing, but to me it was very courageous.

Eddie, seventeen, wrote:

> Bob was always very lively and joyful and no matter who else was with us, he always had time to say hello to me and ask me how I was. That time we went to the All-Star football game in Buffalo when I was 12, he and his kids were presented with autographed footballs, but when he saw that I didn't have one, he gave his to me. When we floated down the Colorado, he was the first to ride the rapids on a rubber mattress.

Concern for the kind of world the children would inherit appeared repeatedly in his speeches and influenced many of his actions. Through their laughter and their tears, through their questioning eyes, he kept his eyes on the future. "We must leave the world a better place than we found it," he would say. One of his favorite quotations was by Albert Camus: "Perhaps we cannot prevent this world from being a world in which children are tortured. But we can reduce the number of tortured children."

John Glenn, the astronaut and a close friend of Bob's, remembers a certain day during the California primary campaign:

> We had walked through a very poor area where several hundred people, mostly children, black, brown and white, surrounded Bob. The children ran, jumped, laughed and sought his hand. He in return talked and joked

with them as we walked through the midst of squalor—unpainted homes and unpaved streets.

Now, he stared out the window of the jet, introspective, lost in his thoughts, saying nothing, and hearing nothing of the typical campaign plane sounds. I sat in the empty seat beside him and remarked, "Something's really on your mind." He turned, did not say anything for a few seconds, then quietly replied, "I just keep thinking of those kids."[1]

One of the first things he did as Attorney General was to begin exploring how the federal government could do more to diminish juvenile delinquency. He asked his friend from prep school, David Hackett, to get ideas and recommendations from persons experienced in the field. But that would not be enough. He wanted to investigate on his own. He was going to New York on March 5, 1961, to participate in a CBS televised panel discussion on the challenge of international Communism. Hackett made arrangements through John Gomez, a New York City youth worker, for Bob to meet with three Harlem street gangs. Bob made one provision: there must be no notice to the press.

The weather was unseasonably warm for so early in March, and after the show Bob and I walked in our shirtsleeves, suit coats slung over our shoulders, from 65th Street and York Avenue to 105th Street and Third Avenue, where he was to meet Gomez. However, he was early, and while he waited, he sat on the curb. He had been recognized by many passers-by as we walked, but in the dusk he sat unnoticed and silent. That night he met separately in a school yard or on a street with two Negro gangs, the Aces and the Redwings, and an Italian gang, tough, cagey youths from sixteen to nineteen years old. One boy had been arrested for selling narcotics. Another had been in prison for murder. A third was out on bond for armed robbery.

Each meeting began with the same question: "What are you doing here?"

"I came because I'm interested," Bob replied. He questioned them about where they lived, what they did with their time, where

---

1. From a eulogy which Glenn gave after Bob's death and which was included in the book *"An Honorable Profession"—A Tribute to Robert F. Kennedy.*

they worked. Few of them worked. There was much talk of violence and of their need to protect their "turf." One of the Aces spoke with pride about how the gang had beaten a boy who was sitting on a bench in a park in their neighborhood. Bob couldn't get that through his head. Fights, he could understand; a gang beating a lone boy, he couldn't. But the youth explained that they had asked the stranger what he was doing there and had been told, "None of your business." That started the fight and everyone joined in, he said.

"Why?" asked Bob.

"Because we all wanted to get into it," the youth replied.

Bob asked the members of each gang what they thought the government should do to help them. Hesitantly, thoughtfully came the answers: provide more jobs and more facilities for recreation. Nothing more.

Bob returned to Washington impressed with Gomez and other youth workers he met—strong-minded men in their twenties who appeared to have gained the gang members' confidence and were attempting to keep them out of trouble and provide direction to their lives, though they themselves were paid less than $5,000 a year.

"They are unsung heroes—maybe they're the best answer," he said as the plane landed at Washington National Airport. He had no ideas more definite than that, but after more talks with young toughs and meetings with experts assembled by Hackett, the President's Committee on Juvenile Delinquency and Youth Crime came into being with Bob as chairman.

The purpose of the committee was to demonstrate that the President was more than just concerned, that he was directly interested in helping communities do more to cope with the complex, interwoven problems of juvenile delinquency. Over the next three years, the committee, working on a small budget, provided assistance to a number of programs from New York to Oregon and gathered data that formed the basis for parts of President Johnson's War on Poverty, particularly the Community Action concept—that a community or an entire area should mobilize its resources and develop its own programs for improving economic opportunity and education for the disadvantaged, with those to be helped involved in planning what was to be done.

Within two years Bob was recognizing the limitations in the Community Action approach that he had recommended—of programs calling for "maximum feasible participation of residents" that were not actually giving the poor a real voice; of lethargy and foot-dragging by local officials in matching federal grants and in providing vigorous leadership. However, unlike many leading political figures in both parties, he did not react with rancor or criticism, but spoke about facts and needs and proposed new approaches. One was the two-corporation approach in Bedford-Stuyvesant—one composed of the black residents of the ghetto and the other of leading New York bankers and businessmen to work together to create more jobs, improve housing and raise educational standards. It is a testimonial to the uniqueness of his leadership that when the Nixon Administration was considering applications from Community Action programs for federal grants in 1970, Bedford-Stuyvesant was one of the few still going that was deemed worthy of federal support. It was given $10 million—25 percent of the special impact funds available.

In 1962 Bob began visiting the beleaguered Washington senior and junior high schools to see conditions in them for himself. He would go on the spur of the moment, seldom giving school officials much advance notice. He never gave a speech. He would begin by saying he was glad to be there and ask if any of the students wanted to ask him any questions. If there were none, he would ask some historical questions: How many knew the names of the two generals who led the Union and Confederate armies at Gettysburg? Who was the Governor of Maryland? How many knew who drafted the Bill of Rights? Soon a student would ask a question. Then another and another. One question often asked was: "Why did you come here?"

Frequently, he would ask a prominent Negro athlete or entertainer to accompany him. Bobby Mitchell of the Washington Redskins went with him frequently. The late Nat King Cole and Rafer Johnson, the Olympic Games gold medal winner in the decathlon, were among the others. He never preached or promised anything, but always urged the students to stay in school and complete their education. He hoped that by showing that the brother of the President had enough interest in the poor black children of Washington to visit them, he would raise their hope for the future or kindle hope where there had been none. But he was far too pragmatic to let it go at that. On one visit, he asked Superintendent Carl F. Hansen to go with him, and afterward, while driving Hansen back to his office, Bob asked: "How many students do you have dropping out of high school?"

"About thirty-five hundred," Dr. Hansen said.

"How many do you suppose drop out for economic reasons?"

"Between seven and eight hundred—but we have a fund to help them."

"How many students are you helping?"

"Only about fifteen."

When Bob returned to the Justice Department, he called a number of people to discuss the problem. Then he had a meeting, and as a result of the discussions he decided to raise $50,000 through a benefit performance to provide Dr. Hansen with a larger fund to pay students for office or custodial work and enable them to stay in school. Twelve dollars a week was set as the maximum any student could earn. Bob arranged for a movie to be previewed at the benefit, and the first year Ella Fitzgerald performed. The next year Sammy Davis, Jr., came. Black and white leaders of Washington worked together to arrange the benefits, and Dr. Hansen reported that each year about four hundred students remained in school because of the extra money they were able to earn.

There was nothing novel about this approach, nor did it require vast amounts of energy to raise the money. The need had existed for a long time, and when Bob realized it, he acted—just as he did in spearheading an effort to open summer jobs to underprivileged youths (1,120 jobs the first summer, 1,000 of them in government offices) or in converting a block of federal property, filled with impounded cars, into a playfield.

But no one ever needed to explain to him that those were only stopgap efforts, the fairly easy meeting of obvious needs. He knew that the Negro youth who took his advice and finished high school was more likely to be unemployed than a white youth who dropped out of school—or was more likely to find only menial work at lower pay.

Summer job programs would help. Bedford-Stuyvesant community development corporations would help, but only a little as long as millions of Americans suffered indignity, disappointment, punishment and deprivation because of their poverty or because of their race. The plight of the Negro in the central city was the most immediate and pressing urban problem, he thought, and providing employment should have the highest priority in dealing with it. He would devise a series of special programs, many of them far-reaching, and despite setbacks and disappointments he would remain hopeful and he would not rest.

"We are all in this together," he said in Bedford-Stuyvesant after the program had been under way for eight months. "If there is to be a better future here, we will all have to stay together. . . . We are striking out in new directions, on new courses, sometimes perhaps without a map or compass to guide us. We are going to try as few have tried before. . . .

"If this community fails, then others will falter, and a noble dream of equality and dignity in our cities will be sorely tried. But if the dangers are great, and the challenges great, so are the possibilities for greatness. . . . I believe that we can succeed, that we can fulfill the commitment, and thereby help others to do so."

As much as anything, it was this spirit, his indomitable will to keep going despite setbacks, despite the odds (which he had analyzed carefully and usually quite accurately), and his extraordinary capacity to give hope to so many people, that set him apart. Perhaps no one has expressed it more eloquently than Deborah Rooks, who lives on the Pine Ridge Reservation in South Dakota, in a letter she wrote after his death:

I remember April 16th [1968], the date he came, very clearly. It was chilly, a rather cloudy and dismal day. We were let out of school early and all of the students were waiting around outside for Mr. Kennedy. When he did come, I felt rather sorry for him. He looked tired and sad, yet he kept smiling and shaking hands with all of us.

He stood up on a platform and spoke to us. He told us of our Indian heritage; he spoke of the good in the Indian people. It looked as though some of the kids were going to cry; he made us feel proud of our race, not ashamed. . . .

Some were looking at him in awe; others with hope; others with faith. They felt that someone had finally realized that we were here and someone was going to help them, not push them away until later. Here was someone great who could help us and wanted to help us. . . . That day was one of the happiest days at Holy Rosary [Mission] because a dream came true. We wouldn't be labeled "dirty Indians" anymore because he cared.[2]

The essence of his character also showed in the self-confidence that allowed him to admit his mistakes, and it was a measure of his leadership that often, without a second thought, he took responsibility for the mistakes of others. Sometimes it cost him greatly, as it did when FBI agents awakened three newsmen in Philadelphia and Wilmington before dawn on April 12, 1962, to question them about a news story.

Opponents of the Administration reacted with righteous indignation, and some went so far as to liken the incident to the Nazis' infamous "knock on the door"—the dreaded SS coming in the middle of the night to hustle Jews off to concentration camps. A year and a half later, the Republican Congressional Committee was referring to it as a "Gestapo-like raid." It was a thoughtless act, nothing more, but it tended to confirm the worst suspicions of those who feared Bob because of his association with Joseph McCarthy, or felt uncomfortable about his pursuit of Jimmy Hoffa, or who recoiled at his single-minded management of John Kennedy's campaigns. And he never fully recovered. Writers always mentioned it in evoking the stereotype of the ruthless, power-hungry Robert Kennedy, and it was a reason, along with his service on the McCarthy and McClellan committees, that liberal Democrats gave for opposing him in the New York Senate race in 1964 and in the 1968 Presidential primaries.

Early in April, 1962, the steel companies and the United Steel-

2. From *That Shining Hour*, a privately printed book containing remembrances of Bob written by his friends and family and collected and edited by his sister, Mrs. Patricia Lawford.

workers Union reached agreement on a contract providing for no general wage increase and fringe benefits costing about ten cents an hour—the most modest steel settlement in the postwar era and the first without a crippling strike since 1954. The President, determined to hold the line on prices and costs to curb inflation and improve the nation's balance of payments, had taken a strong hand in the negotiations. With steel prices "a bellwether, as well as a major element in industrial costs," as the President described them, there was widespread concern that an inflationary steel settlement would signal another siege of inflation at home and make steel and other products less competitive in foreign markets. The President —working through Secretary of Labor Arthur Goldberg, who had been the Steelworkers' general counsel, but taking a hand directly at times—had persuaded the union to forgo a wage increase. By implication it was understood that, in return, industry would not raise prices.

On the afternoon of April 10, after the last major contract had been signed, Roger Blough, chairman of the board of U.S. Steel, called at the White House and handed the President a press release, announcing that the nation's largest steel company intended to raise prices $6 a ton. There had been no advance warning of the purpose of Blough's call, nor had there been any indication during the negotiations that a steel price increase would be forthcoming if the union agreed to hold the line on wages. The President felt he had been double-crossed. His first reaction was one of anger, and then he became coolly determined to see what he could do about it.

In meetings that evening and the next day, he sought to marshal every shred of power at his command to put pressure on U.S. Steel to rescind the raise. On the morning of the eleventh, five companies including Bethlehem Steel, the second largest, had followed U.S. Steel's lead, but a number of companies had not yet done so. If they could be persuaded to hold out, U.S. Steel and the others would have to back down.

Each department, particularly Defense, Treasury, Commerce, Labor and Justice, had been asked to come up with ways to help.

When Bob returned from the White House on the afternoon of the eleventh, discussion with his staff centered on starting a grand jury investigation to see whether the steel companies had violated the antitrust laws by conspiring to fix prices. FBI agents were assigned, as was customary, to make the preliminary inquiries.

Almost as an afterthought, it was decided to have the FBI also contact three reporters who had covered a Bethlehem stockholders' meeting in Wilmington, Delaware, on the day Blough handed the press release to President Kennedy. Bethlehem President Edmund Martin had made a comment to the effect that because of competition, particularly from foreign industry, it was time for American steel to cut prices. At least one reporter interpreted the remark to mean that Bethlehem would not increase its prices, but there was some confusion about Martin's exact words. The *Wall Street Journal* reported that Martin had declined to answer questions about a possible price rise.

However, if he had been quoted correctly, if he had said one day, "We should be trying to reduce the price of steel, if at all possible," and the next morning had gone along with the price increase, then there were grounds to suspect a case of administered prices—that Bethlehem and the others were following the leader regardless of competitive or market conditions. Thus the FBI was asked to confirm the accuracy of what Martin had said.

It was about 6 o'clock in the evening, and as Nicholas Katzenbach, Courtney Evans, an assistant director of the FBI, and I walked out of Bob's office, Katzenbach cautioned Evans to be sure that the steel executives were interviewed at their offices, not at their homes. Bob was not within hearing of the discussion. Neither Katzenbach nor I thought to give similar instructions about the newsmen.

For some reason, never explained, the request to interview the reporters took until after midnight to clear through the FBI office in Philadelphia. About 5 A.M., John Lawrence of the *Wall Street Journal* received a call from an agent, who said, "The Attorney General asked us to call you." Lawrence refused to be questioned except under a subpoena. About the same time, agents called on Lee Linder of the Associated Press and James L. Parks, Jr., of the Wil-

mington *Evening Journal.* Linder promptly filed an account of the
interview, stressing that he had been awakened, and by the time
Bob arrived at the Justice Department the press was clamoring for
an explanation.

Several suggestions were made that he make light of it, expressing
incredulity that any reporter would mind being awakened at any
time if it resulted in a story, or that he simply say that there had
been a misunderstanding on the part of the FBI.

"No," Bob said. "I get some credit when FBI agents do something
good. I'll take the heat when they goof."

He issued a brief statement saying that he took "full responsibility" for what had happened.

The next afternoon, in face of the Administration's hard reaction
and with the refusal of the Inland Steel Company, Kaiser Steel and
the Armco Steel Corporation to raise prices, U.S. Steel and Bethlehem capitulated and rescinded their increases. A few business
leaders and writers grumbled that the President had overreacted,
but most businessmen, economists and the public generally praised
the President's decisiveness and credited him with having won an
important victory in the fight against inflation. Awakening the
three newsmen was the only black mark that the Administration
received, and Bob bore it.

The years of dueling with Hoffa, Beck and the hundreds of other
reluctant witnesses who came before the McClellan Committee
made Bob sharp and sure-footed in answering questions. He enjoyed the give-and-take of a question-and-answer session. The
harder the questions were, the better he liked it. When the questions
were soft, monosyllabic answers would betray his boredom. One of
the reasons he liked to speak at colleges was because students usually asked tougher questions than adults. When the questions were
difficult, his face would become animated and his answers spirited
and detailed.

In Japan in 1962 he was questioned sharply and critically by five
Japanese labor leaders led by Akira Iwai, who described himself as
a neutralist and a Marxist, but not a Communist. For an hour the

labor leaders asked questions critical of the United States, and their statements, following Bob's answers, indicated skepticism and that they believed Communist propaganda about life in the United States.

Near the end, Bob asked: "You call the United States imperialistic. Based on what happened in Tibet and Hungary, then do you consider the Soviet Union and China imperialistic?"

"There were some mistakes made," Iwai replied.

"Do you consider them imperialistic?"

"We don't use the term."

"Why do you use it for the United States and not for them?"

"Well, we determine it in the United States as monopoly capital."

"So, I understand. It is permissible to send troops in and kill people? Then one is not imperialist? I mean, honestly, you know that the United States, run by this Administration, is not made up of a lot of monopolistic capitalists. Did you gather that from Arthur Goldberg, who visited Japan some months ago and who came from the Steelworkers Union? Or, for instance, from me? Or from a country that raised the minimum wage to a dollar and a quarter an hour and passed all the other social legislation? Does that make us imperialists? Capitalistic imperialists? And the Soviet Union puts a wall up to keep their people in this workers' paradise, and they march into Hungary as they did, and you don't call them imperialists? As an amateur in diplomacy, it confuses me."

"I am not making an issue of whether you come from a monopolistic capitalist country," said Iwai. "Of course, the United States has shown some very good results in social security, housing and these things. But the basic characteristic of your nation is capitalism. Isn't that true? With Morgan, Rockefeller and all of these in control?"

"You are talking about the United States a hundred years ago. Do you think we have stood still? And do you think the labor movement of the United States is run by capitalist imperialists? They are supporting President Kennedy. Walter Reuther—is he a capitalist? This is a different country now.... We are not run by the Rockefellers or the Morgan bank. I don't want to be facetious with you.

. . . But I ask that you examine the facts. Analyze what the United States is about."[3]

Formal speeches were something else. Bob had no natural speaking gifts. His voice was high-pitched and had a nasal quality. He got by in the early days on thorough mastery of his subject and dogged conviction. In the late 1950's when he spoke about the work of the McClellan Committee, his information was detailed and well organized in his mind, and he held his audiences' attention by reeling off examples of corruption that had been uncovered and by concluding with a strong explanation why reform legislation was needed. Even in the later years when his appearance aroused wild excitement and he could deeply move an audience as he did in Indianapolis the night Dr. King was assassinated or that memorable night in Atlantic City when he spoke to the Democratic National Convention about President Kennedy, he was never completely at ease when he gave a speech.

While he was Attorney General, he worked diligently to become a better speaker. Once he took speech lessons for a few weeks, but gave up partly because he became impatient with the practice drills and partly because he thought the teacher was overcharging him. He would practice his speeches in front of a mirror. Often at a banquet, after eating and while waiting to speak, he would be hunched over his reading copy, silently going over his text.

It was impossible to tell beforehand how he would do. Sometimes he would enthrall his audience with a speech that was run-of-the-mill. Other times when he had a text that appeared to be eloquent and significant, he would bore everyone. His effectiveness seemed to have more to do with the chemistry of the audience or the occasion than with what he was going to say or how he felt. If he sensed rapport with his audience, he usually did well. If the occasion presented a special challenge, as when he outlined the Administration's civil rights policy at the University of Georgia Law School, he usually rose to it, but not always.

In November 1961 he sought to duplicate the Georgia speech by

---

3. A full account of this and similar encounters on the 1962 trip is contained in Robert Kennedy's book *Just Friends and Brave Enemies.*

outlining the Administration's antitrust policy before the Economic Club of New York, a blue-ribbon group of executives who met twice a year in the Grand Ballroom of the Waldorf-Astoria Hotel. The speech was written, rewritten and honed. Morton Lachman, one of Bob Hope's chief writers for many years, worked over the text and suggested a number of punch lines. Theodore Sorensen, the President's special counsel and a fine writer, added more humor.

Bob was changing into his tuxedo at the Waldorf when his father came in. The Ambassador eyed the room, which was not luxurious by Waldorf standards, and commented, "I see you're living it up, really in the tall cotton, aren't you." "My father's a millionaire," replied Bob. Ambassador Kennedy carefully read the final draft of the speech and predicted that it would be well received. It wasn't. When Bob spoke following enthusiastic applause for a speech by the Ambassador from the Republic of China, the reaction was frigid. The title of Bob's speech, "Vigorous Anti-Trust Enforcement Assists Business," was outrageous to that audience. It was like trying to tell those business executives that bankruptcy would be good for them, and Bob was in trouble from the beginning.

"Thank you, Mr. Chairman, and good evening, gentlemen," he began. "I sincerely hope you enjoyed your dinner. I have been given to understand that I am responsible for a certain amount of acid indigestion in your midst."

Silence.

"I would like to begin tonight by reading a telegram which I received recently. It said: 'Thanks for a good swift kick in the pocketbook. I knocked myself out to help you in the election. Got in Dutch with my boss and other employees and generally took it on the chin with a smile. But, oh, what a different story after a few months. You pointed the finger at every industry in the country— two of which I have stock in. They are not guilty as charged, but the effect on the stock market cost me and the government plenty. I would vote for you boys again, but take it a little easy.'

"What I would like to know is which one of you wrote that telegram?"

Silence.

"Look, I'm personally not against business. Hardly. I am one of its beneficiaries. And I have reason to believe that the President feels very much the same way I do."

Silence.

Bob made it clear, as he did at the University of Georgia, that the Justice Department would enforce the law "in every field of the law," including the antitrust laws, but he sought to show that the Administration was not gunning for business, that the Department had been restrained in filing antitrust actions and that 300 of 439 complaints of antitrust violations had come from businessmen. Thus, Bob argued, the antitrust laws helped and protected business by keeping it competitive.

"This Administration is not antibusiness primarily because there is every reason we should be probusiness," Bob struggled on. "The United States must have a strong and rapidly expanding economy to survive, and this Administration and any Administration has no choice but to be 'probusiness.' An expanding, healthy economy is the backbone of our American system. . . ."

When Bob finished, the applause was scarcely perfunctory. It was the club's custom to have a brief question-and-answer period, with each speaker responding in turn. Each time the Chinese Ambassador answered, the applause was deafening. Bob's answers were received in silence. As a final question, one man demanded: "Mr. Kennedy, a lot of people think your brother talks like Churchill and acts like Chamberlain. What do you have to say about that?"

Bob responded by saying that his family was no stranger to war. Their brother Joe had been killed on a volunteer air mission. Their brother-in-law, the Marquis of Hartington, husband of their sister Kathleen, had been killed in action in France. The President had been injured in the war. He had participated in landing a force of Marines on Choiseul Island and a few days later had taken his PT boat in to rescue some of them. He had seen the war close up, and he was determined to do everything possible to avoid sending other men to war.

"My brother intends to walk the last mile to keep the peace," Bob concluded, and for the first time that long evening the applause for him was generous and there were even a few cheers. But as the executives were walking out, a stout man with a cigar clenched between his teeth was overheard to say to two companions: "I don't give a damn what you say. I'll bet all those Kennedy kids had to be drafted!"

Few of Bob's speeches turned out as badly as that. If he didn't reach his listeners' emotions, he gave them facts and proposals to ponder, and he often disarmed them with candor. However, he often was dissatisfied with his performance and fretted over how to improve.

A big change came during the 1964 Senate campaign in New York. His format—one-line openers making fun of himself or his family; an outline of the subject; facts; a program of action; an appeal for reason with appropriate quotes from Jefferson, Camus, Aeschylus, George Bernard Shaw, Oliver Wendell Holmes, Tennyson or John Kennedy—was set. But campaigning for himself for the first time, feeling the gentleness of the people in the small upstate towns and the surge of the huge city crowds, and winning them— winning the election on his own—removed some of the worry and self-doubt.

Increasingly in the final three and a half years, tones of intensity infused his speeches. There were passion and impatience as well as facts, reason and faith in the country as he felt more and more keenly that the course of the war in Vietnam was wrong, as he identified closely with the dissatisfactions of the young and as he tried to give voice to the blighted hopes of the blacks, the Mexican-Americans, the Indians and the poor of all races—the victims of the twentieth century, as Arthur Schlesinger, Jr., described them.

At Kansas State University, March 18, 1968, two days after he announced for the Presidency, he said:

I am concerned that at the end of it all there will only be more Americans killed; more of our treasure spilled out . . . so that they may say, as Tacitus said of Rome: "They made a desert, and called it peace." I don't think that is satisfactory for the United States of America. . . .

I am willing to bear my share of the responsibility, before history and before my fellow citizens. But past error is no excuse for its own perpetuation. Tragedy is a tool for the living to gain wisdom, not a guide by which to live. Now as ever, we do ourselves best justice when we measure ourselves against ancient tests, as in the *Antigone* of Sophocles: "All men make mistakes, but a good man yields when he knows his course is wrong, and repairs the evil. The only sin is pride." . . .

If it becomes necessary to destroy all of South Vietnam to save it, will we do that, too? And if we care so little about South Vietnam that we are willing to see its land destroyed, and its people dead, then why are we there in the first place?

So I come here today, to this great university, to ask your help; not for me, but for your country, and for the people of Vietnam. . . . Our country is in danger: not just from foreign enemies but, above all, from our own misguided policies—and what they can do to the nation that Thomas Jefferson once said was the last, best hope of man. There is a contest on, not for the rule of America, but for the heart of America. In these next eight months we are going to decide what this country will stand for—and what kind of men we are.

So I ask for your help, in the cities and homes of this state, into the towns and farms, contributing your concern and action, warning of the danger of what we are doing, and the promise of what we can do in the future not just in Southeast Asia, but here at home as well, so that we might have a new birth for this country, a new light to guide us. And I pledge to you, if you will give me your help, if you will give me your hand, I will work for you, and we will have a new America!

He finished with his right fist raised in the air, and the fourteen thousand students, jammed into Ahearn Fieldhouse, gave him a thunderous, ear-splitting ovation. He could command an audience as never before. Thousands came to hear him. Probably only a few ever noticed that as he spoke his large hands trembled.

Through all the times, good and bad, he was fun to be with. When it was all ended and those who had known him well either talked or wrote about him, they remembered his humor and his compassion and his courage, but most of all how much they enjoyed his company. He was serious about everything he did, but he never took himself seriously. He wasn't a teller of jokes or stories, but he had a wry wit. When things were tense or unpleasant, he always came up with a remark, sometimes with a gallows ring, sometimes needling and often self-depreciating, which usually was unanswerable, but which made whoever was with him laugh.

Nicholas Katzenbach would remember Bob's final words as Nick was rushing out the door, heading for Ole Miss: "If things get rough, don't worry about yourself; the President needs a moral issue."[4]

James Whittaker, the first American to reach the summit of Mount Everest, would recall a rainy day in Oregon during the 1968 campaign:

> Our convertible approached a town and people were lining the sidewalks. Bob said, "Put the top down." I said, "It's pouring, Bob." He said, "They're getting wet!" Forty minutes later, the top still down, our car crept out of town. Soaking wet we picked at some chocolate cake a constituent had given him, and that had turned out to be our lunch! Bob gave me a look across the seat and remarked: "Name something you have done that was more fun than this!"[5]

February 1963 was the month of the fifty-mile-hike fad. President Kennedy started it all when he came across a long-forgotten Executive Order in which President Theodore Roosevelt decreed in 1908 that every Marine captain and lieutenant should be able to hike fifty miles in twenty hours, carrying a full field pack. The hike could be stretched over three days, T.R. said, but officers were to do the last half-mile at double time and sprint the final two hundred yards. President Kennedy, who had talked a great deal about physical fitness after entering the White House, sent the order to the Marine Commandant, General David M. Shoup, and appended a note:

> Why don't you send this back to me as your own discovery? You might want to add a comment that today's Marine Corps officers are just as fit as those of 1908, and are willing to prove it. I, in turn, will ask Mr. Salinger for a report on the fitness of the White House staff.

Once the document was made public, people around the country started walking fifty miles in one stretch. Marine officers at Camp Pendleton crossed the finish line on a dead run after eighteen hours and forty-four minutes. The Marines at Camp Lejeune and other

---

4. From *That Shining Hour, op. cit.*
5. *Ibid.*

bases made ready to prove their worth, and at the White House the portly, affable Salinger made a gallant effort to get in shape, but was clearly looking for an escape.

On a Friday afternoon, before the Marines were ready and while Salinger, who had now recruited the White House press corps to make the hike, stalled and prayed for a miracle, Bob decided on the spur of the moment that he'd hike fifty miles the next morning. Louis Oberdorfer, James Symington, who was Bob's administrative assistant then, and I had the misfortune of being in his office when he decided. "You're all going with me, aren't you?" he said mischievously, and there was no escape. He told his brother, but, except for the President and our wives, no one else knew we were going. Bob said he didn't want the hike to look like a publicity stunt and that it would be better if newsmen weren't around "in case some of *you* don't make it."

The next morning at 5 A.M. the three of us and David Hackett met Bob where the towpath along the old Chesapeake & Ohio Canal dips under the Chain Bridge in Washington. Our plan was to hike along the towpath toward Camp David, the Presidential retreat in Maryland, where our wives would meet us.

It was a frigid winter morning. The temperature was 20 degrees. The tree-lined towpath was packed with ice and snow.

Hackett had been a paratrooper and a member of the U.S. Olympic hockey team. Oberdorfer had been an Army artillery officer, and Symington had been a Marine. I had been in the infantry. We knew something about forced marches and wore heavy shoes and carried extra pairs of socks. Bob wore a pair of shiny oxfords. We told Bob that the sensible thing was to march at the infantry pace—106 steps a minute—for fifty minutes and then take a ten-minute rest. Bob didn't say anything, and we set out in the predawn darkness, trudging on the snow and slipping on the ice. When it came time for the first break, we sat down, but after three or four minutes Bob said, "Let's go," and that was the closest thing to a ten-minute break that we had.

The sun came out in the morning, but there were few open stretches on the towpath, so there were few places where the snow had melted. The temperature never went above 25, and it never occurred to our leader or any of us to leave the towpath and walk on a road nearby which was clear of snow.

One by one, Hackett, Oberdorfer and Symington dropped out, and by late afternoon Bob and I and his huge, overly friendly Newfoundland dog, Brumus, were hobbling adjacent to a large field. A helicopter swooped low, the pilot waved, and flew on.

"Maybe your brother is worried about you and sent a helicopter out to check on you," I said.

"No," Bob said grimly. Then he brightened: "Maybe there's a national emergency and I'll have to go back."

The helicopter made another low pass. The pilot waved. We waved back and the helicopter flew away. We plodded on, rounding a turn and saw the helicopter on the ground and two men waiting for us. They turned out to be a reporter and photographer from *Life*.

As darkness fell and the temperature dropped, my legs stiffened so that I could not continue. We had gone about thirty-five miles, not counting the slipping and sliding, according to the reckoning of a National Park Service Ranger. Bob would have completed fifty miles if he had had to crawl, and the *Life* photographer agreed to stay with him to the finish. As Bob started to leave, he bent down and whispered to me: "You're lucky, your brother isn't President of the United States."

Chapter 12

Johnson and Hoover

"THERE'S SO MUCH BITTERNESS I thought they would get one of us, but Jack, after all he'd been through, never worried about it."

Bob walked back and forth on the broad lawn behind his house.

"I'd received a letter from someone in Texas last week warning me not to let the President go to Dallas because they would kill him," he said. "I sent it to Kenny O'Donnell, but I never thought it would happen. I thought it would be me. There's been so much bitterness and hatred, and so many people who might have said something have remained silent. . . ."

His flat, drained voice trailed off. An hour earlier, the world had turned upside down. Trying to think of something comforting, I suggested that perhaps the country would unite, that people would learn from the enormity of what had happened and there would be less bitterness in the land.

"No," he said slowly, "this will make it worse."

In the numbing grief of that tragic afternoon, he could not begin to perceive how Americans would react—no one could—but he sensed that a terrible malevolence had been unleashed.

After the funeral, Bob and Ethel went to Florida for a few days, and when he returned, it was painful to see him. His eyes were haunted, his complexion ashen and his mood desolate and stoic. The center of his life had been shot away; the brother whom he idolized, to whom he had given so much and with whom he had worked so hard. For a dozen years he had been immersed in advancing his brother's career and the causes for which his brother stood, with no thought about what he would be doing at thirty-five, or forty-five, or fifty. ("I don't think about the next job," he always said. "I try to do what I'm doing now well, and if I do that, the next job will take care of itself.") Now an uncertain future faced him, suddenly, shockingly.

His friends wanted to reach out with a touch of the hand or words to ease the pain, but only Ethel, his brother and sisters and Jacqueline could bridge the gulf of grief. We could talk to him. We could discuss matters with him and he would respond, sometimes with a suggestion, sometimes asking for more details, and he strained to show interest, but it was hard, so very hard. There was the matter of his own security. Within an hour after the assassination, the Fairfax County police came without being called and took up positions around Hickory Hill. They remained until after the President's funeral, and then marshals from the District of Columbia and the Northern District of Virginia took over. A few days after returning from Florida, Bob called and asked why the marshals were still on duty. "I appreciate what they're doing, but I don't want them here any more," he said.

"It's only a precaution, Bob," I said.

"We don't need them—now," he replied.

"But you might, you have to consider that," I said. "Every marshal in the District and in northern Virginia volunteered. They can help you. They can get the children to and from school. They can be around if you or Ethel need them."

"Well, I don't want a lot of people guarding me when I go anywhere. I'm not going to change how I do things, I'll just tell you that."

"We're not asking you to. We'd just like to keep the marshals at the house for a while and with the children when they go to school."

"All right," he said resignedly. "For a few weeks, but that's all."[1]

1. Shifts of four marshals at a time remained on duty at the house until Ethel and

It was, perhaps, that he held his grief inwardly so tightly that made it so hard for others to bear. If he had only let all the dark thoughts and sorrow out, but that was not the Kennedy way. He bore it all, as Ethel would do in 1968, with taut self-control, and with his example, and thoughtfulness, consideration and, at times, cheerfulness, gave strength to his family and his friends. Many of us learned from him during that crushing time how necessary it was to function and to keep functioning.

On December 5, the day Mrs. Kennedy moved out of the White House, he wrote notes in his small, cramped handwriting on White House Stationery to many New Frontiersmen. One said:

> This is the last day in the White House and I did not want it to pass without thanking you on behalf of the President and myself for all that you have done over the past three years.
>
> > Best,
> > Bob

The next day he returned to the Department of Justice for the first time and slowly picked up the threads of his duties. He took long walks, went home for lunch and not infrequently stared bleakly out the window of his office for long, silent periods. But he took command of preparations for the impending prosecution of Hoffa for jury-tampering. (Hoffa had announced that the assassination had made Bob "just another lawyer" and had denounced his associate, Harold Gibbons, for having the flag at the Teamsters headquarters lowered to half-mast after the President died.) Bob busied himself with details for the second annual Justice Department Christmas party for seven hundred poor children.[2] The play-

---

the children moved to Hyannis Port for the summer. He did not protest, except that he refused to have any personal security. It was the only time we disobeyed him. Chief Marshal James McShane, with advice from the FBI and the Secret Service, established security around his office as long as he remained Attorney General. When he traveled, FBI agents unobtrusively accompanied him. There was no point in discussing it with him. We simply did it, and he never knew—at least he never indicated that he was aware that he was being guarded.

2. Bob cheerfully greeted the children, guided by members of the Washington Redskins, dressed as Santa Clauses, in his office. Later, he traded jokes with Carol Channing when all the children gathered in the Great Hall of the department. The

field that he was having built where impounded cars had been parked was rushed to completion and he dedicated it—the John F. Kennedy Playfield.

A few days later, he stopped by a Christmas party that Mary McGrory, the Washington *Evening Star* columnist, was having in a restaurant for children from an orphanage. He had been there about ten minutes when in the midst of all the laughter and gaiety, a small Negro boy, about six years old, ran toward him and said solemnly: "Your brother is dead!" The laughing voices hushed and the room became awkwardly silent. The boy looked frightened and began to cry. Bob knelt and drew him in his arms, hugged him and said gently: "That's all right. I have another."

In mid-January, President Johnson dispatched Bob to the Orient to try to dissuade Indonesian President Sukarno from carrying out his announced determination to "crush" the new Federation of Malaysia, which shares a common border with Indonesia on the large island of Borneo. Averell Harriman, then Under Secretary of State, suggested sending Bob. A warm, mutual respect had developed between them, and Harriman wanted to involve Bob in new interests to help him emerge from the gloom, but Harriman also knew that Bob had a good personal rapport with Sukarno. Secretary of State Dean Rusk concurred and Johnson was not opposed. However, before he had made a decision, the Washington *Post* learned about the projected trip. The President felt the news leak forced his hand, that he now would have more to lose than gain if he did not send Bob and was annoyed. So the trip began under circumstances that were somewhat ambiguous, but it was generally interpreted as signaling President Johnson's concern for Bob and his desire to keep him involved in major decision-making.

With the exception of our Ambassador to Indonesia, Howard T.

---

year before he had decided a few days before the party that it would be nice to have horse-drawn sleighs to give the children rides. There had been no snow and no snow was forecast. Despite that, the day of the party, there was snow in the courtyard, and the Redskins, dressed as Santa Clauses, drove three sleighs. During the night, an ice company had blown five inches of artificial snow on the roadway. The party was continued annually by Attorneys General Katzenbach and Ramsey Clark.

Jones, no high American official had as good a rapport with Sukarno as Bob. Two years earlier Bob had negotiated with the mercurial, swashbuckling father of Indonesian independence when he threatened to go to war with the Dutch over possession of West New Guinea, populated by 700,000 primitive Papuans. Though they had talked sternly to each other, Sukarno apparently had enjoyed Bob's candor and Ethel's vivaciousness, and they had gotten on well. At a critical time, Bob had been an effective catalyst in persuading Sukarno and the Dutch to take the first steps which resulted six months later in a peaceful settlement through the United Nations. Though the settlement, giving West New Guinea to Indonesia, drew criticism at home and in Western Europe as an American sellout to Sukarno—and some of it was directed at Bob personally —a war, which neither country wanted, was averted.

Now another war threatened. Malaysia had been formed in September of the former British territories of Malaya, Singapore, Sarawak and North Borneo and given membership in the British Commonwealth. Sukarno viewed the continued presence of British troops as a remnant of colonialism and saw Malaysia as an obstacle to Indonesia's ambitions for big-power greatness. Border fighting was on the increase in Borneo as Indonesian guerrillas clashed with British and Malaysian troops. The Philippines also were being drawn in since President Diosdado Macapagal, apprehensive of Sukarno and unsure about Malaysia, had staked a claim to North Borneo.

Sukarno was on a visit to Japan and agreed to meet Bob there. If their discussions indicated any prospect that the controversy could be settled through negotiations, Bob would then go to Manila and Kuala Lumpur to sound out the Filipino and Malaysian leaders. President Johnson provided an Air Force B-52, equipped with bunks, comfortable seats and working space, and Bob, accompanied by Ethel, flew to Tokyo with a stop in Anchorage for refueling.

Before meeting with Sukarno, Bob made a sentimental visit to Waseda University and for the first time began to realize the magnitude of admiration for President Kennedy that existed overseas. In 1962 at Waseda about two hundred ultraleftist students had tried to heckle Bob off the stage. He had won wide respect in Japan for standing up to the agitators by inviting the noisiest of them to come up to the lectern and state his complaints directly to his face.[3] Upon his return, ten thousand students, huddled under umbrellas in a soft rain, cheered him mightily.

Tears were in his eyes and in the eyes of many of the Japanese as he spoke, without a text, about all the President had hoped to accomplish, and said that the President had looked forward to visiting Japan that spring.

"He was not only President of one nation," Bob concluded, "he was president of young people around the world. If President Kennedy's life and death are to mean anything, we young people must work harder for a better life for all the people in the world."

It was a moment to remember. Shrill, frenzied cheers reverberated against the walls. The students crushed forward to touch Bob and shake his hand.

He met with Sukarno the next day and his message was essentially simple: "Why not negotiate? If it doesn't work out, you can always go back to shooting and killing."

Sukarno was interested. They met the next morning and agreed to meet again in five days in Djakarta. Meanwhile, Bob would go to the Philippines to meet with President Macapagal and to Malaysia to see Prime Minister Tengku Abdul Rahman. Before flying to Manila, he spent a grueling day visiting American and South Korean troops on the 38th parallel in Korea.

Again in the Philippines, the reservoir of respect for President Kennedy among young people overwhelmed him. As he arrived at the University of the Philippines to speak and receive an honorary degree, hundreds of cheering students surrounded his car. It was

3. Reaction in the United States was mixed. John Lindsay, then a New York Congressman, wrote to Secretary of State Dean Rusk questioning "whether it is necessary for you and your office to be either burdened or embarrassed by freewheeling foreign missions on the part of highly placed amateurs." But another Republican—Richard Nixon—said: "In looking at Robert Kennedy, you have here a man who, except for lack of experience which he is now gaining, has many of the qualifications that would make him a very effective leader in the field of foreign policy. He's tough-minded, he's quick, he's intelligent. He is one who has a tremendous will to win."

necessary for his aides and Filipino detectives to walk alongside his car to clear a path and prevent someone from being run over. Now, with a prepared text, he told the students:

> President Kennedy had a particularly close relationship with young people. He felt that the real answer to the problems around the globe was the educated man . . . the ones who actively become involved in the work and the operations of the community and the country. . . .
>
> There is no question that in these dangerous days for all of us, that this planet has grown so small that we are as one. And that's what President Kennedy offered really, and what he fought for, what he attempted to do. . . .
>
> We can't leave it to others. We must participate ourselves. It is not sufficient just being against, just saying, "Well, I don't think I like the way things are going." We have a responsibility to offer an alternative, to know what we are talking about, to think of our ideals and know what's behind them. . . .
>
> So, if there is anything that can be gained, not just for the people of my own country in the United States, but really the people all over the world, and particularly the young people, by the life and the death of President Kennedy, it's the fact that *we must participate.*

Again the ovation was thunderous and emotional. Again, he stood motionless, smiling sadly. Later, some writers would refer to that speech and the one at Waseda as the time Bob discovered the depth of feelings others had for his brother and began to turn it to himself. They were not only harsh but inaccurate. He was speaking from his heart, not his mind, groping to find some meaning to the President's death, trying to put it into words. He had no idea what he would do with his life. He talked about going to a university or just going away for a while. He didn't know.

Bob was able to patch together a shaky agreement for a cease-fire and negotiations to settle the border dispute. The Thais offered Bangkok as a neutral site for the negotiations, and after meeting in Bangkok with the Thais and with Ambassador Jones and our ambassadors to the Philippines and Malaysia, William E. Stevenson and James Bell, Bob flew to Great Britain to report to a skeptical British Government.

The plane's crew attempted to fly nonstop from Bangkok to London, but ran short of fuel and landed at an American air base near Évreux, France. It was midmorning. Rather than wait while the plane took on fuel, Bob wanted to see the city. Bob and Ethel and the ten newsmen who were traveling with them piled into cars and sped to Évreux. There was a round of drinks in a café, a quick walk and brief time for shopping. It was as if someone had descended from outer space. The townspeople gaped, and then when they decided it really was President Kennedy's brother, they nodded respectfully or came forward to shake his hand. Philip Scheffler, a high-spirited CBS newsman, came out of a department store with a stack of berets and clamped one on Bob's head; he wore it jauntily.

It had been a good trip—a trip with a purpose and long hours of work and many good times. Besides Scheffler, warmhearted Walter Dumbrow, Bob's favorite TV cameraman, Peter Maas of the *Saturday Evening Post,* an old friend, and several other newsmen and Ethel kept the atmosphere aboard the plane lively. And then he had to face going home, back to a Washington without John Kennedy.

When he went to the White House to report to the President, instead of briefing LBJ at a private meeting, he was required to brief him in the presence of ranking members of the Senate Foreign Relations and Armed Services Committees. He thought he had made a start in getting the dispute out of the jungle and to the conference table, even though Sukarno had raised the cry of "Crush Malaysia" again. But the State Department showed little interest in his report or his recommendations, and President Johnson did not talk to him about the controversy again, although it continued to smolder and jungle-fighting broke out sporadically. The President may have been sincere in giving Bob the mission to help him out of the doldrums, but Bob concluded otherwise.

Anyone who writes with certainty about Bob's relationship with Lyndon Johnson does so at his own risk. I would not attempt to do so. There are no balanced views, no neutral observers—only partisans. There is only one undisputed fact about their relationship: they mistrusted each other almost from the beginning, and their mistrust turned to bitter enmity at the end.

The unknown factors, the questions, are endless. In those confused, turbulent hours after John Kennedy offered the Vice Presidential nomination to Johnson, did Bob seek to rescind the invitation or was he only attempting to warn LBJ that he might face a sharp liberal-labor floor fight? Was it Vice President Johnson's reluctance to push himself forward or was it Attorney General Kennedy's indifference to the Vice President's opinions that widened the gulf between them? After the assassination, did President Johnson make a sincere effort to ease Bob's sorrow and win his allegiance—certainly he made some moves in that direction—or, knowing that he could never put his brand on Bob, did he make a show of sympathy while scheming to send Bob into political limbo? And on and on. It is not easy to untangle the facts, and it never will be. Events, time and circumstances forced them apart and then drew them into lethal conflict as much as or more than their differences in age, temperament, character and background. As a partisan on the Kennedy side, I can only set down what I remember of what I observed and of what Bob told me, and I do so now with no disrespect for Johnson and not without some comprehension of the terrible problems he faced immediately following the assassination and in the years of his Presidency.

It was after Bob returned from his trip and began to emerge from his mood of desolation—as events of a Presidential election year began their inexorable course—that the strains of their relationship began to show.

The new year had begun with an outward display of harmony. In issuing a Justice Department report detailing the growing success of the federal effort against organized crime and racketeering,[4] the President had praised Bob's leadership and expressed his appreciation for it. On January 2 he sent Bob the following telegram:

---

4. The report demonstrated with the following statistics on indictments and convictions of Mafia leaders and racketeers that considerable progress was being made:

	1960	1961	1962	1963
Individuals Indicted	49	121	350	615
Individuals Convicted	45	73	138	288

(TL) GOVT NL PD   DH AUSTIN TEX

HONORABLE ROBERT F KENNEDY, THE ATTORNEY GENERAL
WASHDC

I KNOW HOW HARD THE PAST SIX WEEKS HAVE BEEN FOR YOU. UNDER THE MOST
TRYING CIRCUMSTANCES YOUR FIRST THOUGHTS HAVE BEEN FOR YOUR COUNTRY.
YOUR BROTHER WOULD HAVE BEEN VERY PROUD OF THE STRENGTH YOU HAVE
SHOWN. AS THE NEW YEAR BEGINS, I RESOLVE TO DO MY BEST TO FULFILL HIS TRUST
IN ME. I WILL NEED YOUR COUNSEL AND SUPPORT.

LYNDON B. JOHNSON

904A EST JAN 2 64

Then came the assignment in Asia, which seemed to indicate that
Johnson was achieving a working relationship with the Kennedys,
but which left Bob with a bitter taste. After the less-than-private
meeting that he had with the President upon his return, Bob spoke
with LBJ infrequently and saw him less. However, there remained
a direct channel of communication between them in the person of
Kenneth O'Donnell, who stayed on the White House staff and who
was tough-minded and pragmatic and had a gift for speaking candidly.

After the assassination, even before President Kennedy was
buried, there had been printed speculation about Bob's future. Most
of it suggested that he would be Johnson's running mate or return
to Massachusetts to seek the governorship. But as February approached, the only decision that he had made was that he wanted
somehow to remain in public service and carry on his brother's
work. Meanwhile, he planned to continue as Attorney General as
long as LBJ wanted him. He was as aware as anyone that a Presidential candidate picks his own running mate. He felt it highly unlikely
that Johnson would choose him, unless the polls were running
against the Democrats. He planned not to make any decision, do
anything or say anything for several months, at least. But a stirring
of open support in New Hampshire as that first of the nation's
Presidential primary elections neared forced him to change his
plans and deepened his breach with Johnson.

When Kennedy-for-Vice President clubs first appeared in New

Hampshire and then spread throughout the state, there was consternation in the White House. When Paul Corbin, Bob's eyes and ears on the Democratic National Committee, became involved, there was deep suspicion in the White House that Bob was making his move. The truth was that Corbin was acting on his own. A blunt, tactless man, Corbin had joined the Kennedys in the Wisconsin primary, and was an anathema not only to the Johnson forces but also to many persons close to President Kennedy and Bob. But he had proved himself to Bob on innumerable occasions to be a gutsy political infighter, and so he was given a position on the National Committee and kept there despite repeated protests from some of President Kennedy's advisers. In return, Corbin gave Bob dogged loyalty that knew no bounds, and that was the trouble. When he took a hand in the New Hampshire primary, he thought he was helping Bob.

On the evening of February 11, President Johnson called Bob to notify him that Corbin was being fired from the committee. Bob remonstrated with the President and said repeatedly that Corbin was "harmless." But LBJ said that Corbin had become "quite a problem" because he was always boosting Bob wherever he went. LBJ said he wanted no one on the committee to take sides in the selection of his running mate. Then he went on to explain that he had sent Bob to Indonesia only because he "had to keep things equal" among those who were in the running for Vice President.

"Don't ever do a favor for me again!" Bob flared, ending the conversation. He stood at the window silently staring into the night for four or five minutes. Then, as he collected some papers to put in his briefcase, he said to me: "I'll tell you one thing, this relationship can't last much longer."

The firing of Corbin had no effect on the Kennedy supporters in New Hampshire, and as their write-in effort gained momentum, there was danger that Bob would draw more votes than the President, which, under the circumstances, would have been a distinct embarrassment for both. Through O'Donnell, Bob offered to issue a statement disavowing the campaign, but the word came back from the White House not to do anything. Support for Bob continued to mount, and five days before the election Bob, now plainly worried that the campaign was getting out of hand, phoned O'Donnell again, and this time the instructions were to put out a statement. It went through several drafts.

The first draft:

> I am very flattered by indications that some of the Democrats of New Hampshire are interested in me as Vice Presidential candidate on the Democratic ticket this fall.
>
> However, the choice of the Vice Presidential candidate will be made, as it should be made, by the Democratic Convention in August guided by the wishes of President Johnson.
>
> Since I am not seeking this nomination, I would appreciate it if the voters in the New Hampshire primary did not write in my name.

Bob decided it was too formal and too pompous. He drew a circle around the phrase "Since I am not seeking this nomination," but it was included in a second draft, which was as follows:

> There have been a number of inquiries about the Attorney General's views on the campaign to write in his name for the Office of Vice President in the primary election in New Hampshire next week.
>
> The Attorney General is not seeking the nomination for Vice President. As he has said, he intends to remain with the Justice Department through November and he has not yet decided what he will do after the election. He has made it clear that the choice of the Democratic nominee for Vice President will be made as it should be made, by the Democratic Convention in August, guided by the wishes of President Johnson and that President Johnson should be free to select his own running mate.
>
> For these reasons, the Attorney General has not been in touch with anyone in New Hampshire or taken any action to encourage the campaign. In fact, he has discouraged any efforts on his behalf.

Bob crossed out the phrase "The Attorney General is not seeking the nomination for Vice President," rewrote the second paragraph, worked over the final paragraph and then eliminated it. The statement which was issued was brief and to the point:

> The Attorney General has said that the choice of the Democratic nominee for Vice President will be made, and should be made, by the Democratic Convention in August, guided by the wishes of President Johnson and that President Johnson should be free to select his own running mate.

The Attorney General, therefore, wishes to discourage any efforts on his behalf in New Hampshire, or elsewhere.

The statement, plus belated efforts by New Hampshire Democratic leaders to turn out the vote for the President, ameliorated the situation for the moment. LBJ polled 29,630 votes; Bob received 25,861.

But the stirring in New Hampshire, the firing of Corbin, Bob's statement and the off-the-record comments emanating from the White House and from Kennedy loyalists in Washington were all grist for the speculation mill. Kennedy-for-Vice President movements started up in New York, New Jersey, Wisconsin and several other states. Almost every day brought a visit or phone calls from politicians friendly to Bob, urging him to give some indication that he would accept the Vice Presidential nomination if it was offered. He went with Jacqueline Kennedy to visit General Douglas MacArthur[5] in New York, and as they were leaving, after MacArthur had regaled them with stories about his career, the old General grabbed Bob's arm and drew him aside.

"Take it!" MacArthur said in his deep, authoritative voice. Bob hesitated, and MacArthur said: "Take it. He won't live. He gambled

---

5. Mrs. Kennedy and Bob called on MacArthur to thank him for his expressions of sympathy when the President died and also to thank him on behalf of the President for successfully negotiating a truce between the Amateur Athletic Union and the National Collegiate Athletic Association. The two organizations have quarreled for years over the sanctioning of athletic events, particularly track meets. In 1963 the dispute threatened to cripple the American team in the 1964 Olympic Games in Tokyo. The State Department tried to arbitrate and failed and then asked Bob to intercede. He thought he had achieved a moratorium until after the games, but it fell apart in a few days. Then he sought advice from Colonel Earl (Red) Blaik, the former Army football coach, who was then head of the Avco Corporation. Blaik suggested that MacArthur might be prevailed upon to perform one more service for his country if the President asked him. JFK did and MacArthur assembled the feuding AAU and NCAA representatives in his apartment in the Waldorf Towers. The meeting began in the morning, continued through the afternoon without a break for lunch, and at 8 P.M. several of the athletic officials, hungry and out of patience, announced they were leaving to have dinner. "Gentlemen," MacArthur commanded, rising from his chair, "sit down! You do not walk out on the President of the United States!" The men returned meekly to their seats. MacArthur took a proposed settlement from his pocket for the first time, and the weary, hungry officials agreed to his terms. It held through the games, but shortly thereafter the AAU and the NCAA reopened the dispute, and it still is basically unresolved.

on your brother and won. You gamble on him and you'll win!"[6]

During this period a great amount of backbiting and rumor-peddling fed the mistrust of both President Johnson and Bob. It did not arise from friction or misunderstanding between Bob's staff and the new men Johnson brought into the White House. The Johnson men with whom we dealt most often—Walter Jenkins, who was the closest to LBJ, Jack Valenti, Bill D. Moyers and George Reedy—were able and cooperative and often went out of their way to be solicitous of Bob and Ethel. The rumors and tales were spread by other persons, some within the government and some outside. Some meant well. Some were malicious, and some sought to curry favor with the President or Bob.

How much effect it all had on either man is problematical, but it didn't help. It appeared to have more effect on the President than on Bob—at least outwardly. Bob, by nature and through his training as an investigator, tended to be skeptical of everything he heard until he'd had a chance to check. With O'Donnell and Lawrence F. O'Brien[7] in the White House and with close connections with most key men in the government, Bob had little difficulty in determining whether a report was fact or gossip. President Johnson, by nature and through experience, also tended to be suspicious. He was particularly so of the Kennedys for outmaneuvering him in 1960. Thus, mistrustful, he fumed and let his suspicions run, especially when some of the tales came from knowledgeable sources like the FBI.

A case in point was a report that grew incredibly from an episode at a party given February 6 to honor John R. Reilly, the evening before he was to become a member of the Federal Trade Commission. Reilly, an attorney with a sharp political mind, had served in the Justice Department as head of the Office of U. S. Attorneys. He often traveled with Bob and also was a close friend of O'Donnell.

---

6. MacArthur died five weeks later. Bob represented President Johnson at MacArthur's burial rites in Norfolk, Virginia.

7. Like O'Donnell, O'Brien was an original member of the group that was most instrumental in securing President Kennedy's nomination and election. During the Kennedy Administration he served as special assistant to the President in charge of liaison with Congress. He continued in that responsibility until August 1965, when President Johnson appointed him Postmaster General.

One of President Kennedy's last appointments was to name Reilly to the FTC, and it was pending in the Senate when President Johnson took office. As a gesture to Bob and O'Donnell, LBJ did not withdraw it, and Reilly subsequently was confirmed.

Myles Lord, the U.S. Attorney in Minneapolis, was in Washington on business, and attended the party, which was held in a Washington restaurant. Reilly had many friends in Washington, and the party was convivial, lasting well after midnight. When Lord returned to Minneapolis, he told friends something that burgeoned into an outlandish story. The story was that a number of Bob's aides, including Nicholas Katzenbach, Louis Oberdorfer, Herbert J. Miller, Jr., and I, had made plans at the party to get the Presidential nomination for Bob. It was ludicrous and untrue.

It is standard procedure in the FBI for the special agents in charge of FBI offices around the country to report to J. Edgar Hoover intelligence not necessarily having to do with national security or law enforcement but which nevertheless may be of special interest to him. The story reached the ears of the special agent in charge of the FBI office in Minneapolis, who duly forwarded it to Washington, and, without any attempt being made to verify its accuracy, a report was sent to the White House. President Johnson complained bitterly to O'Donnell, and despite O'Donnell's assurances that the report was untrue, the President was furious. Bob was amazed that President Johnson would put any credence in such a report, and of course he was miffed at the FBI.

There was no way of knowing for certain whether Hoover authorized sending the report to the President. C. D. DeLoach, an assistant FBI director who was the Bureau's liaison with the White House, denied that the FBI was involved. But O'Donnell was certain that the report had emanated from the FBI, and the upshot was that not only was the gulf between the President and Bob widened a notch, but relations between Hoover and Bob, which had turned from correct to icy after the assassination, were strained further.

It is necessary to digress briefly, for while the tense rivalry between President Johnson and Bob was being waged in the highest councils of the government and was widely reported by the news media, an even more internecine drama was being enacted between Bob and Hoover largely outside the public's view. The latter was much more difficult for Bob to accept.

Bob understood and sympathized to some degree with Johnson's position—his need to be President in his own right and to establish himself without alienating the substantial Kennedy faction in the Democratic Party. He knew that the President would select his own running mate and that it most likely would not be him. He also understood that there had been a radical reduction in his power, that Hoover and other long-time civil servants would go to where the power was. He was prepared for that. What he was not prepared for, and what he could not forgive, was the extreme coolness with which Hoover treated him personally, practically overnight.

Again, one must read with the understanding that I was not an impartial observer. However, it is relevant to point out that I came to the Justice Department with considerable respect for the FBI and a good deal of regard for Hoover. My opinion was formed not so much by what I had read as by observing the FBI in action, for during the fourteen years I was a reporter in Seattle I had worked closely many times with Hoover's men. But like many persons who come from civilian life to the Justice Department thinking nothing but the best about the FBI, seeing Hoover at close range was a revealing and ultimately embittering experience. Despite that, when I left the Department after almost four years, my esteem for the men of the FBI and my respect for the Bureau's capabilities were largely intact. Nor was I inclined to think less highly of many of Hoover's accomplishments: his exceptional ability as an organizer and administrator, the many innovations which the FBI had devised to improve law enforcement, and the dedication which he had instilled in the Bureau. The disenchantment was caused by observing his stiff authoritarianism—particularly the devilish internal inspection system which, as Hoover aged, had become increasingly oppressive to the agents—and his inability to get along with men who honestly disagreed with his views; and finally by his treatment of Bob after the assassination, which seemed to me to be cruel.

It would be an oversimplification to ascribe the deterioration in the relationship between Bob and Hoover to a clash of personalities or to differences of opinion—though these were part of it. A major element was Hoover's full understanding of President Johnson's feelings toward Bob and vice versa. Hoover had survived in Washington through six changes of Administration, and his instincts for entrenching himself with the new men of power were unerring. There were few wry remarks around the Department in the weeks immediately following President Kennedy's death, but one—spoken with traces of bitterness—was that Hoover began moving with the change of power at 1:10 P.M. The President was shot at 1 P.M. Washington time and was pronounced dead a half-hour later. At any rate, Hoover did move extremely rapidly to show President Johnson, whom he had known many years, where his loyalties were. After November 22, Hoover dealt directly with the White House, ignoring the Attorney General's office as he pleased. One incident with which I was familiar had to do with the FBI's first report on its investigation of the assassination. The Warren Commission had been formed and Chief Justice Warren had requested that the report not be made public until the commission had an opportunity to examine it. Deputy Attorney General Katzenbach transmitted the order to Hoover, but within a few hours the report was leaked to several newsmen. All the indications were that it had been done by Hoover's office.

Possibly Hoover felt that his loyalty to the new President had to be untainted by any apparent feeling for Bob. However, many important civil servants in Washington did not think that it would injure their careers to be solicitous of Bob as he struggled with his grief, and they helped him with simple acts of thoughtfulness. One also could not help but note that James Bennett, Director of the Bureau of Prisons, and Ray Farrell, Commissioner of Immigration —both of them, like Hoover, heads of divisions of the Department of Justice—went out of their way repeatedly to assist Bob in the weeks after the President's death. Hoover did nothing.

But one would have to probe the deepest recesses of Hoover's personality to understand his actions fully. No doubt he regarded

Bob and those of us whom Bob brought to the Department as Johnnies-come-lately in the field of law enforcement. However, Bob had worked closely with the FBI during the labor rackets investigation, and there was a firm basis for mutual respect. Hoover had been one of the persons Bob had consulted before agreeing to become Attorney General, and Hoover had urged him to accept. Certainly, in 1960 Bob respected Hoover, and it was mainly at Bob's urging that the first appointments that President-elect Kennedy announced were that Hoover and Allen Dulles, Director of the CIA, would be retained.

No doubt Hoover chafed under the circumstances that made the Attorney General the dominant figure in the Justice Department, in *fact* as well as in name, for the first time in many years. Some of Bob's informality may have grated on Hoover. Unquestionably, Hoover felt it was an intrusion on his prerogatives when the Office of Public Information did not clear his speeches and statements automatically—as had been the Department's time-honored custom —but occasionally required him to make changes in the interest of accuracy or Administration policy. But there was no estrangement while President Kennedy was in office. They were on a first-name basis—Bob and Edgar—and they conferred frequently. Bob defended Hoover when there was public criticism of him. He arranged for Hoover to have lunch at the White House alone with the President on several occasions.

Furthermore, Bob took a deep interest in the work of the FBI— more so than any of his predecessors—particularly in its investigations of organized crime. He visited FBI field offices whenever he traveled. He did not go just to shake hands, but to be briefed and to question agents about their work. He went to the New York office about every six months for lengthy, detailed discussions of organized crime and national security matters. He held similar meetings in Chicago and Los Angeles almost as regularly. Because he was so knowledgeable and concerned about organized crime and because he was the first Attorney General to visit most of the field offices, he raised FBI morale and was highly respected by many agents. How Hoover felt about this was never entirely clear.

While President Kennedy was in office, there were, of course, many disagreements between Bob and Hoover, some minor, some major. Bob regarded them as all part of a day's work. Later, it was evident that Hoover stored his grievances and bided his time, but it would be hard to know for certain now what disturbed him the most, for he never showed his displeasure directly. He did, on occasion, show it indirectly and sometimes in a most complicated way.

The FBI did not concern itself greatly with organized crime until Bob became Attorney General. The man who resurrected the Bureau from the Teapot Dome scandal of the early 1920's, who set new standards for law enforcement and led the FBI brilliantly in tracking down gangsters, kidnapers and bank robbers in the 1930's and in combating foreign espionage and Communist subversion in the 1940's, virtually ignored law enforcement's most difficult problem of the 1950's—the steady expansion of organized crime's power and wealth.

Once the FBI began paying attention to organized crime, under Bob's prodding, it moved with all its legendary vigor and efficiency. Between January 1961 and August 1964, when Bob resigned as Attorney General, the FBI amassed an impressive amount of accurate information about the scope of organized crime and the persons involved in it. Later it developed that a major part of its intelligence had been gathered through the extensive tapping of telephones and use of electronic listening devices, apparently to make up in a hurry for the years when the FBI considered organized crime outside its interest. Eavesdropping is illegal. The FBI had authority, under an Executive Order issued in 1940 by President Franklin D. Roosevelt, to tap telephones, with the written permission of the Attorney General, in national security cases.

As more and more evidence dribbled out in 1964, '65 and '66 that the FBI had been bugging in criminal investigations and the Bureau came under criticism, Hoover sought to shift the responsibility to Bob. This brought their strained relationship out from behind the scenes for the first time. Hoover asserted that Bob not only authorized the bugging but insisted upon it. Bob replied that Hoover "apparently has been misinformed" and said that he had neither authorized it nor was aware that it was being done. The country was confronted, as the columnist Charles Bartlett wrote, with the fact that "Kennedy's deep aversion to falsehood and Hoover's integrity make it almost impossible to believe that either man is misrepresenting his own knowledge of the facts."

Some degree of ambiguity in their relationship was partly responsible, for they dealt in many matters, particularly involving organized crime, through Assistant Director Courtney Evans. Hoover may have believed that Bob had been apprised of the Bureau's intention to bug and had tacitly approved. But the truth was that, though Bob should have known and might have deduced that the FBI was bugging, he didn't. When the facts about the bugging began to come out, Hoover never took the trouble to discuss the problem with Bob, but moved to clear himself of any responsibility.

For the record, I accompanied Bob to every briefing on organized crime that he received at the FBI field offices. On two occasions, once in New York and once in Chicago, recordings of hoodlum conversations were played for him. In both instances the clear impression we received was that the FBI had obtained the recordings from local law enforcement sources. Often after one of these briefings, Bob would comment on the tremendous amount of intelligence the FBI was obtaining. Perhaps we were naïve not to suspect that taps and bugs were being used, and when the controversy broke, Bob thought we had been.

A more neutral comment on the subject, and one with considerable insight, was made by William Hundley in December 1966, several days after Hoover blamed Bob publicly for authorizing the eavesdropping. Hundley served in the Organized Crime and Racketeering Section of the Criminal Division under four Attorneys General from 1954 to 1966.

"Sure, I knew for years that the FBI was making widespread use of electronic bugs in organized crime investigations," he said. "But the top brass of the Bureau would flat-out lie to me, denying it, whenever I officially asked about it.

"And by '61 and '62, when I'd been running the Organized Crime

Section for three or four years, I had learned about the bugs with certainty. But when the Bureau officially kept lying to me about their use, denying it, I figured that this was obviously so delicate that it must be something that was just between the AG and the Director, as it is with national security wiretaps. So I never talked about it."

Hundley said he did not discuss the matter with Bob until he visited him in his Senate office in 1966, and he related the following conversation.

"Bob said to me, 'Say, did you know that the FBI had been using bugs?' and I said, 'Sure, I knew,' and he said, 'Well, why the devil didn't you tell me?' And I explained to him that I assumed that he knew all along."[8]

Hoover was defensive about the fact that until the spring of 1961 the FBI had never admitted that the Mafia existed. The following year, the clinching evidence, if any was needed, was supplied by Joseph Valachi, a graying member of one of New York City's five Mafia family groups, who was in the Federal Penitentiary in Atlanta for trafficking in heroin. Convinced that he had been marked for execution by the Mafia, which suspected him of being an informer (wrongfully, he would insist), Valachi turned to the Bureau of Narcotics in a desperate attempt to save his life.[9] Later, in lengthy, skillful questioning by FBI Special Agent James P. Flynn, Valachi unfolded the full story of his thirty-three years as a close associate of the Mafia chieftain, Vito Genovese. He provided names and amazing detail and earned the distinction of being the first member of the Mafia to break its code of secrecy, revealing its structure and its inner secrets to the law.

8. The most celebrated case of wiretapping occurred when in October 1963 Bob authorized the FBI to tap Dr. Martin Luther King's telephone in Atlanta. The FBI had said that King was continuing an association with a man who the Bureau said was an important American Communist. A full, and in my opinion fair, account of this episode appeared in an article by Victor S. Navasky in the *Atlantic Monthly*, November, 1970.

9. "If I was killed in Atlanta, I would have died branded as a rat anyway without doing anything wrong. So what did I have to lose?" Valachi said in explaining to Peter Maas why he had talked. A revealing account of Valachi's story is detailed in Maas's book *The Valachi Papers*.

After Valachi's information had been carefully checked, the Justice Department debated whether to make it public. Valachi had volunteered to testify before a Congressional committee, and Senator McClellan was anxious to have him as a witness. Valachi's mass of information was so detailed and so harsh that Bob thought it should be disclosed in the hope that it would jolt public apathy and result in more vigorous support for law enforcement in dealing with organized crime. Also, it would show graphically that the Administration's efforts to combat organized crime were getting results. Herbert J. Miller, Jr., head of the Criminal Division, and William Hundley, now chief of the Organized Crime and Racketeering Section, agreed. The only question was whether disclosure that Valachi had turned informer would jeopardize the FBI's ability to develop other informants, particularly if there was a prospect that a Mafioso who gave information to the FBI might find himself appearing in public before a Senate committee.

Miller, Hundley and I put the question to two assistant directors of the FBI. Thus Hoover had the opportunity—and grounds that were unassailable—to block Valachi's testimony or any public release of his information. He chose not to object.

When he didn't, we arranged for Miriam Ottenberg of the Washington *Evening Star* and Maas, writing for the *Saturday Evening Post*, to get the story exclusively. In September 1963, several weeks after their stories were published, Valachi testified before the McClellan Committee.

Hoover in his monthly message "to all law enforcement officials" in an edition of the *FBI Bulletin*, a monthly publication, wrote about the crime syndicate and said, "Recent disclosures in the fight against organized crime serve in a larger sense to magnify the enormous task which lies ahead." The meaning seemed clear enough: that Valachi's disclosures had revealed the viciousness of the syndicate and highlighted the difficulties law enforcement faced in coping with it. However, Joseph E. Mohbat, who covered the Attorney General's office and the FBI for the Associated Press, reported that the statement indicated Hoover was critical of the decision to surface Valachi and interpreted the word "magnify" as meaning

Hoover believed the disclosures would handicap law enforcement.

Mohbat's story put Hoover in disagreement with Bob and therefore was printed widely and broadcast on radio and television. We pressed Hoover to issue a clarifying statement. Was he critical or wasn't he? He refused, saying that the article spoke for itself. It seemed so important then and seems so petty now. However, having had the last word on whether Valachi's story would be revealed, Hoover's refusal to speak out was, to say the least, a contrast with Bob's willingness to assume responsibility when the FBI agents awakened the reporters in the steel crisis.

So Hoover had his catalogue of complaints, and one must conclude that he grew to resent Bob very much. After Bob returned to the Department following the assassination, he talked by phone with Hoover occasionally on business and Hoover came to Bob's office at least once. That was when Bob had a small party to give the members of his staff gold cuff links, engraved with the Department of Justice seal and Bob's initials and those of the recipient. He had intended to give them as Christmas presents and had ordered a set for Hoover. With the change in their relationship, Bob debated whether to invite Hoover, but decided to do so. Hoover came and accepted his gift.[10] Thereafter they communicated only when necessary. Hoover was either unwilling or incapable of showing any compassion for Bob. But it was not that, or that Hoover bypassed him as soon as President Kennedy died, or that messages like the one about Reilly's party kept going to the White House, that made the gulf between them unbridgeable. Bob formed his final judgment of Hoover on the basis of the wiretapping and electronic eavesdropping dispute and a series of other similar incidents.

One evening after Bob had been elected Senator, he had dinner with Burke Marshall, Louis Oberdorfer and me. Hoover's name

10. One of the men in law enforcement most detested by Hoover was the blunt, outspoken Police Chief of Los Angeles, William Parker, who never hesitated to criticize the FBI when he disagreed with it. Hoover's dislike for Parker provided a memorable vignette at the party. Ethel Kennedy maneuvered Hoover against a wall and then said demurely, "Don't you think Chief Parker is a wonderful man? Don't you think that if you ever retired, he'd be the man to replace you?" Hoover reddened slightly and replied meekly, "Yes, Ethel."

came up in conversation, and in the discussion that followed we concluded that the most scathing thing we could say about him was that after working at the top level in the Department of Justice we could no longer believe him.

By mid-March, Bob was learning to live with the disabling loss of his brother. The Asian trip had lifted his morale despite its inconclusive ending. And despite his fragile relations with President Johnson and his troubles with Hoover, he seemed more and more like his old self as he took renewed interest in the work of the Department, particularly in the Hoffa jury-tampering trial[11] and in the progress of the Civil Rights Bill. But just below the surface one often saw signs of a new somberness and fatalism, caused not only by the trauma of his brother's death, but also by the realization that any decision he would make about his future depended on events beyond his control. He still was at loose ends about what he was going to do and still talked about taking a year off and going abroad with his family. However, the first time he ventured before a large public gathering in the United States, he was moved irrevocably to remain in public service, for, as in Japan and the Philippines, he again experienced an overwhelming demonstration of the love for President Kennedy as well as concrete signs that he stood well with the people in his own right.

At the urging of Representative Daniel J. Flood of Pennsylvania, Bob accepted, somewhat hesitatingly, an invitation to make a St. Patrick's Day speech in Scranton. The original plan was that he would make only the speech, staying briefly in the city. However, after he agreed to go, other invitations came from the area and the trip developed into a frenzied, emotional, seven-hour visit with full political-campaign trappings.

When the *Caroline* touched down at Scranton–Wilkes-Barre Airport on a gray afternoon, March 17, more than two thousand people, most of them young, broke through police lines and crowded

---

11. Hoffa was convicted on March 4 on two of three counts of jury-tampering. Shortly thereafter, he went on trial in Chicago on charges of defrauding the Teamsters Central States, Southeast, Southwest Pension Fund and again was found guilty.

around Bob so tightly—jumping, screaming, laughing as they tried to touch him—that he could not move from the bottom of the ramp until police rescued him. He officiated at ground-breaking ceremonies for the new John F. Kennedy Elementary School and drove to nearby Yatesville to speak briefly at a St. Patrick's Day dinner. As he was driven back to Scranton, ten thousand persons stood along the road in a heavy, wet snowfall to catch a glimpse of him in the darkness. Frequently, he stopped his car to get out and shake hands with well-wishers huddling under umbrellas. It was Bob's first visit to Scranton, but "he was welcomed like a returning hero," a local newsman reported. The crowd around the Casey Hotel, where he was to speak, tore heavy doors from their hinges as they crushed around him to shake his hand and touch him. The speech that night was one of the most difficult he ever made.

He had drafted a sentimental Irish speech, not unlike ones President Kennedy had given on other St. Patrick's Days. For an ending he had written:

I like to think—as did President Kennedy—that the emerald thread runs into the cloth we weave today, that these policies in which he believed so strongly and which President Johnson is advancing are the current flowering of the Irish tradition. They are directed toward freedom for *all* Americans here and for all peoples throughout the world. And I like to think that these policies will survive and continue as the cause of Irish freedom survived the death of "The Liberator," Owen Roe O'Neill.

As you'll recall, O'Neill was one of the great figures of Irish history. It was of the period after his death, when the entire Irish nation was overwhelmed with grief, that the following lines were written:

> Sagest in the council was he,
>   kindest in the Hall;
> Sure we never won a battle
>   —'twas Owen won them all
> Soft as woman's was your voice, O'Neill:
>   bright was your eye,
> Oh! why did you leave us, Owen?
>   Why did you die?
>
> Your troubles are all over,
>   you're at rest with God on high,
> But we're slaves, and we're orphans, Owen!
>   —why did you die?

> We're sheep without a shepherd,
>> when the snow shuts out the sky—
> Oh! why did you leave us, Owen?
>> Why did you die?

So, on this St. Patrick's evening, let me urge you one final time to recall the heritage of the Irish. Let us hold out our hands to those who struggle for freedom today—at home and abroad—as Ireland struggled for a thousand years.

Let us not leave them to be "sheep without a shepherd, when the snow shuts out the sky." Let us show them that we have not forgotten the constancy and the faith and the hope of the Irish.

When I worked some changes he wanted into the speech, I eliminated the poem. When he read the redrafted text, he asked: "Why did you do that?"

"You'll never get through it," I said. "You don't have to put yourself through that."

"I've been practicing," he said. "I've been practicing in front of a mirror. I can't get through it yet—but I will."

And in Scranton he did—just barely.

The poignant experience in Scranton stirred Bob deeply, and it was not lost on the Democratic politicians in the White House and elsewhere around the country. Sometime in early April—if any time might be fixed—the rising tide of political activity, with its strong undertow of haunting, pervasive memories of President Kennedy, began to sweep him into an unannounced, restrained campaign for the Vice Presidential nomination. He allowed himself to drift into it even though he felt instinctively—and correctly—that Lyndon Johnson didn't want any part of him; and even though he believed that if he became Vice President he was not temperamentally suited to wait in the wings, not doing much more than that, unless the President wanted him to. "I'd be climbing the walls in three months," he said.

But other forces were carrying him along. The polls showed him steadily building strength for the nomination among rank-and-file Democrats. The Gallup Poll for April 12 estimated that he was the choice of 47 percent, up from 34 percent in January, while Adlai

Stevenson's support dropped from 26 to 18 percent and Hubert Humphrey's fell from 14 to 10 percent in the same period. The calls and visits from Democratic politicians who had been identified with the Kennedys increased. Many members of his family, including Ethel and Jacqueline Kennedy, were urging him to seek the post as a means of keeping alive the effort and idealism which President Kennedy had brought into the government. Some of his closest friends were advising him to make an open fight for the nomination. Others were telling him that, having achieved a place at the center of power, he should not abandon it. Finally, he was so unsure of what he wanted to do that he decided only to keep all his options open. He felt a deep obligation to those who had worked so hard to elect President Kennedy and who had served in the government with him and to young people, but he would see. He would let events take their course.

But beginning in the latter part of April, through May, June and early July, he became exceedingly active. Beginning appropriately in Charleston, West Virginia, he traveled and spoke in all parts of the nation, visited West Berlin, called on West German Chancellor Ludwig Erhard in Bonn and spent four tumultuous days in Poland. His purpose was not to take his case to the people and force the President's hand. He was much more realistic about that than were most of his advisers. His purpose was to demonstrate the public and key political support that impresses occupants of the White House and, in this instance, might lead President Johnson to conclude that Bob's vote-pulling power in the North and West would more than offset the liability he would be in the South. At the same time he sought by what he said and did to get along better with the President, following the advice of one adviser who said: "He is President —you and your brother settled on him—but, most important, you will have far more leverage for the things you believe in if you take the initiative on this. It would be neither a sign of sellout or weakness, but a source of strength to you."

But by late spring President Johnson was rolling along. He was leading the country through the postassassination period with strength and energy, and while he was keeping his own counsel about who would be on the ticket with him, we know now from Theodore White's *The Making of the President—1964* and other accounts that he was seeking ways to make sure it wouldn't be Bob.

While Bob undertook his campaign with reservations, he warmed up to it somewhat, for clamor and excitement surrounded him wherever he went and he encountered touching indications of affection for President Kennedy and constant reminders of needs unfilled, of work to be done.

In West Virginia, leaving the press behind, we accompanied a neighborhood worker, Tex Williams, up the winding hollows of Dry Branch and Wet Branch, where the people lived in pathetic poverty. He went to every cabin, and in almost all of them President Kennedy's picture, cut from a magazine or newspaper, was tacked on the wall. An unemployed coal miner, Greenie Mullens, gave him a bear hug and said: "We loved your brother. That sure was a dirty trick they did." Farther up the rutted road, a young mother of six, whose husband had deserted her, sat in a musty, decaying two-room shack. One of her children, a four-year-old girl, was crippled with cerebral palsy. Bob took the child on his lap, talked softly to her and clipped his PT 109 tie clasp on her worn dress. And he heard the depressing statistics of the two hollows: almost 100 percent unemployment; most of the children had never known their fathers to go to work. "If we can't break into this cycle, we've had it," he muttered, half to himself. "It will never end."

Again, in Kansas City, Missouri, at an old people's home and in a black ghetto housing project, he came upon the photographs of his brother and the evidence of neglect, poverty and despair. And on across the country. Even at West Georgia College in Carrollton, Georgia, where he dedicated the John F. Kennedy Interfaith Chapel, and at conservative Hampden-Sydney College in southside Virginia, students acclaimed him and the townspeople received him courteously.

He did not confine himself to speeches at colleges, tours of poverty areas and dedications in memory of his brother. He spoke before bar associations, the American Jewish Committee, the Business Council, the U.S. Conference of Mayors, the United Auto Workers' national convention and the American Society of Newspaper Editors.

The campaign was great therapy for him, but he could conceive that President Johnson might ask him to be on the ticket only if a Republican moderate like Governor Nelson Rockefeller of New York, Ambassador Henry Cabot Lodge or Governor William Scranton of Pennsylvania won the GOP Presidential nomination. When Senator Barry Goldwater defeated Rockefeller in the California primary in early June and thus sewed up the nomination, Bob was certain that President Johnson would not need him. Still, he went ahead, partly to keep faith with those who were urging him to do so and partly to force Johnson to make the decision.

On June 8, after the California primary, he visited Los Angeles for the first time in almost a year and was engulfed by a fervent crowd when he visited Roosevelt High School in a predominantly Mexican-American neighborhood. He visited two youth training and employment centers funded by the President's Committee on Juvenile Delinquency and Youth Crime; visited a predominantly black junior high school; helicoptered to a fund-raising luncheon for the JFK Memorial Library; stopped by a political luncheon that Jess Unruh was hosting and then traded questions and answers with students at California Institute of Technology. That evening at Cal Tech he spoke about "the opening to the future":

The United States must continue to expand its efforts to reach the peoples of other nations—particularly young people in the rapidly developing Southern continents. Governments may come and go, but in the long run the future will be determined by the needs and aspirations of these young people.

Over the years, an understanding of what America really stands for is going to count far more than missiles, aircraft carriers and supersonic bombers. The big changes of the future will result from this understanding —or lack of it.

We have made some progress in reaching the peoples of other countries. . . . But the critical moves—the moves that will determine our success—are the kinds of political choices this country makes in picking its friends abroad—and its enemies.

Far too often, for narrow tactical reasons, this country has associated itself with tyrannical and unpopular regimes that had no following and no future. Over the past twenty years, we have paid dearly because of support given to colonial rulers, cruel dictators or ruling cliques void of social concern. This was one of President Kennedy's gravest concerns. . . .

Ultimately, Communism must be defeated by progressive political programs which wipe out the poverty, misery and discontent on which it thrives. For that reason, progressive political programs are the best way to erode the Communist presence in Latin America, to turn back the Communist thrust in Southeast Asia, and to insure the stability of the new African nations and preserve stability in the world. . . .

To say that the future will be different from the present is, to scientists, hopelessly self-evident. I observe regretfully that in politics, however, it can be heresy. It can be denounced as radicalism or branded as subversion. There are people in every time and every land who want to stop history in its tracks. They fear the future, mistrust the present and invoke the security of a comfortable past which, in fact, never existed. . . .

The danger of such views is not that they will take control of the American Government. In time, the consensus of good sense which characterizes our political system will digest and discard frozen views and impossible programs. But there is a *short-term* danger from such voices. . . .

The answer to these voices cannot simply be reason, for they speak irrationally. The answer cannot come merely from government, no matter how conscientious or judicious. The answer must come from within the American democracy. It must come from an informed national consensus which can recognize futile fervor and simple solutions for what they are —and reject them quickly.

Three weeks later he flew to Germany, but several days before he left he wrote a letter to President Johnson volunteering to serve as Ambassador to Vietnam if Lodge decided to leave Saigon as was rumored. The President turned down the offer with a warm expression of gratitude.

The purpose of the German trip was to accept an invitation from Mayor Willy Brandt to unveil a plaque of President Kennedy in the square facing the Schöneberger Rathaus, West Berlin's City Hall, where the year before the late President had made his memorable declaration: "All free men, wherever they may live, are citizens of Berlin, and, therefore, as a free man, I take pride in the words 'Ich bin ein Berliner.'" In part to show his popularity with

Polish-Americans, Bob added a four-day visit to Poland to the trip.

More than 250,000 West Berliners lined the streets to applaud and cheer as Bob and Brandt drove by. Eighty thousand more packed in the square where Bob also had spoken in February 1962.

"A new President leads our land," he said, "but our course is unchanged, for under President Johnson as under President Kennedy we are committed to your freedom."

Applause and approving shouts lasted for minutes. He said that when President Kennedy left Berlin he had remarked that he would leave a note for his successor telling him in a moment of discouragement or despair to "go to Berlin."

"I know what he meant because I have done so," Bob exclaimed. "I see again what he meant because I look out on all of you. I know what he meant when he surveyed the Wall of Shame and measured it against your courage and said, 'Ich bin ein Berliner.'"

That night, in a speech at the Free University of Berlin, that moved Ethel to tears, he put into words really for the first time what the weeks of soul-searching and travel had meant to him:

There were many who felt a light had been snuffed out, that the torch-bearer for a whole generation was gone, that an era was over before its time, that with him there died idealism and hope and what was clean and best in all of us.

But in traveling through my own country, through the Far East several months ago and now in Germany, I have come to understand the hope President Kennedy kindled is not dead but alive. It is not a memory but a living force. The torch still burns, and because it does there remains for all of us the chance to light up the tomorrows and to brighten the future. For me, that is the challenge that makes life worthwhile; and I hope it will be the same for all of you.

The Polish Government did not invite Bob. Marshal Tito of Yugoslavia was touring the country on a state visit, but even if he hadn't been, the Polish officials, remembering the outpouring of pro-American sentiment when Vice President Nixon visited there in 1959, were discreetly opposed to his coming. They were not going to ban the brother of the dead President, but they made no announcement that he was coming until two days after he was in the country. The Poles, however, heard about it from Radio Free Europe, the BBC and the Voice of America. Several hundred were waiting outside the Hotel Europejski in Warsaw and applauded vigorously when Bob, Ethel and their three oldest children, Kathleen, Joe and Bobby, arrived. That was the first sign that the visit would be extraordinary.

The next morning, a Sunday, word had spread through the city, and thousands jammed an ancient cathedral and the square outside when the Kennedys went to Mass. When they left the church and struggled through the crowd into Ambassador John M. Cabot's car, the Poles showered them with flowers and pressed so tightly around the car that it could not move. Then, for the first time, Bob used a tactic that was to become a trademark of his campaigns. He pushed a door open, grabbed Ethel's arm and pulled her out, lifted her to the top of the car and climbed up himself. The crowd went wild. Then, with aides and two startled members of the Polish secret police forcing a narrow path, the car moved slowly through the cheering, singing crowd, with Bob and Ethel, and now the children, standing on the roof waving. Inside, the astounded Ambassador, a proper Bostonian, leaned gingerly out a window and, tapping John Nolan, Bob's administrative assistant, said, "I say there, would you tell the Attorney General that the roof is caving in!"

That afternoon Bob and Ethel were scheduled to visit an orphanage. When they arrived with arms full of presents, all the children had been taken away. From that moment on the trip became a battle of wits between Bob and the Polish officials. Determined that the government would not get the best of him, Bob and Ethel drove directly to a children's hospital where they were not expected and spent several hours slowly visiting all the wards.

The day's events not only angered Polish officials but caused a sharp disagreement between the American Embassy and Bob. Ambassador Cabot and his senior aides were extremely uneasy. They thought Bob would leave behind a good deal of fence-mending for them and possibly upset relations between the United States and Poland. But Bob didn't believe it.

"If they think they can shut us off from the people, they're wrong," Bob told Cabot. He asked where he could find a crowd early the next morning before flying to Cracow. No one in the embassy knew.

"All right," Bob said. "We'll show you how it's done."

The next morning he drove to a small outdoor market. There were a handful of shoppers when Bob started walking through. In a few minutes several hundred Poles were crowded around. In a few minutes more than a thousand were hemming Bob and Ethel in, kissing them, cheering, and then, as happened at every stop, the townspeople began singing "Sto Lat," an old Polish wish, "May you live a hundred years."

In Cracow, students at the six-hundred-year-old Jagiellonian University lifted him on their shoulders when he arrived. After touring the university, he and Ethel and the children climbed on top of a Soviet-built Volga car, provided by the Polish Government, and rode to the Renaissance town square where fifteen thousand persons were waiting. The Poles sang "Sto Lat," and Bob replied, "Now we will sing something for you." After a hurried consultation the Kennedys sang "When Polish Eyes Are Smiling," and the crowd roared its approval.

Later, in the office of Cracow Mayor Zbigniew Skolicki, Bob mentioned Lee Harvey Oswald's name for the first time publicly. Student and civic leaders were asking him questions, when one youth asked for Bob's personal opinion about the assassination, apologizing for raising "this delicate subject."

"But," he said, "the name of the Kennedy family is so popular here that we would like to know the truth from a basic source."

Bob stiffened, took a deep breath and said: "I believe it was done by a man with the name of Oswald, who was a misfit in society, who lived in the United States and was dissatisfied with our government and our way of life, who took up Communism and went to the Soviet Union.

"He was dissatisfied there. He came back to the United States and was antisocial and felt that the only way to take out his strong feelings against life and society was by killing the President of the

United States. There is no question that he did it on his own and by himself.

"He was not a member of a right-wing organization. He was a confessed Communist, but even the Communists would not have anything to do with him."

There was silence for several minutes before someone asked another question.

Returning to Warsaw that evening, he was an hour late arriving for a dinner with Polish officials at Ambassador Cabot's residence. The officials were indignant at being kept waiting, but were more upset over his rapport with the crowds and his intention to go the next day to Częstochowa to call on Poland's Catholic Primate and symbol of opposition to the Communist regime, Stefan Cardinal Wyszynski. Deputy Foreign Minister Józef Winiewicz attended the dinner only so that he could scold Bob for stirring the crowds, and to express the government's feeling that it would be "ill-advised" for him to visit the Cardinal. Winiewicz told Bob that Wladyslaw Gomulka, the Polish Communist chief, never played to the crowds.

"Maybe that's the problem," Bob replied curtly.

Ambassador Cabot supported Bob in his intention to visit the Cardinal, and had urged him to go. It would give strong support to the Church, be popular with the people and indicate to the Polish Government that the welfare of the Catholic Church in Poland was a matter of concern to the American Government and the American people, Cabot said. After Winiewicz let Bob know that the visit would displease the Polish Government more than anything else he might do, Cabot and Bob reconsidered whether he should go. However, they concluded there was nothing in Winiewicz's remarks that would be a reason for not going.

Bob met alone with Cardinal Wyszynski for an hour. He never made a public statement about what was said, but it was clear that his visit had been important to the beleaguered Cardinal, who had had no contact with Americans and was trying to avoid open conflict with the Polish Government.

The trip was a personal triumph for Bob. His crowd-pleasing tactics "were scenes out of the Pied Piper except that the adults were there with the kids," Gene Kramer of the Associated Press wrote later. But it was more than that, if only for the visit to Cardinal Wyszynski, which bolstered the Church in a small but important way. But there were other dividends. The enormous admiration in Poland for the United States and for the name "Kennedy" was demonstrated by the Polish people in a most convincing way. Despite Ambassador Cabot's misgivings, Bob gave at least some of the embassy officers new confidence in making contacts. It shook the Polish regime to the point that three years later when Richard Nixon sought to make a private visit, the government declined to issue him a visa.

The day after Bob left, Deputy Foreign Minister Winiewicz sought to exploit the tension between Cabot and Bob by saying, "We know what happened was not the Ambassador's or the embassy's fault." The Polish press, without mentioning the enormous crowds Bob had drawn, told its readers Bob had not conducted himself properly. One paper ran a photo of Bob and Ethel on the roof of a car, cropped so that no crowd would show, with a caption: "Is This How They Travel in America?" But the Polish officials could not have helped but notice the difference in public reaction when Khrushchev, President Antonin Novotny of Czechoslovakia and the East German Communist leader, Walter Ulbricht, visited Warsaw three weeks later. Ambassador Cabot reported to the State Department:

I have just observed through my office window the "triumphal" procession of Khrushchev, Novotny and Ulbricht through the streets of Warsaw. Accompanied by Gomulka and preceded by an Agitprop sound truck announcing approach of a "Leninist hero and fighter for peace," Nikita Khrushchev, the procession was greeted by a minimum of perfunctory clapping from the thin line of Poles along the sidewalk. Even the reception accorded Ulbricht during his September solo visit seemed greater than today's pitiful and yet most expressive display.

Today's silence does not in itself suggest unrest or potential social action. It does underscore, however, the Polish people's total lack of enthusiasm for the self-proclaimed leaders of the "Socialist camp." The contrast to the welcome given Attorney General Kennedy was particularly striking.

Sometime in June, perhaps after the California primary, perhaps earlier, President Johnson decided firmly that he would not need Bob on the ticket to win re-election. Undoubtedly, he had many reasons—all good ones from his point of view—but one must believe that almost certainly, in the last analysis, calculation of his chances against Goldwater outweighed other considerations: his personal feeling toward Bob, his resentment over the pressure that Bob's travels and grass-roots Democratic sentiment were putting on him, and his eagerness to establish a Johnson Administration without having to share it with a Kennedy. If he had chosen Bob, he would have, in effect, had to concede the South to Goldwater, and he was not prepared to do that. In any case, all the polls projected that he held a commanding lead over Goldwater and would run well against him whoever was his running mate.

Thus, as summer began, President Johnson was in a strong position, and out of an abundance of caution and suspicion, he moved to eliminate Bob from any possible consideration well before the Democratic Convention convened in Atlantic City in the last week of August. Since Johnson has not revealed what precipitated his next action, perhaps the clearest insight has been provided by the careful reporting of Theodore White. In *The Making of the President —1964* White wrote:

Early in June, planning for the Democratic Convention had begun. It was to be entertained by various films which might amuse delegates otherwise bored. One film was to be the story of Lyndon Johnson. Another would be a tribute to John F. Kennedy—and to the makers of this film, instructions came from the White House: no clips of Bobby Kennedy in the film. By late July another change had come about: the memorial film to John F. Kennedy would be shown *after* the nomination for Vice President, not before. But then a counter-jolt; the press speculated that Jacqueline Kennedy herself might come before the Convention to plead the cause of her brother-in-law, the Attorney General for Vice President.

Jacqueline Kennedy had told Bob that she would do anything she could to help him get the Vice Presidential nomination, and if it meant an appearance at the convention, she would go, but he never considered having her do it. He was absolutely adamant about not making an open bid for the nomination. Powerful Democrats in populous states like Jess Unruh of California urged him to let them make the bid for him. Others, like Mayor Richard J. Daley of Chicago and Representative William Green of Pennsylvania, while stating they would support the President on any candidate he selected, told Bob they would support him if he would fight for the nomination. But he wouldn't. He felt strongly that such an effort would savagely divide the Democratic Party and reflect poorly on the memory of President Kennedy. But, more important, remembering 1960, he was not going to trespass openly on President Johnson's right to choose his running mate.

However, President Johnson was not about to take any chances. On Monday, July 27, he telephoned Bob and asked him to come to the White House the next day. Bob said he was scheduled to be in New York and offered to cancel his meetings. No, the President said, there was no urgency; Wednesday would be fine, and they agreed Bob would come at 1 P.M.

"He's going to tell me I'm not going to be Vice President," Bob said as he put down the phone. "I wondered when he'd get around to it."

Thus Bob was not surprised when President Johnson got to the point. He told Bob that he had been thinking about the Vice Presidency for a long time; that he wanted someone who would help the country, help the party and work with him and that he had decided that Bob didn't fit that description. Bob said he accepted that and offered to support the President and campaign for him.

They talked for forty-five minutes. Bob chose his words carefully, believing that they were being taped. The President said he thought Bob should be President someday and was well qualified, but didn't particularize on how he would help Bob get there. Instead, he talked about the forthcoming campaign. He said he would have trouble with the youth and with minority groups; that he didn't have a campaign strategy worked out. The President asked Bob to be his campaign manager and afterward he could have whatever post he wanted—in the Cabinet or as Ambassador to Great Britain, the

Soviet Union, France or Italy. Bob said he would have to confer with other persons before deciding.

When he returned to his office, he called Ethel and then Jacqueline. He was miffed, disappointed and relieved. "Now I have to decide what to do—either run for the Senate in New York or work for Lyndon," he said.

Their conversation had ended with Bob saying as he left,"I could have helped you, Mr. President." There had not been any discussion of how the President would let his decision be known. That afternoon, however, he prevailed upon McGeorge Bundy to call Bob and urge him to issue a statement taking himself out of consideration or to give a story to the *New York Times* to that effect. Bob was curt with Bundy. He refused to do so, adding that it was up to the President to make any statement. That evening the President invited several Washington newsmen to dinner and regaled them with a long account of his conversation with Bob, which Bob had understood would be in confidence. The next day when the news began to leak, Bob went to the White House to protest. The President said he hadn't discussed their conversation with anyone, and Bob replied bluntly that the President wasn't telling the truth.

At noon the President called an unscheduled press conference in his office and announced his criterion of a Vice Presidential candidate. He would be someone who "is well received in all the states of the Union among all our people," but gave no hint of his decision. During the afternoon he tried through O'Donnell to prevail upon Bob to issue a statement, offering to let Bob select the Vice Presidential candidate. Bob continued to hold out, and in the evening the President called another press conference. He announced that he was eliminating from consideration all members of his Cabinet and all who met regularly with the Cabinet, disqualifying Ambassador Stevenson, Secretary of State Rusk, Defense Secretary McNamara, Agriculture Secretary Orville Freeman, Peace Corps Director Sargent Shriver—all of whom had figured prominently in speculation —as well as Bob.

The day before, after Bundy's call, Bob, expecting that the President's decision would be leaked to the press, called a meeting of those of his assistants who were in their offices at the time—Burke Marshall, John Douglas, Ramsey Clark, Harold Reis and John Nolan—so that they would hear the news from him. After he had finished telling them, there was an embarrassed silence.

"Ah, what the hell, let's go form our own country," Bob said, laughing.

Chapter 13

The Senate Race

THE IDEA THAT Bob might run for the Senate in New York began germinating in February after he returned from meeting with Sukarno and as he began halfheartedly to think about his future. His brother, Edward, his brother-in-law, Stephen Smith, and Averell Harriman talked to him about it, and overtures came from several New York Democratic leaders. The most persuasive were Peter Crotty in Buffalo, who had played a key role in President Kennedy's election, and John English, a younger breed of Democratic boss whose political savvy had engineered impressive Democratic victories in the Republican stronghold of Nassau County on Long Island. By April, Bob was giving it serious thought.

"It would be a load off my mind," he told me one afternoon. "If Lyndon Johnson hadn't been such an s.o.b. about everything, things might have been different. Being his Vice President could be a real dead end. He could put me in cold storage and I'd suffocate.

"But if I were elected to the Senate, I'd have some impact along with the other younger Senators—Teddy, Birch Bayh and Joe Tydings and Pierre [Salinger][1] if they're elected. As a group, we could

1. Salinger, as White House press secretary, had resigned to run for the Democratic nomination for Senator in California. He won and was appointed to the Senate after Senator Clair Engle died July 30, 1964, but was defeated in November by screen actor George Murphy, the GOP nominee. Tydings, who had been U.S. Attorney for Maryland during the Kennedy Administration, was elected in November.

have some effect. He would have to listen to us."

Then he matter-of-factly analyzed his chances. The biggest liability would be that he was from Massachusetts. But, somewhat offsetting that, he had excellent contacts with Democratic county leaders throughout New York and his family had more than a passing identification with the state.[2] He thought his most effective argument would be to ask New Yorkers if they wanted two Republicans, Keating and Senator Jacob Javits, representing them in the Senate. The *New York Times* and the *Herald Tribune* would be against him, but he could overcome that through television and he could stage a very effective campaign. If he decided to go, he would have to make an accommodation with New York Mayor Robert Wagner, who long had coveted a seat in the Senate, and he would have to decide soon, but he hoped he could wait until the Civil Rights Bill passed.

"So many friends have talked to me about being Vice President," he said. "I have an obligation to them not to take myself out of it yet, but I just want to be in a position where I can turn it down or accept it. If there is some way I can avoid serving under Lyndon and maintain some political base and strength, I think I'd do it. New York is one way."

He paused and then, grinning, said: "It would be awful if I lost!"

During May and early June, Steve Smith, the least known of the Kennedy in-laws, whose slender build and boyish face belied an inner toughness and a shrewd political mind, along with Crotty, English and several other Democratic leaders including State Chairman William H. McKeon, quietly canvassed the state for support. The only Democrat openly seeking the nomination was Representative Samuel Stratton, a hard-working but sometimes abrasive Congressman from upstate Amsterdam, who was not acceptable to either the Democratic bosses or the Reform Democratic leaders in

2. Bob was born November 20, 1925, in Boston. Two months later the family moved to Riverdale, New York, on the west side of the Bronx and in 1928 moved to Bronxville in Westchester County. That was his home up to and including the years his father was Ambassador to the Court of St. James's from 1937 to 1940. His family had maintained an apartment in Manhattan from that time on and had substantial real estate holdings in New York City, Albany and White Plains.

New York City. But long years of bitter factionalism between the regulars and the reformers had fragmented the Democratic machine. It was most unlikely not only that the two factions would agree on a candidate, but also that they would be able to agree among themselves. Many reformers were urging Ambassador Stevenson to make the race. Mayor Wagner was standing in the wings. Dr. Ralph J. Bunche, Under Secretary General of the United Nations, New York County District Attorney Frank Hogan, who lost to Keating by only 132,000 votes in 1958, Queens County District Attorney Frank O'Connor and Harriman also were being boosted. Meanwhile, there was growing speculation that Bob might seek the nomination.

In June and early July statewide polling which Smith had authorized indicated that Bob was the only potential candidate who could defeat Keating. Significantly, it showed that Bob was the only candidate who ran ahead of Keating in upstate New York, which had 43 percent of the vote and normally voted Republican. The poll rated Stevenson and Keating as an even match and gave Keating a strong edge over the others, with Wagner running weakest. Bob received the first returns of the poll the week before he was scheduled to leave for Germany and Poland. Ethel and the three oldest children had gone ahead for a visit in France and Italy, and he went to Hyannis Port to visit the other children and think about what he should do. While he was there, disaster again struck the family. On the night of June 19, Edward Kennedy's back was broken in a small-plane crash near Southampton, Massachusetts, and an aide, Edwin Moss, and the pilot, Edwin Zimmi, were killed. Coming so soon after the President's death, it was a shattering blow. As we walked in a park near the hospital the next afternoon, waiting for the doctors' findings, Bob brooded about the tragedies that had stalked his family and was deeply concerned for his mother and father.

"How much more do they have to take?" he asked. "I just don't see how I can do anything now. I think I should just get out of it all. Somebody up there doesn't like us."

The doctors' report was more optimistic than Bob had anticipated. There was no paralysis or neurological damage. Three vertebrae had been broken, and there would be an eight-to-ten-month period of recuperation, but there was a chance that Ted's back would mend without the necessity of an operation. The news brought color to Bob's haggard face and buoyed his spirit, but the next afternoon he decided to announce that he would not be a candidate in the New York race. He did so the following Monday. His mood was such that he also could have taken himself out of consideration for the Vice Presidential nomination. Perhaps he held a slender hope that he would be chosen, but after Goldwater's victory in the California primary he discounted his chances almost completely. It was hard to tell. His actions that weekend seemed governed by emotion rather than calculation. With Ted's accident he momentarily lost interest in the New York race, but he could not bring himself to give Johnson an easy out. The decision was one the President would have to make.

Intuitively, Smith thought Bob might reconsider and quietly passed that word to the Democratic leaders, like Crotty and English, who had committed themselves publicly and to those who remained uncommitted. Consequently, when President Johnson on July 30 eliminated Bob from consideration for the Vice Presidency, and the warring Democrats were unable to agree on a candidate, the door to New York was still open. Stevenson had all but formally taken himself out of the race. Stratton had been unable to generate support outside his home area. Wagner, having won as the bosses' candidate for Mayor in 1953 and then having split bitterly with them in winning a third term in 1961, faced deep-seated opposition among the regulars in the city and was not strong upstate.

It took Bob about a week to make up his mind. As he decided, he talked again, as he had in the spring, about the Senate offering a chance to establish an independent base where he could continue working on domestic problems and have some impact on national policy. At the center of his thinking was the conviction, reinforced by his travels of the spring and summer, that he was obligated to do what he could to see that the hopes that his brother had kindled around the world did not die. He did not delude himself about the meaning of the outpouring of emotion that he had received. It was for his brother, not for him. But as he had told Ben Bradlee, Washington bureau chief of *Newsweek*, in a conversation which he thought was off the record but which was published: "People are still looking for all that idealism. It permeated young people all over the globe. And I became sort of a symbol, not just as an individual. If I could figure out some course for me that would keep all that alive and utilize it for the country, that's what I'd do."

But he had doubts about his ability as a campaigner. He had been a skillful campaign manager for his brother, but managing a campaign and being the candidate are two different things and no one was more aware of that than he was. Doubt about how he would do as a candidate brought worry that he would be the first Kennedy to lose an election. But there was a good chance that he could defeat Keating. His family, his closest associates and an increasing number of influential Democrats were urging him to run. What finally tipped the balance was that circumstances, and President Johnson as well, had narrowed his alternatives. The New York Senate race was the only immediate opportunity for him to win elective office and thus retain his independence, his only chance to continue to have some direct influence on national policies. If running in New York had its hazards and did not totally appeal to him, the prospect of spending the fall campaigning for Johnson and then ending the year out of government and facing a restless, uncertain future, appealed to him much less.

When he had made his decision, he very accurately predicted how the campaign would go.

"I'll draw huge crowds as I go to different parts of the state for the first time," he said. "All the attention will be on that, and it will last for about three weeks. I'll hit a low point around the first of October. The question will be whether I can turn it around and regain the momentum."

Bob delayed making a formal announcement of his decision until he could obtain Mayor Wagner's express approval. The Mayor was not only the titular head of the New York Democrats but also an important bridge to the reformers, who, for a variety of reasons, mostly stemming from Bob's association with Joe McCarthy and his pursuit of Hoffa, opposed his candidacy.[3] Wagner never indicated that he was against Bob, but it was his custom to be cautious and careful, and he held his cards close to his chest. They met on August 7 and again on August 17. The Mayor wanted to be convinced that Bob would listen to all Democratic voices in the state, the voices of the reformers as well as those of the bosses who had taken the lead in working for his nomination. He also wanted Bob's word that Bob would work with him and not try to impose his leadership on top of the Mayor's. He got those assurances, and in between their meetings Wagner spent a weekend at the White House, where, according to reports, Johnson urged the Mayor to announce for Bob and promised him that he still would have a strong say about political patronage in New York even if Bob was elected. On Saturday, August 22, the Mayor threw his support to Bob.

(It must be pointed out that once Wagner made his decision, he supported Bob unstintingly. He gave Bob the full-time services of one of his principal aides, Bernard Ruggieri, whose enthusiasm and intricate knowledge of New York politics were invaluable. Wagner counseled with Bob frequently and in the closing days delivered a speech attacking Keating's record as a Republican liberal that without question was the most effective oratory of the campaign.)

While waiting on Wagner, Bob rapidly recruited a campaign staff and took a crash course in New York problems. William vanden Heuvel, a New Yorker who had supervised the Prince Edward County free school project, assembled a sheaf of position papers from experts in the federal government, New York professors and

---

3. At the outset of the campaign, Bob made several dogged but not wholly successful attempts to bridge the gulf of emotion and suspicion that separated him from the reformers. With the help of Arthur M. Schlesinger, Jr., philanthropist Mrs. Mary Lasker, industrialist Abraham Feinberg and other prominent liberals, several meetings were arranged so that small groups of leading reformers could question him. Each of the meetings was tense and edgy, and near the end of one an elegantly groomed lady stood and said: "Why don't we quit stalling around and say what's on our mind? Mr. Kennedy, we're afraid that you'll come in here and take over the party, and then what will happen to our power?" As the campaign developed, however, many reformers put their fears aside and worked hard for Bob. Few stayed neutral. Some formed a Democrats for Keating Committee.

state and city officials. Each paper—there were thirty-six in all—stated the problems, outlined what had been done and gave proposals for what should be done. The subjects ranged from agriculture and education to off-track betting and Massachusetts vs. New York. The writers of the papers came to Hickory Hill or Bob met them in New York for lengthy discussions.

Inevitably during the briefing sessions there were comments—some needling and some patronizing—about his lack of detailed knowledge of the state he hoped to represent. In one of the briefing papers someone had placed a travel-folder description of the East River:

> The East River is a body of water fifteen miles long and up to 3½ miles wide extending from the Upper Bay of New York Harbor to the southwestern end of Long Island Sound at Throgs Neck and Willets Point. On the west shore of the river are the boroughs of Manhattan and the Bronx and on the east are . . .

Bob stood and recited the full three-paragraph description as though he were in an elementary school elocution class. After he finished, he looked sardonically at vanden Heuvel.

"That's right, Bill," he said. "You've brought all these experts down here, and what I really need is someone who can lead me around New York."

Putting together a campaign staff was easier. Bob had only to reach out through the Justice Department for people who were anxious to help, among them John Nolan, Walter Sheridan, Angela Novello, Charles Z. Smith and David Hackett. Many who had worked in the 1960 campaign felt the same way, and he was besieged with volunteers. The biggest problem, and one that persisted throughout the campaign to some degree, was to fuse the Kennedy loyalists with the New York State and county professionals. Friction was bound to occur, but it was minimized to a great degree by dividing key responsibilities between the two groups. R. Peter Straus, president of radio station WMCA and a leading advocate of reapportionment of the New York legislature, held the title of campaign chairman for the entire Democratic ticket, but worked closely with Steve Smith. Justin N. Feldman, a New York lawyer and veteran politician with close ties to the reformers, worked side by side with John Nolan, hammering out Bob's daily schedule and supervising the teams of advance men who would go to a city to make detailed arrangements several days before Bob was to arrive. Debs Meyers, Mayor Wagner's politically sagacious former press and executive secretary, shared with me the responsibility for press relations.

Only speech-writing and research on issues and Keating's record remained almost purely Kennedy functions, and these tasks were handled by vanden Heuvel, Milton Gwirtzman, a Washington lawyer who was close to Edward Kennedy, and two young attorneys from the Justice Department, Adam Walinsky and Peter Edelman.[4] However, they were assisted by Benjamin Altman of the Democratic State Committee. Gerald Gardner, a political satirist and professional writer for television, drafted several speeches and provided a series of one-line jokes. William F. Haddad, a former Peace Corps official, ex-New York newspaperman and unsuccessful candidate for Congress, undertook a major part of the research work while directing a Volunteers for Kennedy organization.

Most of these persons and many others were fully involved in the campaign within a few days after Bob formally announced his candidacy. The announcement was made on Tuesday, August 25, from the steps of Gracie Mansion, the official residence of New York City mayors, with Ethel and Mayor Wagner standing beside him.

In his statement he validated the off-record quote he had given Bradlee and met the carpetbagger issue head on, saying:

Our traditional aspirations for peace and prosperity, justice and decency, are being questioned. All that President Kennedy stood for and all that President Johnson is trying to accomplish, all the progress that has been made, is threatened by a new and dangerous Republican assault.

No one associated with President Kennedy and with President Johnson —no one committed to participating in public life—can sit on the sidelines with so much at stake.

I have an obvious problem in coming in from out of state. It's going to

---

4. Walinsky and Edelman were Bob's legislative assistants throughout his service in the Senate.

be tough to win. I recognize that some voters have misgivings about considering a man for high office who has left the state and who has only recently returned.

I understand this, but it is appropriate to point out that my candidacy would fulfill the requirements for membership in the United States Senate which were set forth after solemn consideration by the men who drafted the Constitution of the State of New York as well as by those who drafted the Constitution of the United States.

There may be some who believe that where a candidate voted in the past is more important than his capacity to serve the state. I cannot in fairness expect these people to vote for me, even though my mother and father had a home in New York since 1926 and I attended New York schools for six years.

But I do not base my candidacy on these connections. I base it on the belief that New York is not separate from the nation in the year 1964. I base it on the fact that the greatest state in the Union must play a leading role at the federal level and I wish to play a part in that effort.

That afternoon he and Ethel flew to Atlantic City to meet with New York party leaders who were attending the Democratic National Convention, and went to a reception in his honor. On Thursday he returned to Atlantic City. President Johnson and Hubert Humphrey had been nominated the evening before, and it was a day when the Democratic Party bid an emotional farewell to the brief Kennedy era. That night after visiting many state delegations to thank them for supporting President Kennedy four years earlier, he sat on the wooden steps behind the convention rostrum, nervously writing last-minute changes in a speech he would give introducing the memorial film of his brother's life. Then followed an unforgettable scene.

As Senator Henry Jackson of Washington introduced Bob and he stepped to the microphone, the delegates and the audience stood and wave after wave of applause and cheers reverberated through the great auditorium. It was a moment apart in the history of American politics. For twenty-two minutes the heart-tugging ovation continued. At first Bob smiled wanly. He tried repeatedly to begin speaking: "Mr. Chairman . . . Mr. Chairman . . ." but the cheering only intensified. Then he turned and looked helplessly at Jackson. Then he stood, tears glistening in his eyes, waiting for all the pent-up emotion to subside. As he began to speak, a young woman dropped to her knees in an aisle near the rostrum and clasped her hands in prayer. A reverent silence gripped the hall as he eulogized his brother and spoke of his hopes and his accomplishments and then said:

> I realize that as an individual that we can't just look back, that we must look forward. When I think of President Kennedy, I think of what Shakespeare said in Romeo and Juliet: "When he shall die, take him and cut him out in little stars, and he will make the face of heaven so fine that all the world will be in love with night and pay no worship to the garish sun."
>
> And I realize, as an individual really, he realized this as an individual and even more important for a political party and for the country to be conscious of the past we must look to the future.
>
> So I join with you in realizing that what has been started four years ago, that everyone here started four years ago, that that's to be sustained, that that's to be continued. The same efforts and the same energy and the same dedication that was given to President John F. Kennedy must be given to President Lyndon Johnson and Hubert Humphrey.
>
> If we make that effort, it will not only be for the benefit of the Democratic Party. Far more importantly, it will be for the benefit of this whole country.

"Mr. Chairman! Erie County casts 88 votes for the next Senator from the State of New York, Robert F. Kennedy!"

The calling of the roll at the New York State Democratic Convention signaled the beginning of a new Kennedy saga just as Bob's speech in Atlantic City five days earlier had marked the ending of another. Yet, if one shut his eyes and listened to the clerk's voice, one could think back to 1956, when John Kennedy contested for the Democratic Vice Presidential nomination, or to 1960 in Los Angeles.

"New York County casts 98 votes for Kennedy, 16 votes for Stratton. . . . Nassau County casts 70 votes for Kennedy. . . ."

There in the dark, dingy 71st Regiment Armory on Park Avenue —sweltering, stifling without air conditioning—it began anew. Bob was nominated with 968 votes to 153 for Stratton.

The next morning he opened his campaign in keeping with New York tradition by visiting the Fulton Fish Market on the Lower East Side of Manhattan at 5 A.M. He returned to Washington to resign as Attorney General. There was no time for formal good-byes at the Department of Justice, but he stopped by Cardozo High School, where representatives of the Washington schools—more than three thousand in all—had gathered with their bands and their homemade signs to wish him an emotional, touching farewell. As a result he was twenty minutes late for a courtesy call at the White House, but the President was in a buoyant mood and they talked cordially for sixty-five minutes. Then he returned to New York to begin a grueling three-week tour of the state, drawing enormous crowds wherever he went. During this period, he issued a series of position papers, almost daily giving his views on New York problems. The press ignored them. The crowds, the color, the hysteria were the story.

He began at the state fair in Syracuse, continuing through the Catskill resorts to the Nassau County beaches jammed with people on the Labor Day weekend. The morning after Labor Day he headed upstate again, bound for Buffalo, with stops at Binghamton, Johnson City, Endicott, Elmira and Jamestown. By midnight 200,-000 people had turned out to see him. At each stop there was a rally at the airport, a cavalcade into town, a meeting with local officials and a rally at a downtown square or on the steps of the city hall.

At the Jamestown Airport a small jet plane landed just as Bob began to speak, drowning out his voice. "Goldwater sent it," he shouted. The jet rolled to a stop nearby and let off a passenger. Bob resumed speaking, and the jet throttled up and taxied for a take-off. "He's on his way back to Phoenix to report," Bob shouted, and the crowd roared. The town square in Jamestown was jammed with four thousand people where two hundred had turned out two weeks earlier to hear the Republican Vice Presidential candidate, Representative William E. Miller of upstate New York.

Darkness had fallen and Bob was two hours behind schedule when he arrived in Buffalo. A huge crowd was waiting at the airport, and 150,000 persons lined his route into the city. As his open car approached, the crowd swarmed into the streets. Policemen, barely able to balance their motorcycles, struggled alongside the car to keep a narrow path open. Still, the people grabbed for his hand, tore at his clothes, and it took four men, clinging to his legs and grabbing his belt, to keep him from being pulled from the car.

He was three hours late for a meeting with businessmen at the Buffalo Club. To them he said:

> I've been all over the state talking Medicare today, and when I came into Buffalo tonight I thought I needed it myself. . . . The Kennedys always felt Buffalo was a second home. My brother felt that way. President Kennedy ran on the idea of getting his country moving. We are now in the longest period of prosperity this country ever enjoyed—forty-two months. People said we weren't the businessmen's friends. How in the hell could you have a better friend?
>
> My brother used to say when the market went down, it was a Kennedy market. When it went up, it was due to free enterprise. Well, we made an effort to get going in the past three and one-half years. We made a start. We must continue with other programs, health, education, too.

There were two more meetings to address: the Buffalo Area Council AFL-CIO and a kickoff rally of the Erie County Democratic Committee in Kleinhan's Music Hall, where four thousand exuberant Democrats filled the hall to capacity and overflowed into the street. He had not eaten since breakfast at 6:30 in Manhattan. As we waited alone in his hotel room for steaks and chocolate ice cream to be served, I remarked what a tremendous day it had been. "I've never seen crowds like you're getting, they've got to be a good omen."

He looked at me pensively. "Don't you know?" he said. "They're for him—they're for him."

The next day Bob toured Niagara Falls, Batavia and near evening arrived in Rochester, Keating's home town. Again the crowds were large and enthusiastic. The following morning he was shaking hands at 7:30 A.M. with men and women going to work at a General Motors plant. Then he hedgehopped eastward across the northern reaches of the state, glistening and peaceful in the Indian summer weather: Fulton, Oswego, Watertown, Ogdensburg and Massena, where Edward Kennedy had been scheduled to speak the day after his accident. Signs had been printed: "Welcome Senator Ted

Kennedy." Now the signs waved in the air with "Bob" stapled over "Ted." Bob had one of the sign holders take "Bob" off so the audience could see it. "See," he said, "there's one advantage—elect me and it will be cheaper for everybody. We can interchange signs with Massachusetts."

Then to Saranac Lake, Lake Placid and Plattsburg, where four Keating signs taunted him. One said: "Don't Use Me to Further Your Own Political Ambitions." Pointing to the sign, Bob quipped: "Don't worry, I won't."

The last stop was Glens Falls (population: 21,000), the picture of an all-American small town. He had been scheduled to arrive at 8 P.M. As the *Caroline* was in its final approach, Bob, who never wore a wristwatch, asked the time. "We're five hours late," someone said. "This is crazy," he said. "Everybody's gone to bed." But they hadn't.

As the plane came to a stop, a band started playing and a thousand persons, many holding children in their arms, cheered and crowded around the ramp. "Thank you for waiting," he said and groped for the next words. Then he grinned and said dourly, "Well, here we are, five hours late. That's the smooth, hard-driving, well-oiled Kennedy machine for you."

The ride into town was deeply affecting. Men in bathrobes, women in nightgowns and children in pajamas stood along the road or came out of their homes, waving and shouting greetings: "Good to see you, Mr. Kennedy." "Good luck, Bob." At the town square, four thousand people were waiting. He stood on a small platform, gripping a railing tightly and shaking his head in wonder as the crowd cheered lustily. It was 1:30 A.M.

"I'm not going to make a speech," he said, and someone shouted, "Aw, come on, Bob, say what's on your mind."

"I'll just say this," he replied. "I'd like to make my very first commitment of the campaign. I promise that, win or lose, the day after the election I'm coming back to Glens Falls!"

So it went, day after uproarious day. There was little time to think and plan, no way to stay on schedule. Local Democratic professionals were ecstatically translating September crowds into

November votes. The Keating camp and local Republican leaders were apprehensive, and newsmen, viewing the outpouring of emotion and enthusiasm even in traditional Republican strongholds, wondered what it forecast for November or whether it meant anything at all. The report of one disinterested and perceptive observer, Eric Sevareid, is worth reprinting in full:

> This is what happens in the second most interesting political contest in the season.
>
> The rally in New York's Central Park is for Inter-Faith day. The man introducing Republican Senator Kenneth Keating winds up his peroration by shouting, "The day merit goes unrewarded, that will be the end of civilization!"
>
> Keating, silver-haired, ruddy-faced, looks every inch a senator. He delivers an excellent little speech in strong and resonant tones. The applause is very good.
>
> Republican Congressman John Lindsay takes over the podium. Lindsay never quite finishes his speech. Suddenly, no one in the crowd of some 1,500 is listening. In a rippling wave, they mount their chairs and benches and crane their necks to the far edge of the crowd where something is going on. The woman next to me says, "It's him, it's him!"
>
> Bobby has arrived, and the magic chemistry takes over again, as it did in the garment district, all around Brooklyn, up in Spanish Harlem, in every hotel lobby we followed him through.
>
> In no sense is this a normal political contest. The objective issues involving policy do not matter in the slightest; the press hardly bothers to print the candidates' policy proposals; not one voter in a thousand knows wherein the two men differ on policies. Not even university audiences ask Bobby Kennedy questions about foreign or high domestic policy.
>
> Bobby himself is the issue, as Barry Goldwater himself is the biggest issue in the Presidential contest. The people are for him or against him, no matter what Keating has done or what he says. Keating not only has the Goldwater albatross on his back, not only the Conservative Party which will draw away some votes; but he, a palpable, flesh and blood human being, is fighting witchcraft, a symbol of adulation and sorrow, memory of the deepest mass emotion of recent years, a fabulous ghost returned to earth.
>
> For a stretch through night-time Brooklyn, I rode in Kennedy's open convertible, as the half-hysterical crowds, mostly teen-agers, crushed in upon us. The uncomplaining policemen were smashed backwards over the car, kids went down yelping underfoot.
>
> For a few moments I felt a fear akin to panic rising in my chest. The candidate hates it for personal reasons, loves it for political reasons. He

grins his toothy grin, makes his jabbing little gestures, thumb up, like a hitchhiker, and in those pure Kennedy accents quotes Dante and Bernard Shaw and Pericles, even in the most sordid, poverty stained streets of this wonderful and ghastly city.

It doesn't matter whether he properly inherited the Kennedy mystique or not, whether he deserves it or not. He has it, by name and by act of appropriation. In terms of his own long-term political interest, he was right to seize the baton this year, to run for office wherever he can run, whether he beats Keating or not. He may well do so, by virtue of his name and Johnson's coattails, but he isn't sure. It is impossible to be sure about this unprecedented race.

President Johnson is going to take perhaps 50% of the normal Republican vote in New York; Kennedy is going to get none of it and is going to lose some normal Democratic and independent votes, among the Jews, for example, who owe Keating much, feel sorry for him in his predicament but feel sorry for Bobby, also, as the bereaved younger brother.

Statewide, however, his two great handicaps are the carpetbagger label and his image as a ruthless, power-hungry young man. He is trying to melt down these obstacles by shaking every hand, grinning into every face he can get near.

But he's seeing the people and they are seeing him, and everywhere he is the departed ghost become flesh, sending shivers up the spines of the worshipful.

The New York vote will split all over the place. In 1950, these people elected a Republican governor, a Democratic senator and, in the big town, an independent mayor.

Objectively, he has only one real claim: that as a Kennedy, and as a Democratic senator working with a presumably Democratic administration, he can swing more weight on behalf of this state. In their heads, the voters may recognize the force of this; but they are going to vote from their hearts. This is entirely a subjective affair, a matter of mysticism, not fact, and only a mystic could even try to foretell the outcome.

Mysticism and the legend of John Kennedy; Johnson and Goldwater; caricatures of the good Bob and the ruthless Bob; sympathy for Keating and excitement over Kennedy—all these interlaced and exerted their powerful emotions upon the voters, but the election would be decided by what the two candidates did in the final five weeks of the campaign.

In the tumultuous early weeks, Bob succeeded in blunting the charge that he was a carpetbagger. He did not believe that it would be a decisive issue. His poll showed that it bothered only a handful of voters and made no difference to most—86 percent in New York City, 77 percent in the suburbs and 78 percent upstate. Keating, on the other hand, used it as a major weapon throughout the campaign. When Bob entered the race, Keating welcomed him with an offer to furnish him with a road map, a guidebook and other useful literature about the Empire State. Bob countered by saying, "I know where I stand, I'm for Lyndon Johnson and I'm against Barry Goldwater and no other candidate for the Senate can make that statement"—a reference to the fact that Keating had disassociated himself from Goldwater and would not say that he would vote for the Arizonan.[5] But more effectively, Bob joked about being a carpetbagger, brought it up at every stop and turned it inward. At Batavia six girls held up a sign to show that they were from nearby Kennedy, New York. "They talk about me being a carpetbagger," Bob said pointing at the sign, "and I have a city named after me."

He leased a large home at Glen Cove, Long Island, for two years and told his audiences that he intended to live in New York win or lose. At Cornell University, taking note of some Goldwater signs, he said: "I'm glad to see some people for Senator Goldwater here. It gives you the feeling that the two-party system isn't dead. I can't believe those people holding the signs are going to college."

"Go home!" a boy holding one of the signs bellowed.

"I was just down at Long Island," Bob replied.

When he stumped in the Bronx, he quipped: "I've seen signs all over the state which say, 'Why don't you go back where you came from?' Well, I am glad to be back where I came from—which is the Bronx."

The carpetbagger issue receded and other more serious matters

5. Keating's refusal to endorse Goldwater cost him some votes to the Conservative Party candidate, Henry Paolucci, but unquestionably gained him more votes than he lost. Goldwater wrote off New York from the beginning and made only one appearance in the state. Conservative upstate GOP leaders were more concerned about Bob's entry into New York than they were about Keating's defection and closed ranks in backing him. Furthermore, Keating retained the support of independents and liberals who feared Bob and could not stomach Goldwater.

emerged. One was personal. In late September the strain of the eighteen-hour days and the mauling of the crowds began to show. He called a meeting of his key aides and said: "You can keep scheduling me like this and I can get through it. There are six weeks to go and I can survive, but you'll have a zombi at the end. I'll make mistakes. I haven't any time to think, and I'll tell you I don't think it's very satisfactory, but I can keep doing it."

There was an awkward silence. Nolan and Feldman, who had the last word on scheduling, and the rest of us had been under the impression that Bob had wanted to maintain the pace.

"All right, Bob," said Nolan, "we'll knock it off a bit."

Thereafter the daily schedules were shortened, and he was given one day a week off. He usually spent them at Glen Cove, but they were not totally restful. Except for times when he swam or played with the children, he met with advisers, worked on speeches or looked at film of his television commercials. But the pace did slacken, and it was fortunate, for about that time Keating began to gain ground.

Keating was sixty-four years old, an urbane, genial man who had represented his home town of Rochester in Congress for twelve years and had narrowly won election to the Senate in 1958. He was a graduate of Harvard Law School and had been an Army intelligence officer in the Second World War. As a Congressman he had reflected the middle-of-the-road conservative Republican views of his district, but as a Senator he had moved to the left of center in the Republican Party, following the lead of his New York colleague, Jacob Javits. He had assiduously courted New York's large Jewish vote while keeping an anchor to the windward by appearing just as conscientiously at Communion breakfasts and American Legion functions. He was well liked in the Senate and had his name as co-author on several pieces of important legislation, including the 1957 Civil Rights Act and the Constitutional Amendment giving residents of the District of Columbia the right to vote in national elections. But he was best known for spreading the alarm that Soviet missiles were being emplaced in Cuba, acting on the reports of refugees—information which the White House also had but couldn't act upon until it was validated by the U-2 aerial photographs.

Keating's crowds were small, but were attentive and friendly. During the early weeks he was content to play with the carpetbagger issue, talk about his own record and give his young opponent a brush of his hand. In Buffalo, ten days after Bob's frantic reception there, he was asked at a Catholic girls school whether there was any philosophic difference between him and Bob.

"I just don't know his philosophy," Keating answered. "He's not got a record on anything except in the civil rights field. . . . His main case against me is that I'm a Republican, but I don't think the people of New York are so rigid on party voting. I think they're more sophisticated than that."

But as the novelty of Bob's entry into New York began to fade and the momentum appeared to be shifting, Keating took the offensive, with the popular Javits running interference, questioning Bob's record on civil rights and raising the McCarthy issue. Governor Rockefeller's organization and the whole Republican establishment, freed of any commitment to work for Goldwater, pitched in.

On a quiet Sunday afternoon in September, Keating ripped the campaign open by charging at a Chemical Workers Union meeting in Newark, New Jersey, that Bob "made a deal" in the General Aniline & Film Corporation settlement that would return $60 million of the firm's assets to its "former Nazi cartel owners," that the Swiss holding company, Interhandel, which got the money, was a cloak for I. G. Farben, "the chemical arsenal for Nazi Germany." The statement, with its carefully worded key phrases, had only one purpose—to send chills and revulsion through the Jewish Community. And the Jews had become the pivotal ethnic bloc in the election, for, though they traditionally voted Democratic, they were wavering. Many thought Keating had done a good job and felt sympathy for him. Thus they were hesitating to yield to their Democratic leanings and vote for the brother of the beloved John Kennedy. For Bob they had sympathy, too, but they also had some misgivings.

We had anticipated the General Aniline issue would be raised but had not expected Keating to link Bob with "Nazis." We released a statement pointing out that "according to all available information no money would go to any Nazis" and that as a result of the settlement more than $100 million would be used to pay war claims to Americans who had suffered "at Nazi hands." But Bob was not satisfied.

"What else can we do to turn this around?" he asked.

Several of us thought the attack was so clearly a smear and such a heavy-handed appeal for the Jewish vote that it would repel many Jews. However, Richard Neustadt, author of *Presidential Power* and a consultant to President Truman and President Kennedy, had another thought. "It gives you the justification for attacking him for a change," Neustadt said, and the next morning Bob did.

Gone was the boyish smile. Gone were the deferential references to Keating.

"I never have heard of a charge as low as this one," Bob said grimly at a press conference in his suite at the Carlyle Hotel. "I really expected more from Mr. Keating.

"I must say, his charges were received by me with a good deal of bitterness. I'm not pro-Nazi. I lost my brother and my brother-in-law to the Nazis. I'm not about to make any deals with Nazis. What possibly could be my motive? I have a different opinion of Senator Keating now."

A reporter asked if Bob thought the charge would influence Jewish voters, and he answered:

"In New York, with its heavy Jewish population, there are so many people who have suffered so much from the Nazis, this charge can't help but have an effect. If it were true, I wouldn't deserve to be elected to any public office. The charge isn't true."

Keating had said that he did not know if his statement would affect Jewish voters, and another reporter asked Bob if he thought Keating had been sincere in saying so.

"In my judgment, he was not being truthful," Bob replied.

Then Bob pointed out that Keating had introduced the Senate bill which authorized the sale of General Aniline, had been kept fully informed as the settlement was negotiated and had approved its final terms. Why, then, had Keating waited eighteen months to raise an objection? Bob asked.

Keating had already backed down a bit. Before Bob's press conference, he said: "I have not charged improper motives. . . . I don't think it is my responsibility to tell the Attorney General. . . . I'm not accusing anyone of any heinous crimes . . . I have no proof of improper motives."

Keating continued to mention the case for several days, but, as Frank Lynn of the New York *World Telegram* noted, it seemed obvious that the attack was aimed at New York City's 1.3 million Jewish voters, for Keating did not discuss General Aniline upstate except in answer to press conference questions. Then, apparently sensing that it was beginning to boomerang, he dropped it altogether.

The *New York Times*, which was supporting Keating, called it a "fake issue" and said:

Senator Keating is playing upon what he hopes is voter ignorance in castigating the Justice Department's settlement in the General Aniline and Film case as a payoff to a "huge Nazi cartel." The truth is that neither Senator Keating nor anyone else can be certain whether a portion of the money to be paid . . . may ultimately find its way into the hands of the German owners of the old I. G. Farben.

In the same editorial the *Times* criticized Bob for telling workers at the Brooklyn Navy Yard, which had been marked for closing (and later was), that he would see that the Pentagon provided enough work to keep them fully employed. The *Times* concluded:

New Yorkers know perfectly well that in the long run no politician— not even a Kennedy—can keep a shipyard or an air base in operation if the facility is outmoded or uneconomic. They also know that neither Senatorial candidate is sympathetic to Nazis. Will Mr. Kennedy and Mr. Keating now dispense with the nonsense and get to the issues?

But General Aniline remained a factor in the campaign, though it was never debated and was mentioned only occasionally. Keating had thought he was landing a Sunday punch, but only grazed his opponent below the belt. Thereafter, Keating was either unwilling or unable to mount an effective attack. Bob had been riding on the impact of his screaming crowds. He had been reluctant to attack Keating directly, fearing that, with his reputation for toughness and aggressiveness, he might create sympathy for the white-haired, well-meaning Senator. But that ended when Keating accused him of being party to a deal with Nazis. He had counterattacked and Keating had given ground. The whole tenor of Bob's campaign changed. His strategy shifted, and he was free to carry the fight to Keating.

At this point in the campaign, every indicator of voter sentiment was making it painfully clear that the race would not be won with the roar of the crowd, President Johnson's coattails and the memory of President Kennedy. Bob's own poll, taken in the last week of September, showed Keating with 40 percent of the vote, Bob with 39 percent and 21 percent undecided. Several things could be done immediately.

Polls also showed that President Johnson's lead over Goldwater in New York was mounting to landslide proportions. Bob had said in almost every appearance that he supported President Johnson, but it had been more to take a swipe at Keating's refusal to endorse Goldwater than to identify with the President. His campaign poster, showing him in shirtsleeves, said, "Let's Put Bob Kennedy to Work for New York." A new slogan was adopted: "Get on the Johnson, Humphrey, Kennedy Team," and it appeared with a new photograph of Bob wearing a business suit.

Communication between the Presidential campaign staff and Bob improved. The President triumphantly stumped New York twice with Bob in October, drawing enormous, enthusiastic crowds. Humphrey made three trips to the state, concentrating in the New York City metropolitan area, where his popularity with liberal Democrats undoubtedly made a difference. Humphrey and Bob brought traffic to a halt at noon on Fifth Avenue, campaigned through the garment district and in Westchester County and held an uproarious rally on the steps of the Borough Hall in Brooklyn, where ten Goldwater signs bobbed amid a crowd of five thousand persons. Bob spoke first.

"The Goldwater campaign is so well organized they were able to get ten supporters out to the rally. . . . They flew them in from Albany and several other places." Then he listed measures that Goldwater had voted against and said: "If you want him, you can have him."

Humphrey carried on the attack, and the Goldwater signs were swallowed in waves of laughter. Then he praised Bob's "great contributions to the Kennedy-Johnson Administration" and said he was "a fine man, a fine friend and the leader of a great new political movement in New York."

As Humphrey and Bob walked inside the hall to be photographed with local candidates, Humphrey, smiling broadly, put his arm around Bob's shoulder and said, "Bobby, you really took them on."

"Hubert," said Bob, "you didn't do badly yourself—thanks a lot."

A second thing that could be done quickly was to tighten Bob's campaign organization. Voter registration, a major factor in President Kennedy's election in 1960, had been left in the hands of the New York professionals. As a special four-day registration period approached, it was evident that many local leaders considered new voters a threat to their control and were sitting on their hands. In those areas, particularly in black and Puerto Rican neighborhoods, Kennedy workers marshaled their own registration drives, adding thousands to the rolls. There was similar lack of performance by the regulars in preparing campaign literature to be distributed where Bob spoke. One night, when Bob returned from four rallies in Brooklyn, where there were no leaflets in evidence, he said, "Call Joe Dolan and see if he'll come up here. If nobody can get this job done, I know he can."

Dolan was still serving in the Justice Department as Assistant Deputy Attorney General.[6] He resigned the next morning, arrived in New York at noon and the following evening, working with Bernard Ruggieri, had fifty thousand leaflets ready for distribution.

6. Dolan became Bob's administrative assistant in the Senate.

On one side was Bob's photograph with his signature and on the other a synopsis of his record and his position on issues.

It demonstrated one of Bob's remarkable strengths—the capability to reach out for competent, loyal help in moments of trouble and get fast, effective response. It was only necessary to get on the phone to Dolan and others and say, "Bob needs you," and they came: Gerald Trombley, an experienced advance man who had been a law school classmate of Bob's and a lawyer in Charlottesville, Virginia; E. Barrett Prettyman, Jr., another law school classmate and Washington, D.C., lawyer, to advise on transportation and other problems; Mrs. Polly Fitzgerald of Boston to arrange women's functions; John Douglas to untangle administrative problems and advise on strategy; and many more.

A third decision which could be implemented immediately was to take advantage of the opening Keating had provided and attack him directly on his record as a liberal Republican. Bob opened this front by stating that Keating had voted against such liberal legislation as federal aid to education, federal housing programs, the distribution of surplus food to welfare families and the free school lunch program. On 20 of 23 votes in the House and Senate on public housing, Bob noted, Keating had voted against the position taken by Javits. For the first three weeks of October it was the major theme of Bob's campaign, and with Wagner strongly taking the same line, Keating was forced to spend considerable time defending and explaining his record.

Three other developments caused the tide to shift back in Bob's favor and carry him to victory. They were:

1. *Television.* Bob believed that the voters did not begin to focus finally on how they would cast their ballots until the final weeks of a campaign—"after the World Series." Thus he held back a massive television campaign until the final four weeks, when in twenty-second spots, one-minute spots and several half-hour programs, he was shown doing what he did best—answering difficult questions. Many of the short spots were filmed in shopping center parking lots with the questioners chosen at random from shoppers, but probably the single, most effective footage was a thirty-minute program con-

densed from an hour-and-a-half question-and-answer session with articulate students at Columbia University.

The commercials enabled Bob to be seen as a strong young man with ideas, energy and a sense of humor. In the Columbia film a student asked, "What is your position on birth control?" Bob stumbled for an answer, then turned and looked at Ethel, who had already left her seat and was heading for the door.

All the commercials centered on Bob personally or showed him with Ethel and his children, and he came across with such validity that it was hard to equate the figure on the television screen with the menacing, ruthless, power-hungry stereotype that the Keating camp and the Democrats for Keating were seeking to pass off as the genuine Kennedy.

Keating used television as extensively as Bob did. Some spots showed Keating discussing issues in answer to questions. Some were animated cartoons, raising the carpetbagger issue. Others were singing commercials—"Keating, keep Keating, Keating is our man"—and many were testimonials from liberal Republican Senators—Javits, Margaret Chase Smith of Maine, Clifford Case of New Jersey, Thomas Kuchel of California and George Aiken of Vermont.

Bob's commercials concentrated on the man himself—what he thought and what he felt—and proved to be more effective than Keating's package, which aimed at reminding voters that New York already had a fine Senator and at questioning Bob's credentials.

During the final five weeks the Kennedy campaign purchased the services of a free-lance television news team, which filmed him wherever he went. Every night two planes flew film that the crew had shot to every television station in New York State. No attempt was made to edit the film to Bob's advantage. It was provided to the stations free of charge, and many used it in their evening news shows. On several occasions when his team was the only television crew present at an interesting, unforeseen news break, stations in New York City as well as upstate used the footage. It was expensive, costing about $100,000, but on more than one occasion 98 percent of the New York stations used his film, enabling Bob to get television coverage that couldn't have been purchased and proving that sixty seconds on the 6 o'clock news was more valuable than sixty-minute commercials.

2. *The Black Vote.* The odds are that Bob probably would have received heavy black support, but an incident that occurred midway in the campaign might have cut deeply into the black vote if it hadn't been for Charles Evers, who had taken his slain brother's place as head of the NAACP in Mississippi.

The NAACP was holding its state convention in Buffalo on October 2 and 3. Keating was to speak on the second and Bob the next day. Evers had been invited to be the principal speaker at a dinner meeting on the second. In a prepared text which was distributed to the press, Keating accused Bob of running out on the civil rights drive, saying, "He abandoned his post at the Department of Justice with an unfinished task before him. This task is vigorous enforcement of the 1964 Civil Rights Act, of putting teeth into the new law and defending it against attacks on its constitutionality."

In his actual address, however, Keating softened his attack. He praised Bob's efforts on behalf of civil rights and said nothing about a "run-out." When reporters questioned him about the change, he said he stood by his advance text.

Evers, listening to Keating, was told that the NAACP was prepared to endorse the Republican incumbent. That night Evers discarded his prepared text and defended Bob for thirty minutes and chided the state NAACP leadership for considering endorsement of Keating:

You're fortunate to have a man of Kennedy's caliber even visit New York, much less running for Senator. If he ran for dogcatcher in Mississippi, every Negro in Mississippi would vote for him.

He has done more for minority groups in Mississippi than any other Attorney General. . . . We don't need someone who will talk civil rights and go along, we've had that. We need action. We need young blood and he is the one man who has cared.

In the face of Evers' rigorous remarks and a strong rebuttal to Keating's statement by Bob the next morning, the NAACP decided to remain officially neutral. Later, William Booth, president of the

New York State Conference of NAACP Branches, personally endorsed Keating, but the organization issued a statement stating that it had not endorsed either candidate and added:

> Senator Keating has a long and excellent record of support of civil rights legislation, going back to his days as a Congressman. . . .
> Robert Kennedy was the best Attorney General on civil rights in the whole history of the United States. . . .
> New York State Negro voters must make up their own minds on how they will vote on these two men, both of whom have excellent records on the civil rights issue. It may be that voters will want to consider other factors, but on civil rights the two records are clear.

It may have turned out that an NAACP endorsement of Keating would not have made any difference. Bob thought it would have, reaching beyond the black vote to liberal whites. He felt that it was fortunate that Evers had been invited to the convention and was deeply grateful for what Evers did.

3. *The Debates.* In the early weeks of the campaign when Bob and New York were delighting in discovering each other, Keating challenged him to a debate. But adhering to the politician's maxim that the front-runner doesn't need to debate, Bob didn't accept the challenge. When the tide turned at the end of September, he changed his mind. Most of his closest advisers, including Steve Smith and Bernard Ruggieri, were opposed. The danger they and others saw was that Bob with his direct manner would appear to be attacking the white-maned, courtly Senator as they traded debating points and put himself in a hole from which it would be difficult to recover. Some suggested that he wait a week and see if he continued to decline in the polls.

"Next week will be too late," Bob said. "By then Keating can say that his schedule is set for the rest of the campaign. He can't say that today. We have to decide now."

In the end he overruled his advisers. That night, he said, "The overriding consideration is that if I lose, and hadn't debated, I'll never forgive myself."

But now Keating, asserting publicly that he was forging ahead, lost interest in debating. It was easy for either side to frustrate the other. Keating had originally proposed that they debate head on in the Lincoln-Douglas style. Bob had insisted upon following the format of the 1960 debates, in which newsmen had asked questions which John Kennedy and Richard Nixon answered in turn, with brief opening and closing statements by each candidate. Unless each side agreed to the other's demand there could be no debate, and neither Bob nor Keating, acting through seconds—New York City Council President Paul R. Screvane for Bob and Herbert Brownell, Jr., President Eisenhower's first Attorney General, for Keating— would budge.

When Keating's surge began to wane in mid-October and the first summary of the New York *Daily News*'s usually reliable straw poll showed Bob leading 59 to 38.9 percent, it was Keating's turn again to demand the debate and Bob's turn to demur.

They traded charges until October 28—a week before the election. WCBS-TV had offered an hour of evening time for a debate, an offer that both sides accepted, but neither side would accept the other's proposed format nor could they agree on any other. That was fine with Bob. On the afternoon of the twenty-eighth the negotiations broke down and word reached Bob in the Carlyle Hotel that Keating had purchased a half-hour of CBS time at 7:30 that evening and was going to debate an empty chair. Bob called the station and asked to buy the next half-hour and was refused. Then he called CBS President William Paley in California, pointed out that the CBS outlet in New York seemed to be taking sides, and not long after their conversation CBS officials in New York sold him the half-hour.

Then Bob decided that he would appear and occupy Keating's "empty chair." The decision was a tightly guarded secret, and at 7:29 P.M. Bob appeared at the door of the studio where Keating, with Javits at his side, was about to go on. CBS functionaries blocked the door.

"I'm here to debate—Senator Keating has invited me to debate," Bob insisted.

"I'm sorry, I can't let you in," said a CBS man.

"Senator Keating said he would have an empty chair for me. I'm here and I want to go in."

"Mr. Keating has purchased this time and I can't permit you to enter."

"Then kindly inform Senator Keating that I'm here and ready to go on the air. . . . Why were you waiting for me?"

"We wanted to see you in your proper place."

"This is my proper place," Bob retorted as television news cameras clicked and inside Keating was telling his audience, "I wanted this debate for the benefit of the people of New York and also for my own sake because I know a face-to-face meeting between my opponent and myself would expose his ruthless attempt to destroy my lifetime career."

Bob then asked a CBS man to go into the studio and tell Keating he was there. The CBS man did, and Bob waited along with a score of reporters and news cameramen. When the CBS man reappeared, accompanied by a lawyer, he told Bob that it was a paid political broadcast and he would not be admitted.

"Then kindly remove the empty seat from the stage and ask Senator Keating to withdraw his remark about my not showing up," Bob demanded.

"I cannot," the lawyer replied.

Bob turned and stalked away after saying, "You are obviously being unfair. This is dishonest."

Then he went to the studio which had been reserved for him, fully expecting that Keating would come at the start of the Kennedy half-hour. We planned to admit him and escort him to a microphone. "What will you do?" someone asked Bob. "I don't know," he said. "Maybe I'll talk about the empty chair."

But Keating didn't appear. Instead, he panicked and brushed aside reporters waiting to question him as he emerged from his studio. He broke into a trot, ducked around a corner past stage props—furniture and artificial trees—which Keating aides pulled into the path of a wedge of pursuing reporters and photographers, out a door, down two flights of stairs, past Ethel Kennedy who was entering the building. "Where's my husband?" asked the astonished Ethel. Keating ran and left the building.

It mattered not what either candidate said on their programs. It mattered not that the next day the newspapers impartially reported what had happened. Television cameras had photographed the drama—Bob standing outside the studio door, demanding to be let in, and Keating fleeing the scene with fake palm trees hurtling through the air behind him. Millions of voters *saw* that, and for all practical purposes the race was over.

On election night Bob polled 3,823,749 votes to Keating's 3,104,056. His margin was nearly 2,000,000 votes smaller than President Johnson's over Goldwater, but was 300,000 more than he had expected. More important, he had made the difficult transition from campaign manager to candidate and had stayed alive politically. He was back on his feet, out of his brother's shadow, and he had the great inner satisfaction of knowing that at the crucial moments in a difficult political struggle he had made the right decisions.

In his victory speech to a hall full of campaign workers in the Statler Hilton Hotel, he said: "I believe this vote is a mandate to continue the efforts begun by my brother four years ago—the effort to get something started in this country—and a vote of confidence for Lyndon Johnson and Hubert Humphrey."

Then he thanked his campaign workers, Mayor Wagner, Harriman, Mayor John Burns of Binghamton, Peter Straus, William McKeon and others, with special mention for Smith as the relative "who went far beyond the effort one brother-in-law gives to another," but he forgot to thank President Johnson.

He concluded with a favorite quote from Tennyson: " 'Come, my friends, 'tis not too late to seek a newer world'—that is what I dedicate myself to in the next six years for the State of New York."

From the hotel he went to a victory party in Delmonico's Restaurant on Park Avenue, napped for an hour and started out before dawn to return to the Fulton Fish Market. Then he kept his first campaign promise and flew to Glens Falls.

Chapter 14

Very Gentle, Very Brave

In the spring of 1965 I left Bob to return to newspaper work, joining the staff of the Los Angeles *Times*. On May 1, the evening before I departed, Bob and Ethel gave a party at Hickory Hill for JoAnn and me and Violet and Burke Marshall, who was leaving the government at the same time to become general counsel of IBM.

Bob set the tone for the evening by explaining that he was giving the party to show there were no hard feelings for all the trouble Burke and I had caused him. The atmosphere was buoyant and lighthearted, but saying good-bye was difficult. Bob walked with JoAnn and me to the door. We shook hands. He said, "I'll see you," and I said, "We'll keep in touch." He turned and walked away and we went toward our car. JoAnn was crying and I could hear Bob calling someone in the house.

Thereafter, Bob and I saw each other frequently and talked often by telephone, but others were much closer to the action. Of the last three years, my recollections are a sequence of scenes—a kaleidoscope of memories. Some, like the Manchester affair, I'd just as soon forget. Most are pleasant, and all remind me of his qualities that seemed so special to those who knew him well.

In 1966, Bob asked John Seigenthaler and me to read William Manchester's manuscript for *The Death of a President*. I had been involved in the project from its inception in February 1964. Jacqueline Kennedy hoped at that time to limit exploitative, sensational writing about the President's death by assisting one author in writing a definitive account, and it seemed to be a worthwhile idea. No one whom she and Bob consulted objected. Manchester, a sensitive, experienced journalist, was selected and signed an agreement giving the Kennedys the right to review the manuscript and providing for its publication by spring 1969.

It was a mistake from the beginning. Not that Manchester was not a fully competent author, but for the Kennedys to retain the right of review as a condition for their cooperation, for Manchester to agree to write under those conditions and for anyone to expect that the authorization of an account of an event of such interest and importance would diminish exploitation—all these were errors. But neither Manchester nor Bob nor any of their advisers realized that at the time. Nor did we foresee the emotional strain that re-creating the agony of those dreadful days and the conditions of the agreement would impose on the author. Nor did we foresee that Manchester's vivid manuscript would reflect unfavorably upon President Johnson or that by the time it would be ready for publication Bob would be a strong, independent force, often opposed to the President's policies, and a possible challenger for the nomination in 1968.

The manuscript which Seigenthaler and I read was so strongly critical of President Johnson that it seemed to us that its hostility would destroy the credibility of the book. The substantive changes that we and Evan Thomas, Manchester's editor, suggested were intended to diminish this problem. But when Manchester and Mrs. Kennedy could not agree on much less important details—mostly of personal concern to her—the dispute deteriorated into an undignified lawsuit, demeaning everyone involved, Bob most of all.

No one had to explain to him the unfavorable political repercussions of a court battle, even if Manchester was found partly at fault. But between backing his sister-in-law, right or wrong, or deserting her to avoid damage to his career, Bob chose the former as the only honorable course. That having been decided, he suffered through it, put it behind him and never reproached Seigenthaler and me for what was obvious: he had relied upon us to resolve any difficulties that might arise. Red flags were flying clearly, but we had failed to see them. If we had, we might have been able to spare him and his family—and Manchester—all that agony.

Our fourth child, Diane, was born October 21, 1966, about an hour after Bob arrived in Los Angeles to campaign for Governor Edmund G. (Pat) Brown, whose bid for a third term was destined to fail against the conservative assault of Ronald Reagan. The next morning Bob had the campaign caravan detour to Cedars of Lebanon Hospital. He was Diane's first visitor.

On a trip down the Colorado River in the Grand Canyon, we camped one night at Vasey's Paradise, a shore of sand, rocks and willows. The next morning Bob began studying the canyon walls and turned to Jim Whittaker. "Do you think it's difficult to climb?" Bob asked. "Somewhat," the mountaineer replied. "Okay, everybody," Bob shouted, "let's go!" And almost everyone went, with Whittaker leading and showing us how to inch our way up the steepest parts. It was not as difficult or as dangerous as it appeared from the canyon floor. The children learned about climbing and about courage, but no one except Bob in the party of forty-two would have thought about doing it.

Bob was the speaker for the Democrats at the Washington press corps's annual Gridiron Dinner in March 1967. A fortnight before, he had returned from Paris with what he believed was a peace feeler from Hanoi. The news had been leaked by a State Department official before Bob landed in New York, and there followed an extremely acrimonious meeting with President Johnson in the White House.[1] The President viewed Bob's trip with deep suspicion and resentment. Bob concluded that the President was so hypno-

---

1. A full account of the incident is contained in *The Secret Search for Peace in Vietnam* by David Kraslow and Stuart H. Loory.

tized by prospects of a military victory in Vietnam that a chance for a negotiated settlement was slipping by. On March 2 he broke finally and fully with Johnson on the war when, in a Senate speech, he advocated a bombing halt, a beginning of peace talks and international inspection through the United Nations to report on any further escalation of forces by either side.

The Gridiron custom calls for the Republican and Democratic spokesmen to tell a series of jokes and to conclude with brief, serious remarks. In his speech Bob said:

> Some of you have expressed an interest in knowing the full story about my conference with President Johnson after I returned from Europe. When I walked in, he stood up, looked me right in the eye without a smile and said sternly: "Bob, the time has come for you to tell me one thing— something I have wanted to know for a long time—when are you going to get your hair cut?"
>
> Then we had a long serious talk about the possibilities of a cease-fire, the dangers of escalation and the prospects for negotiations. And he promised me the next time we are going to talk about Vietnam.
>
> You see, all those stories about Mr. Johnson and me not getting along during my brother's years in the White House simply do not square with the facts. We started out during the Kennedy Administration on the best of terms—friendly, close, cordial—but then, as we were leaving the inaugural stands . . . [Long pause.]
>
> Of course, I am more than anxious to settle any disputes the President and I might have. I have made it clear before—and I want to make it clear tonight—that I am willing to go more than halfway to the White House.

Remarks at the Gridiron are off-the-record. By tradition "there are no reporters present." The dinner is given to honor and lampoon the President, who often attends, although Johnson did not that night. Vice President Humphrey was there, as were members of the Cabinet, the Supreme Court, leaders of Congress and other dignitaries, as well as the leading Washington correspondents and their publishers and editors. When it came time to be serious, this is what Bob said:

> Gentlemen: We have our differences; we have our disagreements. But we are all citizens of a wondrous land, united by a common pride in its pro-

gress and by a common obligation to its advancement. No other nation in the history of the world has been so faithful to its word, so generous with its wealth and so restrained in the use of its military might.

And no other group of men in the world has ever borne the awesome burdens that weigh down the men who lead this country. Their task is to manage the unmanageable, to reconcile the irreconcilable and in the end to save mankind from itself. For man has now learned to live in outer space and to live in the ocean depths—but human life is not yet secure and serene between.

Our leaders are neither all-wise nor all-powerful. They are mere mortals doing the best they can. The rest of us—in the Congress and the press and elsewhere—must give them our patient help and our prayers. We can offer both comments and criticism—that is not only our right but our duty. But let us remember the ancient Greek adage, that "None can climb the heights but those to whom the miseries of the world *are* misery and will not let them rest."

Those words were just right for a Gridiron audience—generous to the President and conciliatory—but as Bob spoke, the forces that would drive Johnson from office and propel Bob toward his rendezvous with death were fully in motion.

In 1962 Bob stopped briefly in Saigon on his trip to mediate the West New Guinea dispute. Upon departing, he stated to newsmen: "We are going to win and we are going to stay here until we win."

Following the Bay of Pigs he had become one of the Administration's leading advocates of counterinsurgency. In 1962 he believed that, with the retraining program then under way, the forces of South Vietnam were relying less on conventional tactics and gaining the capability to deal effectively with Vietcong terrorism and guerrilla warfare; and that that, plus the strategic village program to secure the countryside step by step, would end the Communist threat as the British had done in Malaya after fighting for eleven years. But in the fall of 1963 the political situation deteriorated as the regime of Ngo Dinh Diem and his brother, Ngo Dinh Nhu, met opposition from the Buddhists and students with harsh repression and became increasingly separated from the people. The counter-guerrilla program lost momentum, and Bob began to have some doubts, as did others in the Administration.

On September 6 the National Security Council met to consider what steps could be taken to force Diem to make political reforms and regain the initiative on the battlefield. Roger Hilsman, then Under Secretary of State for Far Eastern Affairs, wrote later in his book *To Move a Nation:*

During the Cuban missile crisis, it had been the Attorney General who had asked some of the more fundamental and wiser questions, and he did so again at this meeting. The first and fundamental question, he felt, was what we were doing in Vietnam. As he understood it, we were there to help the people resisting a Communist take-over. The first question was whether a Communist take-over could be successfully resisted with any government. If it could not, now was the time to get out of Vietnam entirely, rather than waiting. If the answer was that it could, but not with a Diem-Nhu government as it was now constituted, we owed it to the people resisting Communism in Vietnam to give [Ambassador] Lodge enough sanctions to bring changes that would permit successful resistance. But the basic question of whether a Communist take-over could be successfully resisted with any government had not been answered, and he was not sure that anyone had enough information *to* answer it. The ensuing debate on whether or not we were winning the war or had ever been winning it produced no agreement.

The meeting was one of several which the National Security Council held through the fall, during which it deliberated inconclusively while the deterioration in Vietnam culminated in a revolt of Diem's generals and the assassination of Diem and Nhu on November 1. The American Government waited for the air to clear. Then came Dallas. It would be one of Bob's deepest regrets that at no time while President Kennedy lived did the Executive Committee of the National Security Council apply the hard, intensive examination to Vietnam that it had to the Cuban missile crisis.

"We were just getting to it," Bob told me ruefully some months later. To put this in context one must understand that no two Presidents operate alike, and though President Johnson retained many of President Kennedy's top advisers, the Ex Comm's makeup and its role in the decision-making process changed after November 22. There was no sense of recrimination in Bob's remark, only regret.

As the nation emerged from the trauma of Dallas and plunged into a Presidential election year, Vietnam was moved to a back burner, smoldering, worrisome, but only a gray cloud on the bright horizon of the Great Society. Yet President Johnson had hardly taken the oath of office for his new term when the political unrest in Saigon that had toppled four governments after Diem's and the declining strength of South Vietnamese forces in the field confronted him with difficult decisions that could not be put off any longer.

In mid-January 1965 word reached Bob from within the Administration that Johnson was leaning toward withdrawal. Bob believed that the United States could not afford to abandon South Vietnam; that it would undermine our commitments to other nations and would be harmful, politically, economically and strategically, as well as psychologically, throughout Southeast Asia. He knew, for example, from his trips to Indonesia that the American effort in South Vietnam and the presence of the Seventh Fleet in Southeast Asia were major factors in sustaining opposition to the powerful Communist Party in that key country. However, he was just as strongly opposed to escalation of the war and thought counterinsurgency still had a chance to force a reasonably satisfactory political solution, such as had been achieved in Laos in 1962.

His views were close to those of Hilsman, who had been an architect of the counterinsurgency program. Hilsman had resigned from the State Department in February 1964 when he judged, correctly, that President Johnson would move toward a military solution and he thought he could oppose it more effectively as a private citizen. With Hilsman's help, Bob began drafting a speech opposing a pull-out. It was not completed when eight Americans were killed in a heavy Vietcong attack on the American barracks at Pleiku, February 7, 1965. President Johnson responded by bombing North Vietnam, and the deadly escalation of the war began.

The bombing deeply troubled Bob. He, of course, knew that it was one of the alternatives under consideration, and in the speech that he never gave there was this paragraph:

We must understand that while bombing targets in North Viet Nam may induce more caution in Hanoi, they will not bring peace to South Viet Nam. In the last analysis, the way to defeat the terrorists is to increase our capability to fight their kind of war.

However, he was convinced that if he raised his voice—a freshman Senator three weeks in office—it would add substance to the stereotype of the ruthless power-seeker and, worse, be interpreted as a personal attack on President Johnson, rekindling the public fight between them, rather than an honest disagreement on strategy. He remained silent, and it was for him, too, the beginning of a long period of escalation—of vexing second thoughts and self-doubts.

He traveled extensively at home and abroad, became deeply involved in the problems of New York and spoke out knowledgeably on the urban crisis, nuclear arms control and many other subjects, but his dilemma over the war held him like a vise. Increasingly, he thought our course was insanely wrong, morally as well as tactically. Yet he was restrained by the belief that if he spoke out it would only be put in the context of a personal struggle with the President, arouse the criticism that he was "only going after headlines" and possibly stiffen Johnson's back. He shook free in February 1966 to propose that, as a condition for getting peace talks started, the Administration should indicate that it was willing to negotiate with the Vietcong as well as with Hanoi. The reaction was worse than he had expected.

"Whatever the exact status of the National Liberation Front—puppet or partly independent," Bob had said, "any negotiated settlement must accept the fact that there are discontented elements in South Vietnam—Communist and non-Communist—who desire to change the existing political and economic system of the country. . . . To admit them to a share of power and responsibility is at the heart of the hope of a negotiated settlement."

In the uproar that followed, Bob's remarks about preventing a Communist takeover of South Vietnam were ignored, and his proposal was generally interpreted as calling for a coalition government. Under Secretary of State George Ball asserted that such a step would lead ultimately to Communist rule. McGeorge Bundy said the proposal would not be a "hopeful or helpful step," and from Wellington, New Zealand, Vice President Humphrey said it amounted to putting a fox in a chicken coop and "there wouldn't be many chickens left." President Johnson made it appear that he was above the battle. Bob tried to clarify his statement and left the impression that he was waffling. Though Walter Lippmann commented that it had remained for Bob "to raise the decisive question about a negotiated settlement," reaction generally was that Bob had floundered, reopened his dispute with Mr. Johnson, undermined U.S. foreign policy and divided his party. Public sentiment appeared to be against him, and he lapsed into a year of restive silence.

The war continued to escalate. American casualties mounted. Devastation became even more widespread. Still, President Johnson's military victory remained a will-o'-the-wisp. From all the information available to Bob—from opponents of the war, but more significantly from Defense Secretary McNamara and other reliable contacts in the Pentagon and the State Department—he saw only a widening conflict ahead unless the United States took the initiative to get negotiations started. Hence his carefully phrased Senate speech a fortnight before the 1967 Gridiron Dinner:

> I do not offer this program as a fixed and frozen formula. They are suggestions to be refined and revised by critical examination of other minds. . . .
>
> If we pursue this program, it will at least help us to know we have done everything we can be expected to do, that we have let neither pride nor fear deter us in the quest for peace. We owe no less to ourselves, to our people, and to those whose land we both protect and ravage. The stakes are very high: they are the home of the child in a jungle village, the hunger of a man driven from his farm, the life of a young American even now preparing for the day's battle. There is great principle, and there is also human anguish. If we can protect the one and prevent the other, then there is no effort too great for us to make.

Thereafter, he spoke out often against the course of the conflict, giving strength to the antiwar movement and becoming one of its leaders in name if not wholly in fact. As President Johnson became less and less believable on the war to more and more people and as dissent gained intensity, Bob came under increasing pressure to challenge him for the 1968 nomination, and the jaws of the vise tightened again.

Because he was Robert Kennedy and because of all the circumstances that formed his rancorous relationship with Lyndon Johnson—now aggravated even more by his opposition to the war—Bob's alternatives were uniquely complicated and especially difficult. Essentially, this was his problem at the outset:

He had, of course, thought a good deal after 1964 about running for the Presidency, but until the fall of 1967 he probably thought in terms of 1972, rather than 1968. He had become fatalistic about life, and when he was asked if he would run for President, he would answer vaguely, "I just don't know. I think we've all seen that it doesn't do much good to plan too far in advance. I just hope to continue in public life some way as long as I can." But as his discontent with President Johnson grew not only over Vietnam, but also over what he believed was a pulling back on the President's commitment to deal with the urban crisis, especially after the Detroit riot in July 1967, his instincts tilted him toward running. Against that was his political logic—the seeming improbability of winning the nomination from a sitting President under any circumstances. But the decisive factor was the added handicap that he was especially vulnerable to charges, certain to be leveled, that his pursuit of the nomination was a self-serving act of vengeance against Mr. Johnson. He was convinced it would put the war issue in the context of a grudge between him and the President and might further entwine Mr. Johnson in the spiral of escalation. He was also convinced that his candidacy would hopelessly divide the Democratic Party, and he believed then—and it can be written only with the utmost irony—that this division would clear the way for the nomination and election of Richard Nixon.

Six detailed accounts of Bob's travail during the winter of 1967–68 have already been written—by David Halberstam in *The Unfinished Odyssey of Robert Kennedy;* Jules Witcover in *85 Days: The Last Campaign of Robert Kennedy;* Jack Newfield in *Robert Kennedy;* Theodore

White in *The Making of the President—1968;* Lewis Chester, Godfrey Hodgson and Bruce Page in *An American Melodrama: The Presidential Campaign of 1968;* and Milton Gwirtzman and William vanden Heuvel in *On His Own: RFK 1964–68.* I can only add a few observations based on my conversations with him—a small percentage of the many conversations he had as he consulted with his family and with a wide range of friends, staff assistants and political allies.

The factors listed above governed Bob's thinking through the end of 1967, causing him to turn down overtures to run, the most persuasive of which came from Allard Lowenstein of New York, a bright, highly principled and deeply committed reformer. Lowenstein, the originator and moving force behind the "Dump Johnson" movement, correctly gauged the ground swell of opposition that was rising against the President and begged Bob to enter the New Hampshire primary. When Bob said he couldn't, Lowenstein searched for another candidate until Senator Eugene McCarthy agreed to go.

Bob continued to weigh his prospects. In the first week of January, I went for a walk with him, Ethel and another man, whom, for reasons personal to him, I cannot identify. Just before we left Hickory Hill, Jess Unruh had been urging Bob to get into the race. We walked in the snow along the banks of the Potomac River debating the alternatives over and over. Each time we came back to what seemed to be the stumbling block: Bob did not think President Johnson could be forced out of the race and that Bob would be blamed for a party split that would benefit only Mr. Nixon. Ethel, who was strongly in favor of Bob's running, said little. As dusk began to darken the trees along the river and we headed toward the house, the other man said: "Bob, it all comes down to this: Do you want to elect Richard Nixon? Is that what you and your brother and all of us worked for all these years?"

"No," Bob replied slowly, and for several minutes we walked in baleful silence.

Those whom Bob consulted divided, roughly speaking, into three groups, and the infinite shadings of each group's views reflected the turmoil and conflict within Bob himself.

There were those to whom the war was uppermost and who believed it was so unpopular and had so destroyed the President's credibility that he could be toppled easily. They argued that Bob, as the strongest voice of dissent against policies that were having grievous consequences at home and abroad, had a moral obligation to risk a fight that overrode political calculations—that if he didn't, he would forfeit his chances to be President.

The second group focused on what appeared to be the political facts of life: the war was not going well, but not badly enough to threaten the President's hold on the Democratic Party; that the President could undercut his opposition by ordering a bombing halt. Whatever their personal feelings were toward Johnson, they believed that Bob's chances of wresting the nomination were not good enough to warrant dismembering the party. They warned that if he opposed Johnson and the Democrats were defeated in November, he would be blamed, rightly or wrongly, and that it would be political suicide.

The third group thought more in terms of Bob as an individual. They shared his views about the war and the President's brand of leadership, but hesitated to advise him to risk everything when the odds appeared to be so much against winning. They wavered between their desire to see him in the White House and their fear that he would be wasting his chances in a lost cause, and through January most of them stopped short of urging him to run.

Then the situation changed drastically with the events of February—the Tet offensive in Vietnam; Governor George Romney's sudden withdrawal from the New Hampshire primary; and on March 1 President Johnson's brushoff of the report of his National Advisory Commission on Civil Disorders, appointed after the Detroit riot. Its basic conclusion was that "our nation is moving toward two societies, one black, one white—separate and unequal" and that white racism was primarily to blame.

On the morning of January 30, Bob had breakfast in Washington with fifteen newspapermen and gave them a statement for attribution that he would not oppose President Johnson "under any foreseeable circumstances." As they were meeting, the Vietcong and

North Vietnamese regulars began the Tet offensive with savage surprise attacks on Saigon and twenty-six other key cities. It would leave a heavier imprint than any other single event on the American political scene of 1968.

For Lyndon Johnson, it was the beginning of the end. The fury of the offensive gutted the Administration's claims that the war was going well and bared its grim realities: that, despite all our troops and firepower, the enemy held the initiative on the battlefield; that the South Vietnamese Government was far from being an effective ally; and that the only alternative to negotiations was an even more massive American commitment, with greater death and destruction and no reasonable assurance of achieving our objectives. Despite Administration claims that Tet had been turned into a Communist defeat, the photographs of American Marines defending the American Embassy in the heart of Saigon, of GI's crouching behind walls in the ancient city of Hué, told a different story.

As Tet eroded Mr. Johnson's credibility, it galvanized Senator McCarthy's campaign. As the opponent of the war who had taken the field against the President, he became the symbol and the hope, not only of the "Dump Johnson" movement, but of millions whose smoldering dissent against the war was ignited by Tet. The trickle of students who had gone to New Hampshire to help McCarthy became a torrent. Older dissenters poured money into his campaign.

For Bob, Tet inflamed his opposition to the war and later, as the Administration debated whether to grant the Pentagon's request for a commitment of 206,000 more troops, he edged toward entering the race. Tet removed his last bit of caution that his opposition to the President's policies would be considered part of their personal feud. He watched with extreme discomfort as young people turned on him and rallied to McCarthy, though McCarthy's rapidly rising strength in New Hampshire indicated clearly that the Democratic Party was deeply split and that Bob was not the cause of it.

On February 28, Romney, with his campaign faltering badly, withdrew from the Presidential race. Though Romney invited the Republican governors to put forward another candidate, presumably Governor Rockefeller, and California Governor Ronald Reagan was pushing himself into the race, Bob interpreted Romney's withdrawal as all but cinching Mr. Nixon's hold on the nomination. That obviated Bob's concern that by entering the race he would help Mr. Nixon toward the GOP nomination.

Then President Johnson received the Civil Disorders Commission report with studied indifference—conspicuously allowing it to be released without the usual White House fanfare and making no statement. For a man as deeply committed to racial equality and narrowing the cleavages between the races as Bob was, that was the last straw.

A few days before the report was issued, he called to talk about whether he should accept an invitation to attend a Mass of Thanksgiving in Delano, California, on March 10, when Cesar Chavez, head of the AFL-CIO United Farm Workers Union, was to end a twenty-five-day fast. Chavez had begun the fast to reaffirm his dedication to nonviolence because of growing militancy within the union as its long bitter strike-boycott against California grape growers dragged on inconclusively. Bob had met Chavez in 1966, admired him for his fight for the impoverished farm workers and had championed the union's cause in Congress.

"Do you think I should come?" Bob asked.

"I don't think it will make much difference," I said. "Those who don't agree with you won't like it. The people who will appreciate it are already with you. It's a long way out here. Why do you want to haul your tail across the country on a Sunday just to go to Delano?"

"Well," he replied, "I guess because I like Cesar."

"Are you going to run?"

"I think I have to. If I don't, I'll have to support Gene McCarthy, and I can't do it in good conscience. A lot of people are still against it. The Democratic Senators who are up for election will be upset, but Tet has changed everything, and if I don't go now and make an effort in the primaries, I think I'll be nothing."

I pointed out that coming to Delano for Chavez might cost him votes in California.

"I know," he said, "but I like Cesar."

When he arrived in Los Angeles on March 10 to take a small plane to Delano, he told me he had decided to run. He said he would have to wait until after the New Hampshire primary[2] two days hence or it would appear that he was undercutting McCarthy. He said he would announce the following weekend.

In Delano, Bob first visited Chavez in a small chapel and then accompanied him to a park, where six thousand emotional followers of Chavez crowded around them at the foot of an altar built on a flatbed truck. Chavez, who had lost thirty-five pounds, was too weakened to speak and slumped in a chair between his seventy-five-year-old mother and Bob, sipping water from a glass. Following the Mass, Chavez broke his fast by taking a bit of semita, a Mexican-type bread. Bob took a piece from the same loaf and now, at the conclusion of the service, said:

"I am here out of respect for one of the heroic figures of our time —Cesar Chavez. I congratulate all of you who are locked with Cesar in the struggle for justice for the farmworker and the struggle for justice for Spanish-speaking Americans. There are those who question the principle of everything that you have done so far—the principle of nonviolence. Let me say to you that violence is no answer."

Bob was the only political figure invited to the ceremony. Returning to Los Angeles, he had dinner with Andy Williams, made one political phone call—to Jess Unruh—and then flew all night to return to Washington and begin his last campaign.

In *A Farewell to Arms* Ernest Hemingway wrote:

If people bring so much courage to this world the world has to kill them to break them, so of course it kills them. The world breaks every one and afterward many are strong at the broken places. But those that will not

2. Closing fast in the final weeks, McCarthy exposed President Johnson's vulnerability by capturing 42.2 percent of the Democratic vote. Johnson polled 49.4 percent, but McCarthy, with a surprising amount of Republican write-in votes, trailed the President 28,791 to 29,021 in the over-all tally.

break it kills. It kills the very good and the very gentle and the very brave impartially. If you are none of these you can be sure it will kill you too but there will be no special hurry.

Bob brought courage to everything he did, and many people drew courage from him, not only those who knew him well, but thousands upon thousands of others, particularly the dispossessed and the young. He had the courage to descend into the widening crevices of American society—between the affluent and the poor, black and white, young and old, hawks and doves—and to see the people trapped in them and to listen to what they were saying. Because he did and because of who he was and what he had done, he gave many the courage to believe that he could do a great deal to make the country better and that he would, if given the chance.

Those hopes are gone, but he would not have thought that Hemingway's passage fitted him. He did not take such a stark view of life, though he was no stranger to tragedy. More appropriate, perhaps, he would have thought, are portions which he often quoted of Thucydides' report of Pericles' funeral oration for Greeks who died in battle:

We are lovers of beauty without extravagance and of learning without loss of vigor; wealth we employ more for use than for show and place the disgrace of poverty not in avowing it, but in declining to struggle against it.

We are a free democracy. . . . We do not allow absorption in our own affairs to interfere with participation in the city's. We differ from other states in regarding the man who holds aloof from public life as useless, yet we yield to none in independence of spirit and complete self-reliance.

But it would be right to esteem those men bravest in spirit who have the clearest understanding of the pains and pleasures of life and do not on that account shrink from danger.

For every land is a sepulcher for famous men; not only are they commemorated by inscriptions on monuments in their own country, but even in foreign lands there dwells an unwritten memorial of them, graven not so much on stone as in the hearts of men.

To a man of spirit it is more painful to be oppressed like a weakling than in the consciousness of strength and common hopes to meet a death that comes unfelt.

After President Kennedy's death, Bob revealed the depth of his feelings only twice in public—on St. Patrick's Day in Scranton and before the Democratic National Convention in Atlantic City. In February 1964 when he wrote a foreword for the memorial edition of the President's *Profiles in Courage,* he said of his brother:

> If there is a lesson from his life and from his death, it is that in this world of ours none of us can afford to be lookers-on, the critics standing on the sidelines.
> Thomas Carlyle wrote, "The courage we desire and prize is not the courage to die decently but to live manfully."

That is how Bob would live out the short span of years left to him, and he would die as he lived—at the center of the action in the public arena, fighting against the odds. He was armed only with a genuine commitment to the impulses which gave birth to the United States—freedom, justice and, as John Adams said, the opportunity to excel: a willingness to serve his country, dissatisfaction with the status quo and a pragmatic belief that the divisions among the people could be narrowed. It was more important to him that his principles and ideas survived than that he survived.

He was a wholly unique figure in our country. Never before had a man so shared the burdens of the Presidency without actually holding the office. Then, after 1964, when the brush-fire war in Vietnam became a conflagration, when black and student militancy turned to violence, when fear and discontent pervaded the land despite all our power and affluence—and America changed—he, more than any other public figure, was able to communicate across the barricades of rising hostility. He was, as Halberstam wrote in *The Unfinished Odyssey of Robert Kennedy,* "at the exact median point of American idealism and American power. He understood the potency of America's idealism and American power. He understood the potency of America's idealism, as a domestic if not an international force, and yet he had also exercised American power."

While he sought out critics of the war in Vietnam and listened to their views, he remained close to his friend in the Pentagon, Defense Secretary McNamara, and drew from him and others in the government who supported the war—as much as from the dissenters—the conviction that the war which he helped perpetuate could neither be won nor advance the best interests of the United States.

No other white politician could have gone into the black ghetto in Indianapolis as he did on the night Dr. King was assassinated, nor has anyone yet been able to bring black militants and white business executives to work in so varied and comprehensive an undertaking as he did in the Bedford-Stuyvesant ghetto in Brooklyn. It is not the whole answer to Bedford-Stuyvesant's massive problems by any means, but with its failures and modest successes, it is a partnership so soundly conceived and so well led that it is still viable three years after his death.

Though many students rallied to the candidacy of Senator McCarthy in the winter of 1968 and scorned Bob for hesitating to challenge President Johnson and then for jumping into the race belatedly, still, he, far more than McCarthy, was sensitive to the causes of their disillusionment, sympathized with them and saw their dissent not as a danger to be repressed but as a highly motivated force that offered hope and direction for the future.

Of the thousands who filed past his casket in St. Patrick's Cathedral and stood along the tracks as his funeral train crept toward Washington, it is the sorrow in the faces of the young and the blacks that one remembers.

However, he was not the apostle only of the young. When he spoke of the spirit of youth, it was not only of those youthful in years, but, as he put it, "a state of mind, a temper of will, a quality of the imagination, a predominance of courage over timidity, of the appetite for adventure over the love of ease. It is the spirit which knows the difference between force and reason. It does not accept the failures of tomorrow. It knows that we can clasp the future and mold it to our will. . . .

"For above all, the spirit of youth is the conviction of possibility: the knowledge that we are not bound in chains of impotence, and that with courage and energy and purpose we can build a better nation and attain a peaceful world."

He has left us these words and the magnificent example of his life:

a man, endowed with all the worldly goods that money could buy, who strove with all his ability to fight against injustice and poverty —poverty of the spirit and poverty of individual freedom as well as material poverty; a man of unlimited courage and capacity who experienced life to the fullest, who grew with every experience and tirelessly sought new challenges. Yet all he had accomplished was only a beginning, for to know anything about him is to know that had he lived and won in 1968, he would have been a great President; that had he lost, he would not have despaired or retreated, but would have fought on as best he could. In either case, he would have called to us as he so often did:

> Come, my friends,
> 'Tis not too late to seek a newer world.
> Push off, and sitting well in order smite
> The sounding furrows; for my purpose holds
> To sail beyond the sunset, and the baths
> Of all the western stars, until I die.
> It may be that the gulfs will wash us down:
> It may be we shall touch the Happy Isles,
> And see the great Achilles, whom we knew.
> Though much is taken, much abides; and though
> We are not now that strength which in old days
> Moved earth and heaven, that which we are, we are;
> One equal temper of heroic hearts,
> Made weak by time and fate, but strong in will
> To strive, to seek, to find, and not to yield.

Index

331

About the Author

Edwin Guthman lives in Los Angeles, where he is national editor of the Los Angeles *Times*. He was born in Seattle, Washington, in 1919, attended public schools there and graduated from the University of Washington in the class of '41. He was drafted in 1941 and served as reconnaissance platoon leader of the 339th Regiment in the Italian campaign. He was wounded and was awarded the Purple Heart and the Silver Star. After being discharged in December 1945, he returned to the Seattle *Star* as a reporter. In 1947 he joined the Seattle *Times*, where, for the next thirteen years, he specialized in political and investigative reporting. In 1950 he won the Pulitzer prize for national reporting for clearing a University of Washington professor of charges by the State Un-American Activities Committee that the professor had attended a secret Communist training school. Guthman found that the committee concealed evidence which disproved the charge. During the 1950–51 school year, Guthman studied at Harvard University as a Nieman Fellow. From 1961 to 1965 he was Robert F. Kennedy's special assistant for public information in the Department of Justice and Kennedy's first senatorial press secretary. He is married and has four children.

71 72 73 74 10 9 8 7 6 5 4 3 2 1